THE POPE BENEDICT XVI
READER

❖

THE POPE BENEDICT XVI READER

FOREWORD BY
BISHOP ROBERT BARRON

WORD ON FIRE
INSTITUTE

Excerpts collected by Daniel Seseske.

Design and layout by Anna Manhart.

24 23 22 21   1 2 3 4

ISBN: 978-1-943243-75-4

Library of Congress Control Number: 2020925449

CONTENTS

❖

FOREWORD

by Bishop Robert Barron

❖

Joseph Ratzinger (Pope Benedict XVI) is, quite simply, one of the three or four most important Catholics of the last hundred and fifty years. As a theologian, he ranks with the greatest Christian intellects of the age: Karl Barth, Karl Rahner, Hans Urs von Balthasar, and Henri de Lubac. But he was also a churchman of extraordinary influence, serving as Archbishop of Munich and Freising, and then, for twenty-three years, as Prefect of the Congregation for the Doctrine of the Faith under Pope St. John Paul II, and finally, for eight years as the successor of Peter. In these properly ecclesial roles, he had an almost unparalleled impact on the life of the Church in Europe and around the world. Since he wrote and spoke on such an extraordinary number of topics in the course of a long career—God, Jesus Christ, the Church, liturgy, anthropology, faith and culture, eschatology, etc.—it is perhaps difficult to gain an adequate appreciation of his thought.

This collection of Ratzinger's writings, from across many years and on a range of themes, is meant to give an overview of his thought to those already acquainted with it and an introduction to those unfamiliar with it. If I were to characterize the life and work of Ratzinger, I would propose these four fundamental themes: he was a man of the Scriptures, a man of the Church Fathers, a man of the Second Vatican Council, and a man of the liturgy. I should like to make just a few simple observations about each of these.

Joseph Ratzinger came of age theologically in the forties and fifties of the last century—which is to say, at the high-water mark of the so-called *ressourcement* (return to the sources) movement. Weary of the somewhat tired scholasticism that dominated Catholic education and of the endless sniping wars between Protestants and Catholics, the leaders of this school of thought, figures such as de Lubac, Jean Daniélou, and Yves Congar, endeavored to recover the great "sources" from which all of Christian theology flows—namely, the writings of the Church Fathers and the Scriptures themselves. Throughout his career, Ratzinger tended away from the rationalism of the scholastics and leaned toward the lyricism of the Bible. This scriptural orientation came to full expression in one of the last works that he produced—namely, the magnificent three-volume study of Jesus of Nazareth that he wrote while pope. To understand his biblical method, I would especially recommend a careful reading of the passage in this collection in which Pope Benedict discusses the limitations of the historical-critical approach to reading the Bible.

The second "source" was no less significant for Ratzinger, for throughout his life, he remained a devotee of the Fathers of the Church, especially of St. Augustine, whom he humbly claimed as his "master." From this great theologian of the Western tradition, he learned to read history in a consistently God-centered manner, and from Augustine's patristic colleagues, he learned the deep integration of theological reflection, biblical inspiration, and personal spirituality. Two of the clearest indications of Ratzinger's patristic formation are his doctoral dissertation on Augustine's notion of the Church as the "house of God" and his follow-up *Habilitationsschrift* on St. Bonaventure's theology of history, which was profoundly marked by patristic thought. But the beautifully crafted and deceptively simple reflections on the Fathers that Pope Benedict gave as Wednesday audience talks during his papacy— many of which are featured in this collection—are perhaps the best introduction to his patristic manner of thinking. I had the very special privilege of hearing a number of these talks in person while I was in Rome as a visiting scholar.

Ratzinger was also a man of the Second Vatican Council. Arriving in Rome in the fall of 1962 as a theological advisor to Cardinal Josef Frings of Cologne, he was, along with Hans Küng, the youngest of the *periti* at the council. During the four sessions of Vatican II, Ratzinger was remarkably active and productive, composing speeches for Frings, editing many of the major conciliar texts, dialoguing with theologians across the ideological spectrum, and helping to explain the determinations of the council fathers to the outside world. In the years after the close of Vatican II, Ratzinger continued to celebrate the achievements of the council in regard to liturgy, ecclesiology, the universal call to holiness, the biblical revival, and the role of the Church in the modern world. Along with Balthasar and de Lubac, he strongly resisted what he took to be a liberal attempt to hijack the council and turn it into a vehicle for the radical transformation of the Church. Thus, from 1965 through the years of his papacy, Ratzinger defended what he called a "hermeneutic of continuity," according to which Vatican II represented indeed a development of doctrine, but not a rupture with the past. At the same time, like John Paul II, he stood against that "traditionalist" interpretation which would see the council as simply a betrayal of the Catholic tradition. He saw his work, both under John Paul II and in his own right as pope, as giving a definitive interpretation to Vatican II, one that would hold off the extremism of both left and right. A number of speeches, interviews, and essays in the present volume vividly present this aspect of Ratzinger's work.

Finally, he was a man of the liturgy. Born on Holy Saturday in 1927 and baptized that same day in the Easter water, Ratzinger saw his life as, from the very beginning, marked by the formal worship of the Catholic Church. From the time he was a child, he loved the rituals, gestures, language, and rhythm of the Mass, appreciating that great prayer as the privileged moment of encounter with Jesus Christ. Accordingly, he remained permanently suspicious of any attempt to turn the liturgy into a celebration of subjective experience or of the sanctity of the community. He strenuously resisted the "closed circle" liturgies of the postconciliar period in which priest and people face one another, with little sense of a transcendent point of reference. Properly enacted and fully understood, the Roman liturgy, he felt, is key to the renewal of the

Church and of the wider society. I will never forget the experience of concelebrating Mass in St. Peter's Square with Pope Benedict and sensing in his voice and body language the truths that I garnered through his writings. To grasp the heart of Ratzinger's theology of the liturgy, I would recommend a prayerful reading of the chapter from *The Spirit of the Liturgy* included in our collection.

As I compose these words in the closing days of the year 2020, Pope Emeritus Benedict XVI is in his ninety-fourth year. I hope that, as this great man comes to the end of his earthly pilgrimage, this book might function not only as a summation of his thought but, more importantly, as a humble tribute to him.

CHRONOLOGY OF THE LIFE
OF JOSEPH RATZINGER

❖

1927	Joseph Ratzinger is born on April 16 in Marktl am Inn in Bavaria, Germany.
1939	Ratzinger enters preparatory seminary in the Archdiocese of Munich.
1941	By law, Ratzinger is forced to enroll with the Hitler Youth, but he refuses to attend meetings.
1951	On June 29, the same day as his brother Georg, Ratzinger is ordained a priest by Cardinal Michael von Faulhaber of Munich.
1953	Ratzinger completes his dissertation on St. Augustine.
1957	After completion of his habilitation on St. Bonaventure, Ratzinger is qualified to serve as a university professor in Germany.
1958	Ratzinger spends a year teaching at Freising College.
1959	Ratzinger becomes a full professor at the University of Bonn.
1962–1965	Ratzinger attends the Second Vatican Council as a *peritus* (theological expert) of Cardinal Josef Frings.
1963–1977	Continuing his professorial career, Ratzinger holds positions at a number of German universities: Münster (1963–1966), Tübingen (1966–1969), and Regensburg (1969–1977).
1972	Along with Hans Urs von Balthasar, Henri de Lubac, and others, Ratzinger cofounds the theological journal *Communio*.
1977	On March 24, Ratzinger becomes the Archbishop of Munich and Freising, and on June 27, he is created a cardinal by Pope Paul VI.
1981	Ratzinger is named Prefect of the Congregation for the Doctrine of the Faith by Pope John Paul II.
2002	John Paul II approves Ratzinger's appointment as Dean of the College of Cardinals.
2005	Following the death of John Paul II, Ratzinger is elected as the 265th pope on April 19, 2005, and takes the name Benedict XVI.
2013	On February 11, Benedict surprises the Church and the world by announcing that he will resign the papacy on February 28.

PART I

LIFE

The excerpts in this part are drawn from Joseph Ratzinger's conversations with Peter Seewald. Seewald is a German journalist who has conducted several interviews with Ratzinger—before, during, and after his papacy—which are published in the following volumes: *Salt of the Earth*, *God and the World*, *Light of the World*, and *The Last Testament*. Seewald's words appear in italics.

CHAPTER I

Early Childhood and Vocation

Joseph Ratzinger was born on April 16, 1927, in Marktl am Inn in Upper Bavaria. In this excerpt, Ratzinger discusses the circumstances of his birth, some memories of family life, and his discernment of a priestly vocation.

Your Eminence, what do you think of this idea: We come into this world and what we want to know, we already know, and where we want to be, we already are?

That is going too far, to my mind. I don't know now where that statement comes from, but man comes into the world as a questioner. Aristotle even says—and Thomas Aquinas says it too—as a *tabula rasa*. In other words, they contest that men have innate knowledge; for them the mind begins as pure readiness to receive. I would nuance that a bit. But at any rate it is correct that man exists first as a questioner, who, however, is, so to speak, open from within to the answers.

To a certain extent I am a Platonist. I think that a kind of memory, of recollection of God, is, as it were, etched in man, though it needs to be awakened. Man doesn't simply know what he is supposed to know, nor is he simply there, but is a man, a being on the way.

Precisely the biblical religion of the Old and New Testament always strongly accentuated the image of the wandering people of God, which in the case of Israel really was a wandering people. This image exemplifies the nature of human existence as such. That man is a being under way and that his way is not a fiction, but that something really happens to him in this life, and that he can seek, can find, but can also miss the mark.

You often use the word "providence." What meaning does it have for you?

I am quite firmly convinced that God really sees us and that he leaves us freedom—and nevertheless leads us. I can often see that things which at first seemed irksome, dangerous, unpleasant, somehow at some point come together. Suddenly one realizes that it was good thus, that this was the right way. For me this means in a very practical way that my life is not made up of chance occurrences but that someone foresees and also, so to speak, precedes me, whose thinking precedes mine and who prepares my life. I can refuse this, but I can also accept it, and then I realize that I am really guided by a providential light.

Now this does not mean that man is completely determined but rather that what is preordained calls forth precisely man's freedom. Just as we hear in the story of the talents. Five are given; and the one who receives them has a definite task, but he can do it in this way or that. At any rate, he has his mission, his particular gift. No one is superfluous, no one is in vain, everyone must try to recognize what his life's call is and how he can best live up to the call that is waiting for him.

You were born on April 16, 1927, in Marktl am Inn in Upper Bavaria. You were born on a Holy Saturday. Does that suit you?

Yes, I'm pleased to have been born on the vigil of Easter, already on the way to Easter, but not yet there, for it is still veiled. I find that a very good day, which in some sense hints at my conception of history and my own situation: on the threshold of Easter, but not yet through the door.

Your parents were named Mary and Joseph. You were baptized just four hours after your birth, at 8:30 in the morning. They say it was a stormy day.

Needless to say, I have no recollection of that. My brother and sister have told me that there was a lot of snow, that it was very cold, although it was April 16. But that is nothing extraordinary in Bavaria.

4

Still, it is uncommon to be baptized just four hours after being born.

That is true. But that has to do with the fact—and this is certainly something that I'm pleased by—that it was Holy Saturday. The Easter Vigil was not yet celebrated in those days, so that the Resurrection was celebrated in the morning, with the blessing of water, which then served throughout the whole year as baptismal water. And because the baptismal liturgy was consequently taking place in the Church, my parents said: "Well the boy's already here," so it is natural that he be baptized too at this liturgical point in time, which is the time when the Church baptized. And the coincidence that I was born at the very moment when the Church was preparing her baptismal water, so that I was the first person baptized with the new water, does indeed mean something to me. Because it situates me particularly in the context of Easter and also binds birth and baptism in a very suggestive way.

You grew up in the country as the youngest of three children. Your father was a constable, the family poor rather than well-off. Your mother, you once recounted, even made her own soap.

My parents had married late, and a Bavarian constable of my father's rank—he was a simple commissioner—was modestly paid. We were not poor in the strict sense of the word, because the monthly salary was guaranteed, but we did have to live very frugally and simply, for which I am very grateful. For thereby joys are made possible that one cannot have in wealth. I often think back on how wonderful it was that we could be happy over the smallest things and how we also tried to do things for one another. How this very modest, sometimes financially difficult situation gave rise to an inner solidarity that bound us deeply together.

Our parents naturally had to make tremendous sacrifices so that all three of us could study. We recognized this and tried to respond. In this way, this climate of great simplicity was a source of much joy as well

5

as love for one another. We realized how much was given to us and how much our parents took upon themselves.

The business about the soap needs some explanation. It wasn't due to poverty but to the wartime situation in which one had to find some way to obtain goods that were not available in sufficient quantities. Our mother was by profession a cook and had many talents, and she knew such recipes by heart. With her great imagination and her practical skill she always knew, at the very moment when there was hunger in the land, how to conjure up a good meal out of the simplest and scantest means.

My mother was very warm-hearted and had great inner strength; my father was more markedly rationalistic and deliberate. He was a reflective believer. He always understood clearly at the outset what was going on and always had an astonishingly accurate judgment. When Hitler came to power, he said: There's going to be war, now we need a house.

[. . .]

How did your vocation happen? When did you know what your destiny was? You said once that "I was convinced, I myself don't know how, that God wanted something from me, and it could be attained only by my becoming a priest."

At any rate, there was no lightning-like moment of illumination when I realized I was meant to become a priest. On the contrary, there was a long process of maturation, and the decision had to be thought through and constantly rewon. I couldn't date the decision, either. But the feeling that God had a plan for each person, for me too, became clear for me early on. Gradually it became clear to me that what he had in mind had to do with priesthood.

[. . .]

After you decided to become a priest—didn't certain self-doubts emerge at some time, temptations or seductions?

They did, to be sure. In the six years of theological study one encounters so many human problems and questions. Is celibacy right for me? Is being a parish priest right for me? Those were indeed questions not always easy to deal with. I always had the basic direction before me, but there was no lack of crises.

What crises emerged? Can you give an example?

In the years when I was studying theology in Munich I had to struggle above all with two questions. I was fascinated by academic theology. I found it wonderful to enter into the great world of the history of faith; broad horizons of thought and faith opened up before me, and I was learning to ponder the primordial questions of human existence, the questions of my own life. But it became clearer and clearer that there is more to the priestly vocation than enjoying theology, indeed, that work in the parish can often lead very far away from that and makes completely different demands. In other words, I couldn't study theology in order to become a professor, although this was my secret wish. But the Yes to the priesthood meant that I had to say Yes to the whole task, even in its simplest forms.

Since I was rather diffident and downright unpractical, since I had no talent for sports or administration or organization, I had to ask myself whether I would be able to relate to people—whether, for example, as a chaplain I would be able to lead and inspire Catholic youth, whether I would be capable of giving religious instruction to the little ones, whether I could get along with the old and sick, and so forth. I had to ask myself whether I would be ready to do that my whole life long and whether it was really my vocation.

Bound up with this was naturally the question of whether I would be able to remain celibate, unmarried, my whole life long. Since the university had been destroyed and there was as yet no place for theology

7

students, we lived for two years in the Fürstenried Castle with its buildings on the edge of the city. There not only professors and students but also male and female students lived at such close quarters that the daily encounter definitely made the question of renunciation and its inner meaning a practical one. I often pondered these questions as I walked in the beautiful park of Fürstenried and naturally in the chapel, until finally at my diaconal ordination in the fall of 1950 I was able to pronounce a convinced Yes.

CHAPTER 2

The Young Professor

Ratzinger was ordained to the priesthood in 1951 (along with his brother, Georg) and continued his preparations for a career in academia. He became a full professor in 1958 at the young age of thirty-one and continued in that role for almost twenty years. In this excerpt, he discusses some of his main influences, noting in particular the importance of the theology of St. Augustine and St. Bonaventure.

You once said, "When I began to study theology I also started getting interested in intellectual problems. This was because they "unveiled the drama of my life and above all the mystery of truth." What did you mean by that?

I would say that's a bit "pompously" expressed. All it means is that when you are studying theology, your intention is not to learn a trade but to understand the faith, and this presupposes, as we said a while ago, using the words of Augustine, that the faith is true, that, in other words, it opens the door to a correct understanding of your own life, of the world, and of men. This study also automatically throws you into the whole intellectual debate of Western history. From the very beginning, the faith is interwoven, on the one hand, with the Jewish heritage and, on the other, with the Latin and Greek heritage. And this obviously applies to its modern history. In that sense, the study of theology was tied to the question: What is really true, what can we know?

In our seminary in Freising there was a very vibrant atmosphere in those days. People had come back from the war, some from six-year-long participation in the war, and they were now filled with a real intellectual and literary hunger. With questions, too, of course, questions posed by what they had just lived through. People were reading Gertrud von le Fort, Ernst Wiechert and Dostoevski, Elisabeth Langgässer, everything that was around in the way of literature at the time. Those who studied in Munich had made the acquaintance of Heidegger and Jaspers via Steinbüchel, who taught moral theology at the time. There was a great intellectual élan, and one got swept up with it.

Which intellectual current interested and fascinated you in particular?

Heidegger and Jaspers interested me a great deal, along with personalism as a whole. *Steinbüchel* wrote a book entitled *The Revolution of Thought [Der Umbruch des Denkens]*, in which he recounted with great verve the revolutionary shift from the dominance of neo-Kantianism to the personalistic phase. That was a key book for me. But then from the beginning Saint Augustine interested me very much—precisely also insofar as he was, so to speak, a counterweight to Thomas Aquinas.

He says: "Reprimand troublemakers, comfort the fainthearted, refute opponents." That's how he defines his office.

He was a real bishop. He wrote huge tomes, too, so that one wonders how he managed to accomplish that next to all the odds and ends he had to do. But as a bishop he had above all to deal constantly with all the quarrels of the state and with the needs of the little people, and he tried to keep this structure together. It was an unsettled time, the barbarian invasions were beginning. In that sense, he was a man who was by no means floating in the clouds. In the organization of the empire at that time, the bishop was also a sort of justice of the peace. He held a certain level of jurisdiction and had to decide routine civil litigations. So he lived amid all that day by day and in doing so tried to mediate to men the peace of Christ, the gospel. In this sense, he is also an exemplar, because although he had such a great yearning for meditation, for intellectual work, he gave himself up to the small details of everyday life and wanted to be there for people.

What moved me then, however, was not so much his office as shepherd, which I was not familiar with in that way, but the freshness and vitality of his thought. Scholasticism has its greatness, but everything is very impersonal. You need some time to enter in and recognize the inner tension. With Augustine, however, the passionate, suffering, questioning man is always right there, and you can identify with him.

You finally became interested in Bonaventure's theology of history. How did that happen?

It was actually by chance. Since my dissertation had dealt with the ancient Church, my teacher, Professor Söhngen, remarked that my post-doctoral work should treat the Middle Ages or the modern period. In any case, I was supposed to do research of some kind on Bonaventure's concept of revelation. Söhngen knew that the Augustinian school appealed to me more than the Thomistic, so he set me to work on Bonaventure, whom he himself knew quite well and venerated.

Fundamental theology has to do with "revelation." What is revelation, actually? Can there be such a thing? And questions like that. After I started and worked through the texts, I discovered that for Bonaventure revelation was inseparable from the Franciscan adventure, and that in turn this adventure was connected with Joachim of Fiore, who foresaw a third age, the Age of the Holy Spirit, as a new period of revelation. Joachim had also calculated the time when this was to begin. And this chronology coincides, strangely enough, with the life of Saint Francis, who really did introduce a quite new phase in the history of the Church. So the Franciscans, at least a significant current of them, soon had the feeling that Joachim had predicted what they in fact were. Here was the new Age of the Holy Spirit; here is the simple, new, poor people of God that doesn't need any worldly structures.

The result was that the concept of revelation wasn't simply put somewhere at the beginning, in some far-off place, but revelation was now bound up with history. It was a process that progressed in history and had now entered into a new phase. So for Bonaventure revelation was no longer an abstract subject but was bound up with the interpretation of his own Franciscan history.

What did that open up for you?

There are two main issues. One could be expressed as follows. If the Christian faith is tied to a revelation that was concluded long ago, isn't it condemned to look backward and to chain man to a past time? Can it then keep pace with the continuing march of history? Does it still have anything at all to say to history? Mustn't it gradually grow old and end up being simply unrealistic? Bonaventure's answer to these questions was to underscore forcefully the connection between Christ and the Holy Spirit according to the Gospel of John. The word revealed in history is definitive, but it is inexhaustible, and it unceasingly discloses new depths. In this sense, the Holy Spirit, as the interpreter of Christ, speaks with his word to every age and shows it that this word always has something new to say. Unlike Joachim of Fiore, Bonaventure doesn't project the Holy Spirit into a future period, but it's always the age of the Holy Spirit. The age of Christ is the age of the Holy Spirit.

This brings up the second question on the agenda, the question of eschatology and utopia. It's hard for man to hope only for the beyond, or for a new world after the destruction of the present one. He wants a promise in history. Joachim concretely formulated such a promise and so prepared the way for Hegel, as Father de Lubac showed. Hegel, in turn, furnished the intellectual model for Marx. Bonaventure objected to the kind of utopia that deceives man. He also opposed an enthusiastic, spiritual-anarchical concept of the Franciscan movement and prevailed with a sober and realistic concept, something that offended many, and still does. But he saw the answer to the question of utopia precisely in such non-utopian communities that were nonetheless driven by the passion of faith. They don't work for a world beyond tomorrow; they work instead so that there may be something of the light of paradise present in this world today. They live in "utopian" fashion, as far as possible, by renouncing possessions, self-determination, and eros and its fulfillment. So a breath of fresh air comes into the world, breaking through its constraints and bringing God very close, right into the midst of this world.

CHAPTER 3

A *Peritus* at Vatican II

In 1962, Ratzinger was invited by Cardinal Josef Frings to accompany him as a *peritus* (theological expert) at the Second Vatican Council. In this conversation from 2016, Benedict XVI looks back on some of the highlights of his time in Rome, laments the misinterpretations that followed the council, and affirms the council's continued importance for the Church today.

When the Council was announced—do you remember now how you heard of it, and where you were?

Not exactly, no. I'm certain I heard about it on the radio. Then, of course, we spoke about it among the professors. It was a profound moment. The announcement of the Council had already provoked questions—How will it go? How can it all be carried out correctly?—but also great hopes.

Were you there from the first to the last day, in all four sittings?

Completely, yes. I was formally put on leave as a professor by the ministerial authorities in Germany.

You probably didn't see any of the sights of the city during the Council.

Very little time, one was very much made use of. Of course I took my walk every day, but that stayed within the vicinity of the Anima, where there is indeed much to be seen. The French national church, St. Luigi, the Pantheon, St. Eustace, the Sapienza and so forth, Palazzo Madama, but I could not see much otherwise.

The Council involved an unbelievable amount of work?

I don't want to exaggerate. So, it didn't break my back. But there was certainly lots to do, especially because of all the meetings.

Were you still able to get any sleep?

Yes, yes, that is non-negotiable for me. [Laughs] I'll never let that be infringed upon.

How did you actually communicate? You could only speak a little Italian.

A little, yes. Well, I functioned with it, somehow. I had reasonable Latin. Although I must say I had never studied theology in Latin, never spoke Latin like the Germanikers (German-speaking theology students that study at the Collegium Germanicum in Rome, founded in 1552 by Pope Julius III). We did everything in German. So for me to speak in Latin was something quite new. Therefore the possibilities for contributing that were at my disposal were limited. I could speak Français reasonably well, of course.

You hadn't yet gone on an Italian course?

No. [Laughs] I had no time, there was so much to do.

Did you take a dictionary with you?

Certainly, yes.

So you practiced "learning by doing"?

Precisely.

And which experience do you remember most fondly?

We travelled to Capri with the cardinal on All Saints' Day. We looked around Naples beforehand, the various churches and so on. To make the journey to Capri was very adventurous back then. We took a boat, which swayed from side to side in an alarming way. We all vomited, even the cardinal. I had always been able to master it until then. But then Capri was really lovely. It was a real sigh of relief.

14

Which camp did you belong to at that time: the progressives?

Yes, indeed, I would say so. At that time progressive did not mean that you were breaking out of the faith, but that you wanted to understand it better, and more accurately, how it lives from its origins. I was of the opinion then that that was what we all wanted. Famous progressives like de Lubac, Daniélou, etc. thought likewise. The change of mood was indeed already noticeable by the second year of the Council, but it only began to loom clearly with the passing of the years.

Recent research shows that your contribution on the part of Cardinal Frings was even greater than you have revealed yourself. We've already mentioned the Genoa Speech. In addition there was a first lecture for the German-speaking bishops in the Anima, just before the opening of the Council, a kind of briefing. In accordance with Frings's instructions, a plan was made to torpedo the election of ten Council commissioners on October 13, to oust the favored candidates the Roman Curia had put forward.

Well, that was on his own initiative. I haven't interfered with business, technical, or political matters. That genuinely was his idea; he first had to get to know the people there at Council, in order for him to select committee members from his own ranks.

How did that actually come about? Frings was certainly not known to be a revolutionary.

No, absolutely not. He was known to be very conservative and strict. Everyone was surprised and astounded that he now took on a leading role. He even saw it that way himself; we spoke about it. He explained that, when exercising governance in the diocese, a bishop is responsible for the local church before the Pope and before the Lord. But it is something different if we are called to a Council to exercise shared governance with the Pope. A bishop then assumes his own responsibility, which no longer consists simply in obedience to the papal teaching office but rather in asking what needs to be taught today, and how that teaching is to proceed. He was very aware of this. He distinguished

15

between the normal situation of a Catholic bishop and the special situation of a Council Father, in which one is fully involved in shared decision-making.

Did he come to Rome with precise ideas already?

I wouldn't say so, no. He had sent all the *schemata*, which I had by no means judged as negatively as they were judged subsequently. I sent him many corrections, but I had not laid hands on the substance of the whole, except in the case of the decree on revelation. That could have been improved. We agreed that the basic orientation was there, but on the other hand there was much to improve. Primarily, that it be less dominated by the current Magisterium, and had to give greater voice to the Scriptures and the Fathers.

You were awarded a leading role in the "coup meeting" in the German priests' college, the Anima, on October 15, 1962. A new text, an alternative to the Roman draft edition, was brought to the table and then reproduced in 3,000 copies and distributed to the Council Fathers.

To call it a "coup meeting" is too strong. But we were of the opinion that something different had to be said precisely about the theme of revelation, different from what was taking shape in that first edition. The draft still maintained a neo-scholastic style, and didn't take enough account of our findings. For me, "revelation" was of course a predetermined topic, because of my post-doctoral work. So I'd already worked with it but everything was contributed by invitation of his Eminence, and within his sights. Afterwards I was accused of deceiving the cardinal or some such. I really must repudiate that. We were both convinced in unison that we had to serve the cause of the faith and the Church. Also, in order to address this cause in a new terminology, in a new way, we wanted to clarify the proper relationship between Scripture, Tradition, and the Magisterium, so that this relationship could really be understood and justified. That was then picked up.

How many people were involved at this meeting?

I can remember there was a discussion among cardinals only, and another with professors, but I cannot say exactly now.

It must have been dominated by an enormous tension.

No, actually we weren't really aware that we were doing anything stupendous. We didn't make any decisions there, but developed ideas. How it then got spread about the whole Council, I do not know. Of course we were awash with polemics: that we produced a typically freemasonic text and such things.

You were charged with that?

[Laughs] Yes, yes, although I really shouldn't be held in suspicion of being a freemason.

It was your arguments, it was your text, which Cardinal Frings presented to those assembled in the Council chamber erected in St. Peter's Basilica on November 14, 1962, and brought everything to a tipping point. The original draft was on the table, and everyone had blocked it. Unrestrained dispute could now begin.

The question being put to the vote was very complicated. Those who wanted new things had to vote no. And those who wanted old things, had to vote yes. Anyway, it was a very close vote. Those who won were those who wanted to stay with the original *schema*. So from a legal perspective there was a very slight majority in favor of maintaining the first draft of the text. But then Papa Giovanni saw that the majority was too thin to be viable, and decided that the vote should be reopened.

It is said that there was thunderous applause for Cardinal Frings in the Council chamber.

I wasn't inside then. I also don't believe it.

There was no phone booth in front of St. Peter's, let alone mobile phones in those days. How did you learn of these things back then?

Well after the Council sitting, the cardinal came over. I can't remember now if he told us about it himself. We were all very excited about what the Pope would do. And very happy that he said that even if a purely legal perspective would permit the first draft to stay in force, we would begin afresh.

Seven days later, on November 21, the withdrawal of the schema on the "Sources of Revelation" took place, a text you had heavily criticized. The text was, they wrote at the time, "defined by the anti-modernist mentality." It was said to have a tone which was "frosty, almost shockingly so." You yourself saw this withdrawal as the real turning point of the Council.

[The Pope laughs] Now I'm surprised that I spoke in such an audacious manner back then. It is correct that this was a real turn, insofar as the submitted text was put to one side and there was a completely new beginning to the discussion.

How was it meeting Karl Rahner? You initially worked on a few texts together. He was much older than you, thirty years.

Just twenty-three I believe; he was born in 1904 and I was in 1927.

Of course, you're right. Were things complicated with him?

I wouldn't say so. He was someone who consciously wanted to be responsive to young people, to young theologians. That then facilitates someone like me working with him. At that time we had a very good relationship. When we worked on that text, I soon noticed, however, that we belonged to two different worlds of thought. He had completely come out of scholasticism, which was a great advantage for him, because he could engage in the accustomed style of discussion more intensely thereby. While I came from just the Bible and the Fathers.

[. . .]

Your attitude towards the Council had gradually changed. In your book published in 1965, Ergebnisse und Probleme der 3. Konzilsperiode, it states "The Council, and the Church with it, is on the way. There is no reason for skepticism and resignation. We have every reason to have hope, good spirits, patience." But by June 18 this same year, you declare before a Catholic student community in Munster that one is beginning "to wonder, if things were not always better under the rule of the so-called conservatives, than they are able to be under the dominance of progressivism." A year later, in 1966 at the Bamberg Katholikentag, you strike a balance which expresses skepticism and disillusionment. And with a lecture in Tubingen in 1967 you point out that the Christian faith is by now surrounded "with a fog of uncertainty" as had "hardly been seen before at any point in history." Is the new internal split, then beginning within the Church, and basically enduring to this day, to be considered as part of the tragic nature of the Council?

I would say so, yes. The bishops wanted to renew the faith, to deepen it. However, other forces were working with increasing strength, particularly journalists, who interpreted many things in a completely new way. Eventually people asked, yes, if the bishops are able to change everything, why can't we all do that? The liturgy began to crumble, and slip into personal preferences. In this respect one could soon see that what was originally desired was being driven in a different direction. Since 1965 I have felt it to be a mission to make clear what we genuinely wanted and what we did not want.

Did you have pangs of conscience, as a participant, one who shares responsibility?

One certainly asks oneself whether or not one did things rightly. Particularly when the whole thing unraveled, that was definitely a question one posed. Cardinal Frings later had intense pangs of conscience. But he always had an awareness that what we actually said and put forward was right, and also had to happen. We handled things correctly, even if we certainly did not correctly assess the political consequences and the actual repercussions. One thought too much of theological matters then, and did not reflect on how these things would come across.

Was it a mistake to convoke the Council at all?

No, it was right for sure. One can ask whether it was necessary or not, OK. And from the outset there were people who were against it. But in itself it was a moment in the Church when you were simply waiting on something new, on a renewal, a renewal of the whole. This was not to be something coming only from Rome, but a new encounter with the worldwide Church. In that respect the time was simply nigh.

The objective of the Council was, among other things, that a Pope, as you formulated it at the time, "not only verifies texts from above, but rather helps to shape them from the inside." A new physiognomy of the primacy was to make way for a new style of "togetherness" between Pope and bishops, in turning back to "that spirit of simplicity, which is the seal of their origin." It seems connected, right here fifty years later, as you tried to implement your interpretation of the texts of the Council, in ecclesiastical office, in style, in word, in deed, including even the appearance of the Pope. Correct?

Absolutely, yes.

CHAPTER 4

Prefect of the Congregation for the Doctrine of the Faith

In 1977, Ratzinger was appointed the Archbishop of Munich and Freising. Later that year, he was created a cardinal by Pope Paul VI. In 1981, Pope John Paul II named Ratzinger the Prefect of the Congregation for the Doctrine of the Faith, the Church's congregation for defending and clarifying Catholic doctrine. In this excerpt from 2016, Benedict XVI discusses his time as prefect, offering some insights into his close relationship with John Paul II.

Holy Father, on November 25, 1981, you were appointed Prefect of the Congregation for the Doctrine of the Faith, and hence alongside the Pope as the supreme guardian of the faith of the Catholic Church. On March 1, 1982, you reported for duty in Rome. It is said that the first major meetings you held in office were conducted in Latin.

I couldn't yet speak Italian. I'd only learned to join in conversations. Of course that remained my handicap too. I wasn't able to steer matters when speaking Italian then, so did it in Latin.

In the hope that you would be understood.

Then everyone could really still speak Latin, that wasn't a problem.

How was your first encounter with John Paul II in the Vatican? Was there a conversation about the fundamental orientation of the pontificate, and about your tasks particularly?

No. I did have the weekly audience. That gave plenty of time to interact. We didn't undertake any deliberations on policy. It was actually quite clear what a prefect had to do.

You once said that you got to know this great man better by concelebrating the Holy Mass with him than by analyzing his books. Why was that?

Yes, well, if you concelebrated with him, you felt the inward proximity to the Lord, the depth of faith which he would then plunge into, and you really experienced him as a man who believes, who prays, and who is indeed marked by the Spirit. This was more the case than if you read his books, although they also gave an image of him, but they certainly didn't let the whole of his personality emerge.

You had very different temperaments. Why did things work so well between you both? Or maybe that is precisely why it worked so well.

Maybe that's why, yes. He was a man who needed companionship, needed life, activity, needed encounters. I, however, needed silence more, and so on. But precisely because we were very different, we complemented each other well.

And simply because you liked each other?

Yes.

Because the chemistry was right?

That is correct.

And the same faith was there?

Exactly.

That makes it nice and easy.

Sure. Because you always know that you want the same thing.

Was there private contact too? Outings, meals, walks together?

Meals certainly, but always with a little group. No walks, actually.

And above all, no skiing.

[Laughs] No, I can't, unfortunately.

Did you use "Du"¹ when speaking with one another?

No.

As Archbishop of Munich, or as Prefect in Rome, were you assigned by the Pope to do any tasks in Poland? Tasks to support the opposition movement Solidarność?

No I wasn't.

You went to Poland several times in this period.

Certainly, yes, but not so that . . . There was a direct relationship then.

The state security service of the GDR had you under observation. There is a file on you.

Indeed, yes, but there was nothing to find.

Were you actively involved in the Pope's Ostpolitik?

We spoke about it. It was clear that Casaroli's politics [Cardinal Agostino Casaroli is regarded as the architect of the Vatican's *Ostpolitik* under John Paul II and Paul VI; under Karol Wojtyla he served as Cardinal Secretary of State from 1979 to 1990], although well intentioned, had basically failed. The new approach from John Paul II came from his own life experience, from contacts with these powers and forces. Of course, one could not hope then that this regime would soon collapse. But it was clear that, rather than trying to be reconciled with it through conciliatory compromises, one must strongly confront it. That was John Paul II's basic insight, which I shared.

---

1. "Du" is the German word for "you," used between friends and family members, as opposed to "Sie," a polite term used in more formal settings.

There were also disputes with one another.

No.

But probably differences. The Pope's prayer meeting in Assisi with representatives of the world religions, for example; that just wouldn't have been your favorite idea.

That's right, certainly. But we didn't argue about it, because I knew that he wanted the right thing, and, vice versa, he knew that I took a slightly different line. He said to me before the second meeting in Assisi that it would be very nice for him if I came along, so then I went too. It was also structured better then, because the objections I had were taken on board. It was then structured in a way that meant I could gladly participate.

It is alleged that John Paul II had a saying he used when confronted with a complicated question: "What will Cardinal Ratzinger say about it?" I asked you at the start of our first book, Salt of the Earth, *"Is the Pope afraid of you?"*

No. [Vigorous laughter] But he took our stand very seriously. I can tell you a little anecdote here. Pius XII was once asked by a nuncio whether or not he was allowed to do such-and-such with a certain problem, even if it was not entirely in keeping with the rules. The Pope mulled it over and then said: "You can. If, however, the Holy Office discover it, I cannot protect you." [Laughs]

One of your most sensational publications as Prefect was the declaration Dominus Jesus. *It is about the uniqueness of the Catholic Church, which unleashed fierce criticism. Whether or not you wrote this document yourself is a question being puzzled over to this day.*

I deliberately never wrote any of the documents of the office myself, so that my opinion does not surface; otherwise I would be attempting to disseminate and enforce my own private theology. Such a document should be grown organically, from the soil of the relevant offices responsible. Of course I was a co-worker, and did some critical redrafting, etc. But I didn't write any documents myself, including *Dominus Jesus.*

At the time the impression was conveyed that even the Pope was against this document.

Which is not true. He called me one day and said: "I want to speak about it during the Angelus and make it quite clear that I am in complete agreement with it, so I'm asking if you will write the text for the Angelus yourself, so there can be no doubt that the Pope is at one with you." So I wrote a text. But then I thought I shouldn't write so starkly, it didn't fit. The content was clear, but I made the style more elevated. He then said to me: "Is it really waterproof? Are you sure?"—"Yes, yes." But the opposite was the case. Because of this more elevated style everyone said: "Ah, even the Pope has distanced himself from the cardinal."

How was it with the great confession of guilt in 2000, whereby the Catholic Church apologized for her past failings and offences? Did you oppose this, as is often said?

No. I was there too. I mean, one can certainly ask oneself whether or not corporate confessions of guilt are really something meaningful. But even I maintained that it is something quite proper that the Church, following the example of the Psalms and the Book of Baruch, should also confess her guilt through the centuries.

Did the idea to produce the Catechism of the Catholic Church *come from you?*

Not only me, but I was involved. More and more people asked themselves then: does the Church still have a homogeneous set of doctrines? They no longer knew what the Church actually believes. There were some very strong tendencies, with really good people onside too, saying: a catechism cannot be produced any more. I said: either we still have something to say, in which case one must be able to describe it—or we have nothing left to say. In this way I made myself a champion of the idea, with the conviction that we must be in a position to say what the Church believes and teaches today.

25

Fides et Ratio, *Faith and reason, the 1998 encyclical—how much input did Cardinal Ratzinger have into this? None at all, or a little?*

A little, sure. Let's say, ideas.

Do you have a favorite anecdote from your relationship with John Paul II?

When the Pope was in Munich on his first trip to Germany, I saw what an incredible itinerary he had, that he was continuously busy from first thing in the morning till last thing at night. Then I thought to myself: This really shouldn't be done! You have to introduce a little rest. I then ensured there would be a nice lunchbreak. We had a lovely apartment in the Palais. He had only just gone up there at lunchtime when he called me, saying I should come up quickly. When I came up, he had just prayed with his breviary. I said: "Holy Father, you simply must rest now!" "I can rest in eternity," he said. I think that is very typical of him: I can rest in eternity. In the present he was always restless.

Which perhaps also applies to you a little. When I was able to interview you for the first time in November 1992, in any case, you frankly confessed that you were exhausted, tired, and would actually have liked to resign your office. But fresh vitality was to come.

In 1991 I had this brain hemorrhage, the effects of which were still very intense in 1992. The years 1991 to 1993 were somewhat onerous, I have to say: in terms of physical strength and psychological strength. Then, yes, I pulled myself together again.

As you so often did. When was the first time you asked for your dismissal?

I have to think about that earnestly. I pointed out to the Pope after my first Quinquennium [five years] in 1986 that my tenure was served. But he told me that wasn't the case. I then asked for it urgently in 1991. As I said, I had suffered a brain hemorrhage and was in a decidedly bad way. I said to him: "I can't do any more now." But the response was a "No."

And for the third time?

Before I could ask him about it he had already said: "You don't need to tell me, you don't need to write to me, saying that you want to be set free; it will not be heard. As long as I am here, you must stay."

CHAPTER 5

Habemus Papem

"We have a pope!" On April 19, 2005, Ratzinger was elected as the 265th pope, taking the name Benedict XVI. In this conversation, he recalls some of the events surrounding his election and reflects on the daily life and responsibilities of the pope.

Rarely before in a papal election has the vote been so fast and so unanimous. Even after the first ballots in the Sistine Chapel, the results "moved dynamically toward the new Pope," as Curia Cardinal Walter Kasper reports. You yourself uttered in the conclave a fervent prayer like the one we know from the Garden of Gethsemane: "Lord, don't do this to me! You have younger and better men."

Seeing the unbelievable now actually happen was really a shock. I was convinced that there were better and younger candidates. Why the Lord settled on me, I had to leave to him. I tried to keep my equanimity, all the while trusting that he would certainly lead me now. I would have to grow slowly into what I could do in each given situation and always limit myself to the next step. I find in particular this saying of the Lord so important for my whole life: "Do not be anxious about tomorrow. . . . Let the day's own trouble be sufficient for the day." One trouble a day is enough for man; more he cannot bear. That is why I try to concentrate on clearing away today's trouble and to leave the rest for tomorrow.

On the balcony of Saint Peter's Basilica, you said with a trembling voice during your first appearance that "after the great Pope John Paul II" God had now chosen "a simple and humble laborer in the vineyard of the Lord." It comforted you to think that the Lord "knows how to work . . . even with inadequate instruments." Now was that a papal understatement? After all, there were good reasons for electing you. No one has so publicly and intensively tackled the major issues as you have as a theologian: the relativism of modern society, the intra-ecclesial debate about the structure of the Church, reason and faith in the age of modern science. As Prefect of the Congregation for the Doctrine of the Faith, you helped shape the preceding pontificate. The Catechism of the Catholic Church, *one of the mammoth undertakings of the Wojtyła era, was produced under your direction.*

I did have a supervisory role, but I did nothing alone but was able to work in a team. Precisely as someone, among many others, who collaborates in the harvest of the Lord's vineyard. As foreman, perhaps, but nevertheless as someone who is not qualified to be the first and to carry the responsibility for the whole. So there was nothing left for me but to admit that there must be, besides the great Popes, little ones also, who give what they can. In this sense I said what I really felt at that moment.

For twenty-four years you stood at the side of John Paul II and knew the Curia like no one else. How long was it, though, until you fully realized how enormous the scope of this office really is?

One realizes very quickly that it is an immense office. If one knows that one already has a great responsibility as a chaplain, as a pastor, as a professor, then it is easy to extrapolate what an immense burden is imposed on the one who bears responsibility for the whole Church. But then of course one must be all the more aware that one does not do it alone. That one does it, on the one hand, with God's help and, on the other hand, in a great collaboration. Vatican II correctly taught us that collegiality is a constitutive element in the structure of the Church. That the Pope can only be first together with others and not someone who would make decisions in isolation as an absolute monarch and do everything himself.

Saint Bernard of Clairvaux in the twelfth century, at the request of Pope Eugene III, composed an examination of conscience with the title "What a Pope Must Consider." Bernard had a sincere dislike for the Roman Curia and recommended to the Pope vigilance above all else. In the commotion of business he must find detachment, maintain oversight, and continue to be decisive with regard to the abuses that a Pope in particular finds on every side. He feared most of all, Bernard writes, "that you, surrounded by business matters, the number of which only increases until you see no end to them, might harden your heart." Can you understand these "considerations" now from your own experience?

The "Consideration" by Saint Bernard is of course required reading for every Pope. There are great things in it, too, for example: Remember that you are not the successor of Emperor Constantine but rather the successor of a fisherman. The basic theme is the one that you have noted: Do not become utterly absorbed in activism! There would be so much to do that one could be working on it constantly. And that is precisely the wrong thing. Not becoming totally absorbed in activism means maintaining *consideratio*, discretion, deeper examination, contemplation, time for interior pondering, vision, and dealing with things, remaining with God and meditating about God. One should not feel obliged to work ceaselessly; this in itself is important for everyone, too, for instance, for every manager, too, and even more so for a Pope. He has to leave many things to others so as to maintain his inner view of the whole, his interior recollection, from which the view of what is essential can proceed.

Nevertheless, people have the impression that Pope Benedict is constantly busy, that he never takes a break.

No; well. . . .

You are one of the most diligent, perhaps even the most diligent worker of all the Popes.

But part of that is always meditation, reading Sacred Scripture, reflecting on what it says to me. One cannot simply work only on files. I do read as much there as I can. But I keep in mind the exhortation of Saint Bernard that one must not lose oneself in activism.

30

Paul VI, on the evening of his election as Pope, wrote in his diary: "I find myself in the papal chambers. A profound sense of uneasiness and confidence at the same time. . . . Then it is night, prayer and silence; no, it is not silence: the world watches and overtakes me. I must learn really to love it, the Church as she is, the world as it is."

Did you too, like Paul VI at the beginning, have a little fear of the masses of humanity whom you now must confront? Paul VI had even considered discontinuing the Angelus prayer at the window of the Apostolic Palace. He wrote, "What is this need to see a person? We have become a spectacle."

Yes, I understand the feelings of Paul VI very well. Here is the question: Is it really right for someone to present himself again and again to the crowd in that way and allow oneself to be regarded as a star? On the other hand, people have an intense longing to see the Pope. It is not so much a question then of contact with the person as it is of being physically in touch with this office, with the representative of the Holy One, with the mystery that there is a successor to Peter and someone who must stand for Christ. In this sense, then, one has to accept it and not refer the jubilation to oneself as a personal compliment.

Are you afraid of an assassination attempt?

No.

The Catholic Church is the first and greatest global player in world history. But everyone knows that she is not a business enterprise and the Pope is not a chief executive. How is it different from leading a multinational business empire?

Well, we are not a production plant, we are not a for-profit business, we are Church. That means a community of men standing together in faith. The task is not to manufacture some product or to be a success at selling merchandise. Instead, the task is to live the faith in an exemplary way, to proclaim it and at the same time to keep this voluntary association, which cuts across all cultures, nations, and times and . . . is not based on external interests, spiritually connected with Christ and so with God himself.

Were there mistakes at the beginning?

Probably. But I cannot tell now what in particular. Maybe one makes even more mistakes later, because one is no longer so careful.

Was the feeling of being locked up, though, a little oppressive at first? In other words, does the Pope sometimes, to put it casually, get away once in a while on the sly?

I don't do that. But the fact that one can no longer simply go on an excursion, visit friends, or just be at home, that I cannot simply be in my house in Pending again like I used to, walk together with my brother into the city, and go into a restaurant or look at something by myself is of course a loss. But the older you get, the less one takes the initiative, and in this respect one also puts up more easily with that loss.

Some think that the Pope is in a sort of isolation. That he breathes only filtered air and does not get any real sense of what is going on "out there." That he is not at all acquainted with the cares and needs of people.

Of course I cannot read all the newspapers and meet with an unlimited number of people. But there are, I believe, few people who have as many meetings as I do. Most important of all to me are my meetings with the bishops from all over the world. These are men who have both feet on the ground, and they do not come here because they would like something; they come in order to speak with me about the Church in their locality and about life in their locality. So in this way I can, after all, encounter the things of this world very humanly, personally, and realistically and observe them from an even closer perspective than from the newspaper. In this way I get a lot of background information.

Once in a while a mother comes along or a sister or a friend and would like to tell me one thing or another. There are, then, not just official visits but visits with quite a lot of human features. Then of course I find the papal household invaluable. In addition, friends from old times come to visit. All in all, therefore, I cannot say that I live in an artificial world of courtly personages; on the contrary, through these many meetings I experience very directly and personally the normal, everyday world of this time.

Does the Pope follow the news each day?

That too, of course.

History has already seen instances of Pope and anti-Pope. But seldom— or perhaps never before—have there been two successors of Peter whose pontificates were fused together—into a sort of millennial pontificate, so to speak—as John Paul II and Benedict XVI. Your predecessor was concerned with social problems worldwide, especially in Eastern Europe, whereas today the emphasis is more on the Church herself. Could one say that because of the ways in which John Paul II and Benedict XVI are different, they comple- ment one another perfectly? The one, so to speak, plowed—the other sows. The one opened—the other fills?

That might be saying too much. Time does go on, too. Meanwhile another new generation is here with new problems. The 1968 genera- tion with its peculiarities is established and past. The next generation, which then was more pragmatic, is aging already, too. Today the ques- tion is in fact: How do we manage in a world that is threatening itself, in which progress becomes a danger? Shouldn't we make a fresh start with God? The question about God confronts the new generation again, but in a different way. And the new generation in the Church is different, too; it is more positive than the breakthrough generation of the 1970s.

You have stepped up to devote yourself to an inner renewal of the Church. As you put it, it is necessary "to ensure that [God's] Word continues to be present in its greatness and to resound in its purity, so that it is not torn to pieces by continuous changes in usage." In your book about Jesus we read:

33

"The Church and the individual need constant purification. . . . What has become too big must be brought back to the simplicity and poverty of the Lord himself." In the business world one would say: Back to the beginning, to our core competence. What specifically does this inner renewal mean for your pontificate?

It means finding out where what is superficial and unnecessary is being dragged along—and, on the other hand, learning how we can succeed better at doing what is essential, so that we can really hear God's Word, live it out, and proclaim it in this time.

The Year of Saint Paul and the Year for Priests were two attempts at initiatives along these lines. To draw attention to the figure of Paul is to set the gospel before us in its original vitality, simplicity, and radicality, to make it present again. Precisely at a time when the sacrament of Holy Orders had been defiled so much, the Year for Priests was also supposed to present again in its beauty the unchangeable, unique task of this office, despite all the sufferings, despite all the horrible things. We must try to combine the humility and the greatness, so as to encourage priests again and give them joy in the priesthood.

The synods, too, help with this approach, for example, the Synod on the Word of God. Even the exchanges on this subject were very important. Today it is a question of setting forth the major themes and at the same time—as with the *caritas* encyclical, *God Is Love*—making visible again the center of Christian life and thus the simplicity of being a Christian.

One of your major themes is building a bridge between religion and rationality. Why do faith and reason belong together? Couldn't we also simply "just" believe? Jesus says, "Blessed are they who do not see and yet believe."

Not seeing is one thing, but even the faith of someone who does not see has to have its reasons. Jesus himself made faith thoroughly understandable by presenting it with an inner unity and in continuity with the Old Testament, with all of God's commands: as faith in the God who is the

Creator and the Lord of history, to whom history testifies and about whom creation speaks.

It is interesting that this essential rationality is already in the Old Testament a fundamental component of the faith; that particularly in the time of the Babylonian exile it is said: "Our God is not one or another of many; he is the Creator; the God of heaven; the one God." Thereby a claim is made, the universality of which was based precisely on its reasonableness. This core concept later became the meeting place between the Old Testament and Greek civilization. For at approximately the same time as the Babylonian exile singled out in particular this feature of the Old Testament, Greek philosophy also developed, which now looked beyond the gods and inquired about the one God.

Today it is still the major task of the Church to unite faith and reason with each other, to write looking beyond what is tangible and rational responsibility at the same time. For after all, reason was given to us by God. It is what distinguishes man.

Now what is the special charism that a Pope brings with him from Germany? The Germans for almost a thousand years were responsible for the Holy Roman Empire. Delving deeply for knowledge is one of the fundamental themes in German cultural history, as exemplified by mystics like Meister Eckhart, polymaths like Albertus Magnus, and on down to Goethe, Kant, and Hegel. Germany, admittedly, is also the land of schism, the cradle of scientific communism, which promised paradise, not in heaven, but on earth. And last but not least it is the scene of a truly diabolical regime that called for the total destruction of the Jews, the Chosen People of God.

As you have indicated, in Germany we have a complex, contradictory, and dramatic history. A history full of guilt and full of suffering. But also a history with human greatness. A history of holiness. A history of great intellectual achievement. In that respect there is not simply one German charism.

You pointed out that another particular feature of a German cultural history is thoughtfulness. For a long time this trait was viewed as

characteristic. Today people would probably view talents such as enterprise, energy, or efficiency as typically German instead. I think that
God, if he was going to make a professor Pope in the first place, wanted
this element of thoughtfulness and precisely this struggle for the unity
of faith and reason to come to the fore.

CHAPTER 6

The Resignation

On February 11, 2013, Benedict XVI surprised the Church and the world, announcing that he was resigning the papacy. In this excerpt, taken from his conversation with Peter Seewald in 2016, Benedict XVI explains the circumstances surrounding the decision, denounces claims of blackmail or conspiracy, and affirms that it was the right decision.

Now we come to that decision which in itself already makes your pontificate seem historic. Your resignation was the first time a genuinely ruling pontiff had stood down from his office. No one else has changed the papacy more deeply in modern times than you, with this revolutionary act. The Petrine foundation has come closer to us; it is more modern, and in a certain sense more human. Already in 2010 you explained in your book, Light of the World, *that if a pope is physically or psychologically no longer in a position to maintain office, he has the right and in some cases even the duty to step back from his job. Was there nevertheless a fierce inner struggle with this decision?*

[Deep intake of breath] Of course it was not entirely easy. No Pope has stood down for a thousand years; it was still an exception in the first thousand years of the papacy. It is a decision which was not taken easily, and which had to be mulled over again and again. On the other hand, the evidence was so great that there was no internal struggle. An awareness of its responsibility and seriousness called for the most thorough examination, time and again having to examine yourself before God and before yourself; that took place, yes, but not in the sense that it tore me to pieces.

Had you judged that your decision was also a disappointment, something that would cause bewilderment?

That was perhaps more intense than I thought it would be, because friends, people, were stopped in their tracks at my news. For them it was serious and groundbreaking; at that moment they were really distressed and felt forsaken.

Did you take into account the shock it would cause?

I had to accept it, yes.

It must have expended an incredible amount of energy.

With matters like these one is helped. But it was also clear to me that I had to do it and that this was the right moment. People then also accepted this. Many are grateful that there is now a new Pope approaching them with a new style. Others may still mourn somewhat, but they have also come to be grateful. They know that my hour had passed and I had given all I could give.

When was your mind made up?

I would say during the summer holiday of 2012.

August?

Thereabouts, yes.

Were you in a depression?

Not a depression, no, but things weren't going well for me. I realized the trip to Mexico and Cuba had really taken it out of me. The doctor also said to me that I could not fly over the Atlantic again. As scheduled, World Youth Day was supposed to be in Rio in 2014. Because of the football World Cup it was brought forward by one year. It was clear to me that I must step down in plenty of time for the new Pope to plan for

Rio. In this respect the decision matured gradually after the Mexico-Cuba trip. Otherwise I would have had to try holding out until 2014. But I knew that I could no longer manage it.

How does one manage to carry out a decision on this scale without anyone to talk with about it?

You talk about it extensively with the loving God.

Did you confide in your brother?

Not immediately, but I did. Yes, yes.

Until shortly before the announcement, only four people had been confided in. Was there a reason for this?

Yes of course, because the moment the people knew, the mandate would crumble, since its authority disintegrates then. It was also important that my position was genuinely occupied and my service could be done fully up to the last.

Were you afraid someone would talk you out of taking this step?

No [amused laughter], I mean, there was that, but I wasn't fearful because I had an inner certainty that it had to be done, and that isn't something you can be talked out of.

When and by whom was the text of your resignation speech written?

By me. I couldn't tell you now exactly when, but I wrote it at the most fourteen days beforehand.

Why in Latin?

Because you do something so important in Latin. Furthermore, Latin is the language that I've so mastered that I can write in it properly. I could have written it in Italian, but with the danger that there would be a couple of mistakes in it.

You wanted to resign originally in December, but then settled on February 11, Rose Monday, feast day of Our Lady of Lourdes. Does this have a symbolic significance?

I was not aware of the fact that it was Rose Monday. This caused disturbances in Germany. It was the day of Madonna of Lourdes.[1] The feast of Bernadette of Lourdes is on my birthday though. In this sense there are connections, and it seems right to me that I did it on this day.

So this moment in time has . . .

. . . certainly an inner connection, yes.

How do you remember this historic day? It can be assumed you didn't sleep particularly well the night before.

But it's not all bad. To the general public, of course, it was a new and tremendous step, which is how I saw it. But I had wrestled with it inwardly the whole time, so my inward self was to some extent already weathered. In this sense it was not a day of particular suffering for me.

Did everything go as normal that morning, with the usual routine?

I would say so, yes.

The same prayers . . . ?

The same prayers, and, of course, a couple said intensively for that hour, certainly.

You didn't awake earlier, or eat breakfast late?

No, no.

---

1. Rose Monday (*Rosenmontag*) is in some German-speaking regions the highlight of the Carnival before Lent; it is the Monday before Shrove Tuesday.

Around seventy cardinals sat in a horseshoe shape in the huge hall with the beautiful name Sala del Concistoro.[2] It was a consistory scheduled to announce various canonizations, so as you entered the room no one could have expected what was going to happen.

We had planned a couple of canonizations, yes.

The astonishment began as you started to speak in Latin: "Dearly esteemed cardinals, I have not gathered you together only to let you participate in the canonizations, but I also have something of great importance to tell you." Everyone was already confused. As you continued reciting your statement, some faces came over petrified, others in disbelief, or helpless, astounded. When the dean of the College of Cardinals, Angelo Sodano, first took the floor, all that had happened became clear. Did the cardinals speak to you immediately afterwards, or bombard you, even?

[Laughs] No, that would not happen. After the consistory the Pope goes out solemnly, so no one bombards him. In such situations the Pope is sovereign.

On this day, about which historians still write, what was going through your head?

The question: "What will mankind be saying as I stand there?," of course. It was a sad day in my household, naturally. I brought myself before the Lord in a particular way throughout the day. But there was nothing specific.

In the resignation speech the reason you gave for relinquishing your office was the diminishing of your energy. But is a slowdown in the ability to perform, reason enough to climb down from the chair of Peter?

One can of course make that accusation, but it would be a functional misunderstanding. The follower of Peter is not merely bound to a function; the office enters into your very being. In this regard, fulfilling a

---

2. The "Hall of the Consistory" is in the Apostolic Palace in Vatican City.

function is not the only criterion. Then again, the Pope must do concrete things, must keep the whole situation in his sights, must know which priorities to set, and so on. This ranges from receiving heads of state, receiving bishops—with whom one must be able to enter into a deeply intimate conversation—to the decisions which come each day. Even if you say a few of these things can be struck off, there remain so many things which are essential, that, if the capability to do them is no longer there—for me anyway; someone else might see it otherwise— now's the time to free up the chair.

Cardinal Reginald Pole (1500–58), to whom you referred in a lecture, says in his theology of the cross: the cross is the authentic place of the representative of Christ. There is a martyrological structure of the papal primacy.

That was deeply moving to me then. I'd had a dissertation written about him by one of my students. It is certainly enduringly true, and thus the Pope must each day bear witness, must take up his cross each day and always be a martyr, in the sense of being a martyr to the sufferings of the world and its problems. That is something very important. If a pope were only ever applauded, he would have to ask himself whether or not he was doing things right. The message of Christ is a scandal for the world, beginning with Christ himself. There will always be opposition, and the Pope must be a sign of contradiction. This is a criterion which concerns him. That doesn't mean, however, that he must die by the sword.

Did you want to stop yourself being on display to the world in the way your predecessor was?

My predecessor had his own mission. I am convinced that—after he took it up with mighty force, took all of humanity on his shoulders as it were, and for twenty years bore the weight and the suffering of the centuries, he had proclaimed his message—a period of suffering belonged to that pontificate. And it was a unique message. People have seen it in this way. He's actually held so fondly by them as a sufferer. You come close to people's hearts if you are laid open. This was definitely his significance. However, I was convinced that one may not arbitrarily repeat this. It seemed to me after a pontificate of eight years it was not possible to cling on for another eight years.

You say that you sought counsel on your decision. Indeed, with your ultimate boss. How was that?

You have to lay out all your affairs before Him as clearly as possible and try not to see everything only in terms of efficiency or other criteria for resignation, but to look at it from faith. It was from precisely this perspective that I became convinced that the commission of Peter demanded concrete decisions, insights, from me, but then, when it was no longer possible for me for the foreseeable future, that the Lord no longer wanted me to do it and freed me from the burden, as it were.

There was a report that you had a "mystical experience" which brought you to this step.

That was a misunderstanding.

Are you at peace with God?

Indeed, I really am.

Did you feel that your pontificate was somehow exhausted, that it was no longer moving forward correctly? Or that possibly the person of the Pope was no longer the solution but the problem?

Not in that way, no. I mean, I was certainly conscious that I was not able to give very much any longer. But that I was, so to speak, the problem for the Church, this was not and is not my view.

Did being disappointed by your own people play a role, feeling there was insufficient support?

Not that either. I mean, the Paolo Gabriele affair was a disastrous business. But first, I was not to blame—he was checked by the authorities and put in post by them—and second, one has to reckon with such things in human beings. I am not aware of any failures on my part.

Nevertheless the Italian media speculated that the true background to your resignation is to be found in the Vatileaks affair, not only in the Paolo Gabriele case, but also in the financial problems and intrigues among the Curia. Ultimately you were so shocked at the 300-page investigation report into these things that you could see no other way out other than to make space for a successor.

No, that is not right, not at all. On the contrary, the Vatileaks matter was completely resolved. I said while it was still happening—I believe it was to you—that one is not permitted to step back when things are going wrong, but only when things are at peace. I could resign because calm had returned to this situation. It was not a case of retreating under pressure or feeling that things couldn't be coped with.

In some newspapers there was even talk of blackmail and conspiracy.

That's all complete nonsense. No, it's actually a straightforward matter. I have to say on this that a man—for whatever reason—thought he had to create a scandal to clean up the Church. But no one has tried to blackmail me. If that had been attempted I would not have gone, since you are not permitted to leave because you're under pressure. It's also not the case that I would have bartered or whatever. On the contrary, the moment had—thanks to be God—a sense of having overcome the difficulties and a mood of peace. A mood in which one really could confidently pass the reins over to the next person.

One objection is that the papacy has been secularized by the resignation; that it is no longer a unique office but an office like any other.

I had to accept that question, and consider whether or not functionalism would completely encroach on the papacy, so to speak. But similar steps had already been made with the episcopacy. Earlier, bishops were not allowed to resign. There were a number of bishops who said, "I am a father and that I'll stay," because you can't simply stop being a father; stopping is a functionalization and secularization, something from the sort of concept of public office that shouldn't apply to a bishop. To that I must reply: even a father's role stops. Of course a father does not stop being a father, but he is relieved of concrete responsibility. He remains a father in a deep, inward sense, in a particular relationship which has responsibility, but not with day-to-day tasks as such. It was also this way for bishops. Anyway, since then it has generally come to be understood that on the one hand the bishop is bearer of a sacramental mission which remains binding on him inwardly, but on the other hand this does not have to keep him in his function forever. And so I think it is also clear that the Pope is no superman and his mere existence is not sufficient to conduct his role; rather, he likewise exercises a function. If he steps down, he remains in an inner sense within the responsibility he took on, but not in the function. In this respect one comes to understand that the office of the Pope has lost none of its greatness, even if the humanity of the office is perhaps becoming more clearly evident.

Immediately after the announcement of your decision, the Curia went into their Lenten retreat, as always on Ash Wednesday. Was anything said about your resignation on retreat at least?

No, retreats are places of silence, of listening, of prayer. Of course it was part of the whole plan of the resignation for it to be followed by a week of silence, where everyone is able to work it out inwardly, or the bishops, cardinals and staff of the Curia at least. Because then everyone is taken away from external things and they interiorly face the Lord together. So it was good and poignant for me that, on the one hand, there was seclusion and silence and no one could disturb me—because there were no audiences, everyone was taken out of the hustle and bustle and we were very close on an inner level, all of us prayed and listened together four times a day with each other—but on the other hand everyone stood in his own personal responsibility before the Lord. So, I have to say the planning was very good. In retrospect I think it was better even than I was aware of at first.

Have you ever regretted the resignation even for a minute?

No! No, no. Every day I see that it was right.

So you haven't once yet said to yourself, maybe . . .

No, definitely not. It was considered long enough and spoken about with the Lord.

Were there any aspects to it which you had not thought of? Something which perhaps only became clear in retrospect?

No.

So you also considered whether or not there might in future be legitimate demands against a Pope calling for him to resign?

Of course you are not permitted to yield to demands. I therefore emphasized in my speech that I was acting freely. One is not allowed to go away if one is running away. One cannot submit to coercion. One can only turn away when no one has demanded it. And no one demanded it of me during my time as Pope. No one. It came as a complete surprise to everyone.

But it might have surprised you that through your resignation a turn to another continent was immediately inaugurated.

In the holy Church one must always be prepared for anything.

PART II

GOD

CHAPTER 7

Prolegomena on the Subject of God

In 1968, Ratzinger published *Introduction to Christianity*, which has remained one of his most popular works. The book was drawn from a series of lectures on the articles of the Apostles' Creed that then-Fr. Ratzinger delivered at the University of Tübingen, where he was a professor. The following excerpt is taken from the opening of his discussion of God, where Ratzinger speaks to the questions that have become prominent in modern times.

What in fact is "God" really? In other ages this question may have seemed quite clear and unproblematical; for us it has become a genuine inquiry again. What can this word "God" signify? What reality does it express, and how does the reality concerned make contact with man? If one wished to pursue the question with the thoroughness really needed today, one would first have to attempt an analysis, from the angle of the philosophy of religion, of the sources of religious experience. Such an inquiry would also have to consider how it is that the theme of God has left its stamp on the whole history of humanity and right up to the present can raise such passionate argument—yes, right up to this very moment when the cry that God is dead resounds on every side and when nevertheless, in fact for this very reason, the question of God casts its shadow overpoweringly over all of us.

Where does this idea of "God" really come from? From what roots does it grow? How is it that what is apparently the most superfluous, and, from an earthly point of view, most useless, subject in history has at the same time remained the most insistent one? And why does this subject appear in such fundamentally different forms? So far as this point is concerned, it could of course be demonstrated that in spite of a confusing appearance of extreme variety the subject exists in only three forms (which occur in a number of different variations, of course)—monotheism, polytheism, and atheism, as one can briefly describe the three main paths taken by human history on the question of God. Moreover, we have already noted that even atheism's dismissal of the subject of God is only apparent, that in reality it represents a form of man's concern with the question of God, a form that can express a particular passion about this question and not infrequently does. If we wanted to pursue the fundamental preliminary questions, it would then be necessary to describe the two roots of religious experience to which the manifold forms of this experience can almost certainly be traced back. The peculiar tension existing between them was once defined by van der Leeuw, the well-known Dutch expert on the phenomenology of religion, in the paradoxical assertion that in the history of religion God the Son was there before God the Father. It would be more accurate to say that God the Savior, God the Redeemer appears earlier than God the Creator, and even this clarification must be qualified by the reminder that the formula is not to be taken in the sense of a temporal succession, for which there is no kind of evidence. As far back as we can see in the history of religion the subject always occurs in both forms. Thus the word "before" can only mean that for concrete religious feeling, for the living existential interest, the Savior stands in the foreground as compared with the Creator.

Behind this twofold form in which humanity saw its God stand those two points of departure of religious experience of which we spoke just now. One is the experience of one's own existence, which again and again oversteps its own bounds and in some form or other, however concealed, points to the entirely Other. This, too, is a process with many layers—as many layers as human existence itself. Bonhoeffer thought, as is well known, that it was time to finish with a God whom we insert to fill the gap at the limit of our own powers, whom we call up when we ourselves are at the end of our tether. We ought to find God, he thought, not, so to speak, in our moments of need and failure, but amid the fullness of earthly life; only in this way could it be shown that God is not an escape, constructed by necessity, which becomes more and more superfluous as the limits of our powers expand. In the story of man's striving for God, both ways exist, and both seem to me equally legitimate. Both the poverty of human existence and its fullness point to God. Where men have experienced existence in its fullness, its wealth, its beauty, and its greatness, they have always become aware that this existence is an existence for which they owe thanks; that precisely in its brightness and greatness it is not what I myself have obtained but the bestowed that comes to meet me, welcomes me with all its goodness before I have done anything, and thus requires of me that I *give* a meaning to such riches and thereby *receive* a meaning. On the other hand, man's poverty has also acted again and again as a pointer to the entirely Other. The question that human existence not only poses but itself *is*, the inconclusiveness inherent in it, the bounds it comes up against and that yet yearn for the unbounded (more or less in the sense of Nietzsche's assertion that all pleasure yearns for eternity yet experiences itself as a moment), this simultaneity of being limited and of yearning for the unbounded and open has always prevented man from resting in himself, made him sense that he is not self-sufficient but only comes to himself by going outside himself and moving toward the entirely Other and infinitely greater.

The same thing could be demonstrated in the theme of loneliness and security. Loneliness is indubitably one of the basic roots from which man's encounter with God has risen. Where man experiences his solitariness, he experiences at the same time how much his whole existence is a cry for the "You" and how ill-adapted he is to be only an "I" in himself. This loneliness can become apparent to man on various levels. To start with, it can be comforted by the discovery of a human "You." But then there is the paradox that, as Claudel says, every "You" found by man finally turns out to be an unfulfilled and unfulfillable promise; that every "You" is at bottom another disappointment and that there comes a point when no encounter can surmount the final loneliness: the very process of finding and of having found thus becomes a pointer back to the loneliness, a call to the absolute "You" that really descends into the depths of one's own "I." But even here it remains true that it is not only the need born of loneliness, the experience that no sense of community fills up all our longing, that leads to the experience of God; it can just as well proceed from the joy of security. The very fulfillment of love, of finding one another, can cause man to experience the gift of what he could neither call up nor create and make him recognize that in it he receives more than either of the two could contribute. The brightness and joy of finding one another can point to the proximity of absolute joy and of the simple fact of being found that stands behind every human encounter.

All this is just intended to give some idea of how human existence can be the point of departure for the experience of the absolute, which from this angle is seen as "God the Son," as the Savior, or, more simply, as a God related to existence. The other source of religious perception is the confrontation of man with the world, with the powers and the sinister forces he meets in it. Again, it remains true that the cosmos has brought man to the experience of the all-surpassing power that both threatens him and bears him up as much through its beauty and abundance as through its deficiencies, its terrors, and its unfathomability. Here the resulting image is the somewhat vaguer and more distant one crystallized in the image of God the Creator, the Father.

If one were to pursue further the questions here adumbrated one would spontaneously run up against the problem, touched on above, of the three varieties of theism to be found in history—monotheism, polytheism, and atheism. Then, so it seems to me, the underlying unity of these three paths would become apparent, a unity that of course cannot be synonymous with identity and cannot imply that, if one only digs deep enough, everything finally becomes one and foreground differences lose their importance. Such demonstrations of identity, which philosophical thinking might feel tempted to undertake, take no note of the seriousness of human decisions and could certainly not do justice to reality. But even if there can be no question of identity, a deeper look would be able to recognize that the differences between the three great paths lie elsewhere than is suggested by their three labels, which declare respectively: "There is one God"; "There are many Gods"; and "There is no God." Between these three formulas and the professions contained in them there exists an opposition that cannot be swept aside, but there also exists a relationship of which the mere words contain no hint. For all three—this could be demonstrated—are in the last analysis convinced of the unity and oneness of the absolute. It is not only monotheism that believes in this unity and oneness; even for polytheism the many gods that it worshipped and in which it placed its hopes were never the absolute itself; even to the polytheist it was clear that somewhere or other behind the many powers there stood the one Being, that in the last resort being was either one or at any rate the eternal strife of two principles opposed to each other from the beginning. On the other hand, although atheism disputes the recognition of the unity of all being through the idea of God, this does not mean at all that for the atheist the unity of being itself is abolished. Indeed, the most influential form of atheism, namely Marxism, asserts in the strictest form this unity of being in all that is by declaring all being to be matter; in this view, granted, the one thing that is being itself becomes, as matter, completely separated from the earlier concept of the absolute, which is linked to the idea of God, but it simultaneously acquires features that make its absoluteness clear and thus once again recall the idea of God.

Thus all three paths are convinced of the unity and uniqueness of the absolute; where they differ is only in their notions of the manner in which man has to deal with the absolute or, alternatively, of how the absolute behaves toward him. If—to treat the question very schematically—monotheism starts from the assumption that the absolute is consciousness, which knows man and can speak to him, for materialism the absolute, being matter, is devoid of all personal predicates and can in no way be brought into contact with the concepts of call and answer; the most one could say is that man himself must liberate what is divine from matter, so that he would then no longer have God behind him as something that had gone before him but only in front of him as something to be creatively effected by him, as his own better future. Finally, polytheism can be closely related to both monotheism and atheism, because the powers of which it speaks imply the oneness of a supporting power, which can be thought of in either way. Thus it would not be difficult to show how in antiquity polytheism went perfectly well with a metaphysical atheism but was also combined with philosophical monotheism.

All these questions are important if one wishes to pursue the subject of God in our present situation today. To deal with them adequately would of course require a great deal of time and patience. It must, therefore, suffice here to have at any rate mentioned them; we shall meet them again and again if we now go on to consider the fate of the idea of God in the faith of the Bible, an investigation of which is demanded by our subject. While we thus follow up further the problem of God at one quite specific point, we shall remain confronted with humanity's universal struggle for its God and open to the full scope of the question.

CHAPTER 8

God: The Essential Matter

In his interview book with Peter Seewald entitled *God and the World*, published in English in 2002, Ratzinger addresses a wide variety of topics on Catholic theology and spirituality. In this excerpt, Seewald poses some fundamental questions about the nature of God. Seewald's words appear in italics.

Can we say what [God] is like? The Old Testament tells us of great out-breaks of wrath and subsequent acts of judgment. "For I, the Lord your God," he says then, "am a jealous God: and to those who hate me, I punish the guilt of the fathers in the sons, as far as the third and fourth generation." Is God still as wrathful as he used to be, or has he changed?

The very first thing I would like to do is to complete the quotation. In fact, it says: "I extend the punishment to the third or fourth generation, but my mercy lasts for a *thousand* generations." We can see how this oracle portrays an unequal balance between wrath and mercy. Mercy is a thousand times greater, as compared with wrath, and in this sense the oracle means that although I may have merited punishment and thus have fallen out of God's love, I can always be sure that God's mercy is a thousand times greater.

But this Judeo-Christian God does show himself to be wrathful.

The wrath of God is a way of saying that I have been living in a way that is contrary to the love that is God. Anyone who begins to live and grow away from God, who lives away from what is good, is turning his life toward wrath. Whoever falls away from love is moving into nega-tivity. So that is not something that some dictator with a lust for power inflicts on you, but is simply a way of expressing the inner logic of a certain action. If I move outside the area of what is compatible with the ideal model by which I am created, if I move beyond the love that sustains me, well then, I just fall into the void, into darkness. I am then no longer in the realm of love, so to speak, but in a realm that can be seen as the realm of wrath.

When God inflicts punishment, this is not punishment in the sense that God has, as it were, drawn up a system of fines and penalties and is wanting to pin one on you. "The punishment of God" is in fact an expression for having missed the right road and then experiencing the consequences that follow from taking the wrong track and wandering away from the right way of living.

But does one not necessarily have a feeling of dependence, even of being led by the hand like a child, when it says: "It is God who brings into being within you both the will and the action." What kind of a God is that, who always has to be showing us how we are nothing without him? Doesn't he, for his part, bear some responsibility for us? For who can do anything about the fact that he is living here on earth? There are plenty of people who are not exactly overjoyed about it.

It is important that the Church should draw a large enough image of God and not decorate it with artificial dreadful threats. In the past that did happen in part of catechetic teaching, and perhaps it still happens here and there. In contrast to this, we must present a picture of God, in all his greatness, as seen through Christ, a God who gives us a great deal of free play. Sometimes one would almost rather he spoke to us somewhat more clearly. We would be more inclined to ask: Why does he let us have so much room to maneuver? Why does he let evil have so much freedom and so much power? Why doesn't he intervene more positively?

Let us stay with God, with the question of where and how we can find him. There's a little story about this: Once, a mother brought her son to the rabbi. Then the rabbi asked the boy something: "I will give you a guilder if you can tell me where God lives." The boy didn't need to think about it very long; he answered: "And I will give you two guilders if you can tell me where he doesn't live." In the Book of Wisdom, it says that God "lets himself be found

56

by those who do not tempt him and shows himself to those who do not mistrust him." But where exactly is God?

Let us start with the Book of Wisdom. There we find a saying that seems to me to speak to us today: "God does not let himself be found by those who put him to the test," that is to say, he does not allow himself to be found by those who wish to conduct experiments on him. This truth was already known in the Hellenistic world, and it hits its mark right up to today. If we want to, so to speak, test God—are you there or not?—and undertake certain things to which we think he must either react or not react, if we make him the object, so to speak, of our experiment, then we have set off in a direction that will not lead us to find him. God is not prepared to submit to experiments. He is not a thing we can hold in our hand.

One of my friends says, I don't feel anything, even if I go to church on a Sunday. I merely see there's nothing there.

God is just not something we could ever force to call out at given moments: "Oh, here I am." God is found precisely when we do not subject him to the criteria of falsification used by modern experiments and existential proof, but when we regard him as God. And to look on him as being God means to stand in a quite different relation to him.

I can actively and methodically investigate material things; I can subject them to my control, because they are inferior to me. But even another person is beyond my understanding if I treat him in this way. On the contrary, I only come to know something of him when I begin to put myself in his place, to get inside him, by some kind of sympathy.

This is more than ever true of God. I can only begin to seek God by setting aside this attitude of domination. In its place I have to develop an attitude of availability, of opening myself, of searching. I must be ready to wait in all humility—and to allow him to show himself in the manner he chooses, not as I would like him to do it.

57

But just where is God exactly?

As your rabbinic story shows us quite beautifully, he is not in any particular place. To put it more positively: There is nowhere where he is not, because he is in everything. Or to put it negatively: He is never where sin is. Whenever contradiction exalts nonbeing to a position of power—he is not there.

God is everywhere, and yet there are various stages in his proximity, because each higher level of being is a little closer to him. But wherever understanding and love grow, we reach a new kind of closeness, a new form of his presence.

God is present, then, wherever faith and hope and love are, because they, contrary to what happens with sin, constitute the personal space within which we move into the dimensions of God. Thus God is present in a quite specific sense in every place where something good is happening, a sense that goes beyond his general omnipresence and his comprehension of all being. He may be encountered as a more profound presence wherever we approach those dimensions of existence that most closely correspond to his inner being—namely, those of truth and love, of goodness of any kind.

This "more profound presence"—does that mean that God is not somewhere or other far away out in space, but is right here in our midst? He is within each individual person.

Yes, that is what Paul said in his speech to the Athenians on the Areopagus. In that speech he quotes a Greek poet: In God we live and move and have our being.

That we exist and move within the atmosphere of God the Creator, that is obviously true, first of all, purely from the point of view of our biological existence. And it becomes ever more true, the more we penetrate into the quite specific essence of God. We can put it this way: Wherever one person does something good for another, there God is especially near. Whenever someone opens himself for God in prayer, then he enters into his special closeness.

God is not an entity who can be located in accordance with physical or spatial categories. He is not so many thousands of miles up or at a distance of so many light years. The closeness of God is instead a closeness in terms of categories of being. Wherever there is something that best reflects him and makes him present, where there is truth and goodness, in those cases we are in contact with him, the Omnipresent, in a special way.

But that also means that God is not automatically there; he is not always present.

He is always present in the sense that without him I should be cut off from the aggregate stream of existent being, if you like to put it like that. In this sense, there is a certain presence of God, a simply existent presence, everywhere. But the more profound presence of God, the presence that is a gift to man, can fade or even disappear altogether—or, on the contrary, it can become really strong.

In someone in whom God is present through and through, there is naturally a much stronger presence of God, a greater inner closeness, than in the case of someone who has completely distanced himself from God. Let's consider the Annunciation to Mary. God wishes Mary to become his temple, a living temple, and not merely by physical occupation of her body. But it only becomes possible for God truly to dwell in her because she opens herself to him inwardly; because she develops her inner being to become entirely compatible with him.

But might it not equally be the case that God withdraws himself, at least temporarily. Einstein, for example, revered God as architect of the universe but also in the end held the opinion that God took no further interest in his creation or in the fate of man.

This idea of God as the master builder, as the great architect of the universe, comes from entertaining too narrow an image of God. Here, God is only the marginal hypothesis, the theory we still find necessary in order to explain the origin of the universe. He puts it all together, so to speak, and then it starts working. But since, in relation to the world, he was nothing more than the final cause in a system of physics, quite naturally, therefore, he left the stage after that. And now nature is a complete working system, but God is unable to move, and his relationship to the human heart, to this other dimension of existence, is what this kind of picture of creation is, from the start, quite unable to envisage. In this perspective, he is no longer "the living God," but really a kind of hypothesis, and this hypothesis is intended, in the end, to be likewise redundant.

But still, theologians sometimes talk about an "absence of God."

That is something quite different. We already find in the Holy Scriptures this business of God hiding. God hides from disobedient people. He is silent. He does not send any prophets. And in the lives of saints, too, there is this dark night. They are, so to speak, thrust into a kind of absence, the silence of God, as for instance happened to Thérèse of Lisieux, and they then have to share in the darkness of the unbeliever.

That certainly does not mean that God does not exist. Equally, it does not mean that he has become powerless or that he is no longer loving. Here it is a matter of situations in the history of mankind, or in certain people's lives, in which their inability to perceive God brings about a kind of "darkness" of God, as Martin Buber expressed it. In this inability or unwillingness to perceive God or to relate to him, God then appears to have withdrawn.

CHAPTER 9

One God in Three Persons

At the heart of the Christian faith is belief in the triune God: Father, Son, and Holy Spirit. In this excerpt, taken from his book *The God of Jesus Christ: Meditations on the Triune God*, Ratzinger sheds light on the meaning of this great mystery and its impact on our spiritual lives.

God is as Father, Son, and Holy Spirit, three and one. This is the very heart of Christianity, but it is so often shrouded in a silence born of perplexity. Has the Church perhaps gone one step too far here? Ought we not rather leave something so great and inaccessible as God in his inaccessibility? Can something like the Trinity have any real meaning for us? Well, it is certainly true that the proposition that "God is three and God is one" is and remains the expression of his otherness, which is infinitely greater than we and transcends all our thinking and our existence. But if this proposition had nothing to say to us, it would not have been revealed. And as a matter of fact, it could be clothed in human language only because it had already penetrated human thinking and living to some extent.

What, then, does this mean? Let us begin at the point where God himself began. He calls himself Father. Human fatherhood can give us an inkling of what God is; but where fatherhood no longer exists, where genuine fatherhood is no longer experienced as a phenomenon that goes beyond the biological dimension to embrace a human and intellectual sphere as well, it becomes meaningless to speak of God the Father. Where human fatherhood disappears, it is no longer possible to speak and think of God. It is not God who is dead; what is dead (at least to a large extent) is the precondition in man that makes it possible for God to live in the world. The crisis of fatherhood that we are experiencing today is a basic aspect of the crisis that threatens mankind as a whole. Where fatherhood is perceived only as a biological accident on which no genuinely human claims may be based, or the father is seen as a tyrant whose yoke must be thrown off, something in the basic structure of human existence has been damaged. If human existence is to be complete, we need a father, in the true meaning of fatherhood that our faith discloses, namely, a responsibility for one's child that does not dominate him but permits him to become his own self. This fatherhood is a love that avoids two traps: the total subjugation of the child to the father's own priorities and goals, on the one hand, and the unquestioning acceptance of the child as he is, under the pretext that this is the expression of freedom, on the other. Responsibility for one's child means the desire that he realize his own innermost truth, which lies in his Creator. And naturally, a fatherhood of this kind is possible only if one accepts one's own status as a child. If men are to be fathers in the correct way, they must assent in their heart to the words of Jesus: "You have only one Father, who is heaven" (Matt. 23:9). This has nothing to do with a domination that makes others one's slaves. It is a responsibility born of truth: because I have freely handed myself over to God, I can now free the other to be himself, without egoism, free for the God in whom he has his existence.

Here, of course, another point is important: the fact that the primary biblical image of God is the "Father" also means that the mystery of motherhood, too, has its origin in him and has exactly the same potential as fatherhood either to point to God or, when it is distorted, to point away from him. Here we can grasp what it means in real and very practical terms to affirm that man is "the image of God." Man is not God's image as an abstraction—for that would lead in turn only to an abstract God. He is God's image in his concrete reality, which is relationship: he is God's image as father, as mother, as child ("son"). This means that when we apply these words to God, they are "images"; but they are images precisely because man is an "image," and therein lies their claim to reality. They are images that require "the Image," and this means that they can be the realization of God or his "death." We cannot separate man's becoming man and his knowledge of God precisely because he is "the image" of God. When his humanity is destroyed, something happens to the image of God. The dissolution of fatherhood and motherhood, which some would prefer to relocate in a laboratory[1] or at least reduce to a biological moment that does not concern man *qua* man, is linked to the dissolution of childhood, which must give way to a total equality from the very beginning. This is a program of hubris, which at one and the same time wants to remove man from the biological sphere and enslaves him completely within it; this hubris reaches into the very roots of human existence and into the roots of the ability to think of God, for where he can no longer be depicted in an image, it is no longer possible to think of him. Where human thought employs all its power to make it impossible to depict God in an image, no "proof of God's existence" can ever have anything to say.

Naturally, we must not indulge in wild exaggerations when we criticize the age in which we live. To begin with, we must not forget that there are exemplary fathers and mothers even today, and that great figures such as Janusz Korczak and Mother Teresa demonstrate in our age that the reality of fatherhood and motherhood can be achieved even without the biological dimension. Besides this, we must always remember that the utterly pure realization of the image of God has always been an exception: God's image in man has always been stained and distorted. This is why it is empty romanticism to plead: "Spare us the dogmas, the Christology, the Holy Spirit, the Trinity! It suffices to proclaim God as Father and all men as brothers and to live this without any mystical theories. That is the only thing that matters!" This sounds very plausible, but does this really do justice to the complicated being called man? How do we know what fatherhood is or what it means to be brothers and sisters? What entitles us to put so much trust in these realities? There are indeed moving testimonies in early cultures to a pure trust in the "Father" in the skies, but subsequent development mostly

---

1. [This text was written several years before the birth of the first "test-tube baby" in England in 1978.—Trans.]

meant that religious attention very quickly moved away from him to concentrate on "powers" that were much closer at hand; in the course of history, the image of man, and hence also the image of God, everywhere took on ambiguous traits. It is well known that the Greeks called their Zeus "Father." But this word was not an expression of their trust in him! Rather, it expressed the profound ambiguity of the god and the tragic ambiguity, indeed, the terrible character of the world. When they said "Father," they meant that Zeus was like human fathers—sometimes really nice, when he was in a good mood, but ultimately an egoist, a tyrant, unpredictable, unfathomable, and dangerous. And this was how they experienced the dark power that ruled the world: some individuals are courted as favorites, but this power stands by indifferently while other individuals starve to death, are enslaved, or go to ruin. The "Father" of the world, as he is experienced in human life, reflects human fathers: partisan and, in the last analysis, terrible.

People today bid farewell to the world of the fathers and sing the enthusiastic praises of "brotherhood." But in our de facto experience, is brotherhood really so unambiguous, so full of hope? According to the Bible, the first pair of brothers in world history were Cain and Abel; in Roman myth, we find the corresponding pair of Romulus and Remus. This motif is found everywhere and is a cruel parody—but one written by reality itself—of the hymn to "brotherhood." Have not our experiences since 1789 contributed new and even more dreadful features to this parody? Have they not confirmed the vision that bears the name "Cain and Abel" rather than what the word "brotherhood" promised us?

How, then, do we know that fatherhood is a kindness on which we can rely and that God, despite all outward appearances, is not playing with the world, but loves it dependably? For this, it was necessary that God should show himself, overthrow the images, and set up a new criterion. This takes place in the Son, in Christ. In his prayer, he plunges the totality of his life into the abyss of truth and of goodness that is God. It is only on the basis of this Son that we truly experience what God is. The nineteenth-century critics of religion claimed that the religions came into being when men projected their own best and most beautiful characteristics onto heaven, in order to make the world bearable for themselves; but since they were only projecting something of their own selves onto heaven, this took the name of Zeus and was terrible. The biblical Father is not a heavenly duplicate of human fatherhood. Rather, he posits something new: he is the divine critique of human fatherhood. God establishes his own criterion.

Without Jesus, we do not know what "Father" truly is. This becomes visible in his prayer, which is the foundation of his being. A Jesus who was not continuously absorbed in the Father and was not in continuous intimate communication with him would be a completely different being from the Jesus of the Bible, the real Jesus of history. Prayer was the center out of which he lived, and it was prayer that showed him how to understand God, the world, and men. To follow Jesus means looking at the world with the eyes of God and living accordingly. Jesus shows us what it means to lead the whole of one's life on the basis of the affirmation that "God is." Jesus shows us what it means to give genuine priority to the first table of the Ten Commandments. He gave this center a meaning, and he revealed what this center is.

At this point, however, a question arises. Jesus lives in an uninterrupted prayerful communication with God, which is the foundation of his existence. Without this, he would not be the one he is. But is this communication equally essential to the Father whom he addresses, in the sense that the Father, too, would be someone else if he were not addressed in this way? Or does this prayer pass him by without penetrating him? The answer is that it is just as essential to the Father to say "Son" as it is essential to the Son to say "Father." Without this address, the Father, too, would not be the same. Jesus does not merely touch him from the outside; he belongs to the divinity of God, as Son. Before the world was made, God is already the love of Father and Son. He can become our Father and the criterion of all fatherhood precisely because he himself is Father from eternity. In Jesus' prayer, the inner life of God becomes visible to us: we see how God himself is. Faith in the triune

God is nothing other than the exposition of what takes place in Jesus' prayer. In his prayer, the Trinity is revealed.

The next question is: "Why a Trinity? We have grasped that God is two—after what you have said, this makes perfect sense. But where does this third Person suddenly come from?"

I will devote a meditation specifically to this question; here, I simply wish to indicate where the answer lies. It is impossible for a mere "twofoldness" to exist. Either the contraposition, that is, the fact that there are *two*, will endure, so that no genuine unity comes about; or else the two will melt into each other, so that they are no longer *genuinely* two. Let me try to put this in less abstract terms. The Father and the Son do not become one in such a way that they dissolve into each other. They remain distinct from each other, since love has its basis in a "vis-à-vis" that is not abolished. If each remains his own self, and they do not abrogate each other's existence, then their unity cannot exist in each one by himself: rather, their unity must be in the fruitfulness in which each one gives himself and in which each one is himself. They are one in virtue of the fact that their love is fruitful, that it goes beyond them. In the third Person in whom they give themselves to each other, in the Gift, they are themselves, and they are one.

Let us return to my earlier point: in Jesus' prayer, the Father becomes visible and Jesus makes himself known as the Son. The unity that this reveals is the Trinity. Accordingly, becoming a Christian means sharing in Jesus' prayer, entering into the model provided by his life, that is, the model of his prayer. Becoming a Christian means saying "Father" with Jesus and, thus, becoming a child, God's son—God—in the unity of the Spirit, who allows us to be ourselves and precisely in this way draws us into the unity of God. Being a Christian means looking at the world from this central point, which gives us freedom, hope, decisiveness, and consolation.

This brings us back to the starting point of these reflections. We were baptized in the name of the Father, the Son, and the Holy Spirit before we knew what was happening to us. Today, many people doubt whether this is a good thing. We have the impression that decisions are being anticipated and imposed on the person that only he himself can properly make. Such presumption seems to us a questionable limitation on human freedom in a central sphere of life.

Such feelings express our profound uncertainty with regard to the Christian faith itself. We find it a burden rather than a grace—a burden that one may accept only for oneself. But here we are forgetting that life, too, is something determined in advance for us—we are not consulted beforehand! And life entails so much else as well: when a person is born, not only his biological existence is determined in advance, but also his language, the age in which he lives, its way of thinking, its evaluations. A life without "advance gifts" of this kind does not exist; the question is *what* these advance gifts are. If baptism establishes the "advance gift" of being loved by eternal Love, could any gift be more precious and pure than this? The advance gift of life alone is meaningless and can become a terrible burden. May we determine in advance the life another person is to lead? This is defensible only if life itself is defensible, that is, when life is sustained by a hope that goes beyond all the terrors of earthly existence.

Where the Church is regarded only as an accidental human association, the "advance gift" of faith will be questionable. But one who is convinced that it is a question, not of some human association, but rather of the gift of the love that already awaits us even before we draw our first breath, will see his most precious task as the preparation of another person to receive the advance gift of love—for it is only *this* gift that justifies passing on the gift of life to him. This means that we must learn anew to take God as our starting point when we seek to understand the Christian existence. This existence is belief in his love and faith that he is Father, Son, and Holy Spirit—for it is only thus that the affirmation that he is "love" becomes meaningful. If he is not love in himself, he is not love at all. But if he is love in himself, he must be "I" and "Thou," and this means that he must be triune. Let us ask him to open our eyes so that he becomes once again the basis of our understanding of the Christian existence, for in this way we shall understand ourselves anew and renew mankind.

PART III

JESUS CHRIST

CHAPTER 10

Jesus Christ: The Incarnate Love of God

On his first Christmas as pope, Benedict XVI released his encyclical *Deus Caritas Est* (*God Is Love*). The following excerpt discusses Jesus as the enfleshment of the love of God for the sake of our salvation.

The newness of biblical faith

First, the world of the Bible presents us with a new image of God. In surrounding cultures, the image of God and of the gods ultimately remained unclear and contradictory. In the development of biblical faith, however, the content of the prayer fundamental to Israel, the *Shema*, became increasingly clear and unequivocal: "Hear, O Israel, the Lord our God is one Lord" (Deut. 6:4). There is only one God, the Creator of heaven and earth, who is thus the God of all. Two facts are significant about this statement: all other gods are not God, and the universe in which we live has its source in God and was created by him. Certainly, the notion of creation is found elsewhere, yet only here does it become absolutely clear that it is not one god among many, but the one true God himself who is the source of all that exists; the whole world comes into existence by the power of his creative Word. Consequently, his creation is dear to him, for it was willed by him and "made" by him. The second important element now emerges: this God loves man. The divine power that Aristotle at the height of Greek philosophy sought to grasp through reflection, is indeed for every being an object of desire and of love—and as the object of love this divinity moves the world[1]— but in itself it lacks nothing and does not love: it is solely the object of

---

1. Cf. *Metaphysics*, XII, 7.

71

love. The one God in whom Israel believes, on the other hand, loves with a personal love. His love, moreover, is an elective love: among all the nations he chooses Israel and loves her—but he does so precisely with a view to healing the whole human race. God loves, and his love may certainly be called *eros*, yet it is also totally *agape*.[2]

The Prophets, particularly Hosea and Ezekiel, described God's passion for his people using boldly erotic images. God's relationship with Israel is described using the metaphors of betrothal and marriage; idolatry is thus adultery and prostitution. Here we find a specific reference—as we have seen—to the fertility cults and their abuse of *eros*, but also a description of the relationship of fidelity between Israel and her God. The history of the love-relationship between God and Israel consists, at the deepest level, in the fact that he gives her the *Torah*, thereby opening Israel's eyes to man's true nature and showing her the path leading to true humanism. It consists in the fact that man, through a life of fidelity to the one God, comes to experience himself as loved by God, and discovers joy in truth and in righteousness—a joy in God which becomes his essential happiness: "Whom do I have in heaven but you? And there is nothing upon earth that I desire besides you . . . for me it is good to be near God" (Ps. 73 [72]:25, 28).

We have seen that God's *eros* for man is also totally *agape*. This is not only because it is bestowed in a completely gratuitous manner, without any previous merit, but also because it is love which forgives. Hosea above all shows us that this *agape* dimension of God's love for man goes far beyond the aspect of gratuity. Israel has committed "adultery" and has broken the covenant; God should judge and repudiate her. It is precisely at this point that God is revealed to be God and not man: "How can I give you up, O Ephraim! How can I hand you over, O Israel! . . . My heart recoils within me, my compassion grows warm and tender. I will not execute my fierce anger, I will not again destroy Ephraim; for I am God and not man, the Holy One in your midst" (Hos. 11:8–9). God's

---

2. Cf. Ps. Dionysius the Areopagite, who in his treatise *The Divine Names*, IV, 12–14: PG 3, 709–713 calls God both *eros* and *agape*.

passionate love for his people—for humanity—is at the same time a forgiving love. It is so great that it turns God against himself, his love against his justice. Here Christians can see a dim prefiguration of the mystery of the Cross: so great is God's love for man that by becoming man he follows him even into death, and so reconciles justice and love.

The philosophical dimension to be noted in this biblical vision, and its importance from the standpoint of the history of religions, lies in the fact that on the one hand we find ourselves before a strictly metaphysical image of God: God is the absolute and ultimate source of all being; but this universal principle of creation—the *Logos*, primordial reason—is at the same time a lover with all the passion of a true love. *Eros* is thus supremely ennobled, yet at the same time it is so purified as to become one with *agape*. We can thus see how the reception of the *Song of Songs* in the canon of sacred Scripture was soon explained by the idea that these love songs ultimately describe God's relation to man and man's relation to God. Thus the *Song of Songs* became, both in Christian and Jewish literature, a source of mystical knowledge and experience, an expression of the essence of biblical faith: that man can indeed enter into union with God—his primordial aspiration. But this union is no mere fusion, a sinking in the nameless ocean of the Divine; it is a unity which creates love, a unity in which both God and man remain themselves and yet become fully one. As Saint Paul says: "He who is united to the Lord becomes one spirit with him" (1 Cor. 6:17).

The first novelty of biblical faith consists, as we have seen, in its image of God. The second, essentially connected to this, is found in the image of man. The biblical account of creation speaks of the solitude of Adam, the first man, and God's decision to give him a helper. Of all other creatures, not one is capable of being the helper that man needs, even though he has assigned a name to all the wild beasts and birds and thus made them fully a part of his life. So God forms woman from the rib of man. Now Adam finds the helper that he needed: "This at last is bone of my bones and flesh of my flesh" (Gen. 2:23). Here one might detect hints of ideas that are also found, for example, in the myth mentioned by Plato, according to which man was originally spherical, because he was complete in himself and self-sufficient. But as a punishment for pride, he was split in two by Zeus, so that now he longs for his other half, striving with all his being to possess it and thus regain his integrity.[3] While the biblical narrative does not speak of punishment, the idea is certainly present that man is somehow incomplete, driven by nature to seek in another the part that can make him whole, the idea that only in communion with the opposite sex can he become "complete." The biblical account thus concludes with a prophecy about Adam: "Therefore a man leaves his father and his mother and cleaves to his wife and they become one flesh" (Gen. 2:24).

Two aspects of this are important. First, *eros* is somehow rooted in man's very nature; Adam is a seeker, who "abandons his mother and father" in order to find woman; only together do the two represent complete humanity and become "one flesh." The second aspect is equally important. From the standpoint of creation, *eros* directs man towards marriage, to a bond which is unique and definitive; thus, and only thus, does it fulfil its deepest purpose. Corresponding to the image of a monotheistic God is monogamous marriage. Marriage based on exclusive and definitive love becomes the icon of the relationship between God and his people and vice versa. God's way of loving becomes the measure of human love. This close connection between *eros* and marriage in the Bible has practically no equivalent in extra-biblical literature.

Jesus Christ—the incarnate love of God

Though up to now we have been speaking mainly of the Old Testament, nevertheless the profound compenetration of the two Testaments as the one Scripture of the Christian faith has already become evident. The real novelty of the New Testament lies not so much in new ideas as in the figure of Christ himself, who gives flesh and blood to those concepts—an unprecedented realism. In the Old Testament, the novelty of the Bible did not consist merely in abstract notions but in God's

---

3. Plato, *Symposium*, XIV–XV, 189c–192d.

unpredictable and in some sense unprecedented activity. This divine activity now takes on dramatic form when, in Jesus Christ, it is God himself who goes in search of the "stray sheep," a suffering and lost humanity. When Jesus speaks in his parables of the shepherd who goes after the lost sheep, of the woman who looks for the lost coin, of the father who goes to meet and embrace his prodigal son, these are no mere words: they constitute an explanation of his very being and activity. His death on the Cross is the culmination of that turning of God against himself in which he gives himself in order to raise man up and save him. This is love in its most radical form. By contemplating the pierced side of Christ (see John 19:37), we can understand the starting-point of this Encyclical Letter: "God is love" (1 John 4:8). It is there that this truth can be contemplated. It is from there that our definition of love must begin. In this contemplation the Christian discovers the path along which his life and love must move.

Jesus gave this act of oblation an enduring presence through his institution of the Eucharist at the Last Supper. He anticipated his death and resurrection by giving his disciples, in the bread and wine, his very self, his body and blood as the new manna (cf. John 6:31–33). The ancient world had dimly perceived that man's real food—what truly nourishes him as man—is ultimately the *Logos*, eternal wisdom: this same *Logos* now truly becomes food for us—as love. The Eucharist draws us into Jesus' act of self-oblation. More than just statically receiving the incarnate *Logos*, we enter into the very dynamic of his self-giving. The imagery of marriage between God and Israel is now realized in a way previously inconceivable: it had meant standing in God's presence, but now it becomes union with God through sharing in Jesus' self-gift, sharing in his body and blood. The sacramental "mysticism," grounded in God's condescension towards us, operates at a radically different level and lifts us to far greater heights than anything that any human mystical elevation could ever accomplish.

Here we need to consider yet another aspect: this sacramental "mysticism" is social in character, for in sacramental communion I become one with the Lord, like all the other communicants. As Saint Paul says, "Because there is one bread, we who are many are one body, for we all partake of the one bread" (1 Cor. 10:17). Union with Christ is also union with all those to whom he gives himself. I cannot possess Christ just for myself; I can belong to him only in union with all those who have become, or who will become, his own. Communion draws me out of myself towards him, and thus also towards unity with all Christians. We become "one body," completely joined in a single existence. Love of God and love of neighbor are now truly united: God incarnate draws us all to himself. We can thus understand how *agape* also became a term for the Eucharist: there God's own *agape* comes to us bodily, in order to continue his work in us and through us. Only by keeping in mind this Christological and sacramental basis can we correctly understand Jesus' teaching on love. The transition which he makes from the Law and the Prophets to the twofold commandment of love of God and of neighbor, and his grounding the whole life of faith on this central precept, is not simply a matter of morality—something that could exist apart from and alongside faith in Christ and its sacramental re-actualization. Faith, worship, and *ethos* are interwoven as a single reality which takes shape in our encounter with God's *agape*. Here the usual contraposition between worship and ethics simply falls apart. "Worship" itself, Eucharistic communion, includes the reality both of being loved and of loving others in turn. A Eucharist which does not pass over into the concrete practice of love is intrinsically fragmented. Conversely, as we shall have to consider in greater detail below, the "commandment" of love is only possible because it is more than a requirement. Love can be "commanded" because it has first been given.

This principle is the starting-point for understanding the great parables of Jesus. The rich man (cf. Luke 16:19–31) begs from his place of torment that his brothers be informed about what happens to those who simply ignore the poor man in need. Jesus takes up this cry for help as a warning to help us return to the right path. The parable of the Good Samaritan (cf. Luke 10:25–37) offers two particularly important clarifications. Until that time, the concept of "neighbor" was understood as referring essentially to one's countrymen and to foreigners who had settled in the land of Israel; in other words, to the closely-knit community of a single country or people. This limit is now abolished. Anyone who needs me, and whom I can help, is my neighbor. The concept of "neighbor" is now universalized, yet it remains concrete. Despite being extended to all mankind, it is not reduced to a generic, abstract, and undemanding expression of love, but calls for my own practical commitment here and now. The Church has the duty to interpret ever anew this relationship between near and far with regard to the actual daily life of her members. Lastly, we should especially mention the great parable of the Last Judgement (cf. 25:31–46), in which love becomes the criterion for the definitive decision about a human life's worth or lack thereof. Jesus identifies himself with those in need, with the hungry, the thirsty, the stranger, the naked, the sick, and those in prison. "As you did it to one of the least of these my brethren, you did it to me" (Matt. 25:40). Love of God and love of neighbor have become one: in the least of the brethren we find Jesus himself, and in Jesus we find God.

CHAPTER 11

The Birth of Jesus

In this selection, drawn from his 2012 book *Jesus of Nazareth: The Infancy Narratives*, Ratzinger highlights the "historical and theological framework of the Nativity Story in Luke's Gospel."

"In those days a decree went out from Caesar Augustus that all the world should be enrolled" (Luke 2:1). With these words, Luke introduces his account of the birth of Jesus and explains how it came to take place in Bethlehem. A population census, for purposes of determining and collecting taxes, was what prompted Joseph to set off from Nazareth for Bethlehem, together with Mary, his betrothed, who was expecting a child. The birth of Jesus in the city of David is placed within the overarching framework of world history, even though Caesar was quite unaware of the difficult journey that these ordinary people were making on his account. And so it is that the child Jesus is born, seemingly by chance, in the place of the promise.

The context in world history is important for Luke. For the first time, "all the world," the *ecumēnē* in its entirety, is to be enrolled. For the first time there is a government and an empire that spans the globe. For the first time, there is a great expanse of peace in which everyone's property can be registered and placed at the service of the wider community. Only now, when there is a commonality of law and property on a large scale, and when a universal language has made it possible for a cultural community to trade in ideas and goods, only now can a message of universal salvation, a universal Savior, enter the world: it is indeed the "fullness of time."

Yet the link between Jesus and Augustus goes deeper. Augustus did not want merely to be a ruler like any other, such as had existed before him and would come after him. The inscription at Priene, from the year 9 B.C., helps us to understand how he wanted to be seen and understood. There it is said that the day of the Emperor's birth "gave the whole world a new aspect. It would have fallen into ruin had not a widespread well-being shone forth through him, the one now born . . . Providence, which has ordered all things, filled this man with virtue that he might benefit mankind, sending him as a Savior (*sōtēr*) both for us and our descendants . . . The birthday of the god was the beginning of the good tidings that he brought for the world. From his birth, a new reckoning of time must begin" (cf. Stöger, *Lukasevangelium*, p. 74). From a text like this it is clear that Augustus was regarded not just as a politician, but as a theological figure—which shows that our distinction between politics and religion, between politics and theology, simply did not exist in the ancient world. In the year 27 B.C., three years after his assumption of office, the Roman Senate had already awarded him the title Augustus (in Greek: *sebastos*)—meaning "one worthy of adoration." In the inscription at Priene, he is called Savior, Redeemer (*sōtēr*). This title, which literature ascribed to Zeus, but also to Epicurus and Asclepius, is reserved in the Greek translation of the Old Testament to God alone. For Augustus too, there was a divine ring to it: the Emperor ushered in a changed world, a new era.

In Virgil's Fourth Eclogue, we have already encountered the hope of a new world, the expectation of a return to Paradise. While in Virgil, as we have seen, there is a broader background to this nevertheless the outlook on life typical of the Augustan era leaves its mark: "Now all must change . . ."

There are two aspects of the self-understanding of Augustus and his contemporaries that I would like to single out. Peace, above all, was what the "Savior" brought to the world. Augustus himself left a lasting monument to his peace-bringing mission in the *Ara Pacis Augusti*, the remains of which, even today, manifest most impressively how the universal peace that he established for a certain period made it possible to breathe freely and to hope. Marius Reiser, citing Antonie Wlosok, writes as follows: On September 23 (the Emperor's birthday), "between morning and evening, the shadow of this sun clock moved about 150m straight along the equinox, to the very center of the *Ara Pacis*; there is thus a direct line from the birth of this man to Pax, and in this way it is clearly demonstrated that he is *natus ad pacem* (born for peace). The shadow comes from a ball, and the ball . . . is both the heavenly sphere and the earthly globe, a symbol of dominion over the world which is now at peace" (*Wie wahr*, p. 459).

Here we see the second aspect of Augustus' self-image: the universality that, once again, he himself put on display in a very public record of his life and work, listing specific facts—the so-called *Monumentum Ancyranum*.

This brings us back to the registration of all the inhabitants of the empire, by which the birth of Jesus of Nazareth is linked to Caesar Augustus. There is a long-running dispute among experts regarding this tax collection (population census), but there is no need for us to enter into all the details here.

One initial problem can be solved quite easily: the census took place at the time of King Herod the Great, who actually died in the year 4 B.C. The starting-point for our reckoning of time—the calculation of Jesus' date of birth—goes back to the monk Dionysius Exiguus († c. 550), who evidently miscalculated by a few years. The historical date of the birth of Jesus is therefore to be placed a few years earlier.

There is much debate regarding the date of the census. According to Flavius Josephus, to whom we owe most of our knowledge of Jewish history around the time of Jesus, it took place in the year 6 A.D. under the governor Quirinius, and as it was ultimately a question of money, it led to the uprising of Judas the Galilean (cf. Acts 5:37). According to Josephus it was only then, and not before, that Quirinius was active in the region of Syria and Judea. Yet these claims in their turn are uncertain. At any rate, there are indications that Quirinius was already in the Emperor's service in Syria around 9 B.C. So it is most illuminating when such scholars as Alois Stoger suggest that the "population census" was a slow process in the conditions of the time, dragging on over several years. Moreover, it was implemented in two stages: firstly, registration of all land and property ownership, and then—in the second phase—determination of the payments that were due. The first stage would have taken place at the time of Jesus' birth; the second, much more injurious for the people, was what provoked the uprising (cf. Stöger, *Lukasevangelium*, pp. 372f.).

Some have raised the further objection that there was no need, in a census of this kind, for each person to travel to his hometown (cf. Luke 2:3). But we also know from various sources that those affected had to present themselves where they owned property. Accordingly, we may assume that Joseph, of the house of David, had property in Bethlehem, so that he had to go there for tax registration.

Regarding the details, the discussion could continue indefinitely. It is difficult to gain an insight into the daily life of a society so complex and so distant from our own as that of the Roman Empire. Yet the essential content of Luke's narrative remains historically credible all the same: Luke set out, as he says in the prologue to his Gospel, "to write an orderly account" (1:3). This he evidently did, making use of the means at his disposal. In any case, he was situated much closer to the sources and events than we could ever claim to be, despite all our historical scholarship.

Let us return to the wider context of the moment in history when Jesus' birth took place. By referring to the Emperor Augustus and to "the whole *ecumēnē*," Luke was intentionally creating both a historical and a theological framework for the events he was about to recount.

Jesus was born at a time that can be precisely determined. Later, at the start of Jesus' public ministry, Luke once again offers a meticulously detailed chronology of that particular moment in history: the fifteenth year of the reign of the Emperor Tiberius. He adds the names of the Roman governor that year, the tetrarchs of Galilee, of Ituraea and Trachonitis and of Abilene, as well as the high-priests (cf. Luke 3:1f.).

It was not with the timelessness of myth that Jesus came to be born among us. He belongs to a time that can be precisely dated and a geographical area that is precisely defined: here the universal and the concrete converge. It was in him that the *Lógos*, the creative logic behind all things, entered the world. The eternal *Lógos* became man: the context of place and time is part of this. Faith attaches itself to this concrete reality, even if the resurrection then bursts open the categories of time and space, as the risen Lord, going before the disciples into Galilee (cf. Matt. 28:7), opens up a pathway into the vast expanse of humanity (cf. Matt. 28:16ff.).

There is a further important element. Augustus' instruction regarding the registration, for tax purposes, of all the citizens of the *ecumēnē* leads Joseph, together with Mary, his betrothed, to Bethlehem, the city of David, and thus it helps to bring to fulfillment the promise of the prophet Micah that the shepherd of Israel would be born in that city (cf. 5:1–3). The Emperor unwittingly contributes to the realization of the prophecy: the history of the Roman Empire is interwoven with the history of the salvation that God established with Israel. The history of God's election, hitherto confined to Israel, enters the wider world, it enters world history. God who is the God of Israel and of all peoples, shows himself to be the true guiding force behind all history.

Significant exponents of modern exegesis take the view that when Matthew and Luke say Jesus was born in Bethlehem, they are making a theological statement, not a historical one. In actual fact, these exegetes claim, Jesus was born in Nazareth. By placing the birth of Jesus in Bethlehem, the evangelists are thought to have refashioned history theologically, in accordance with the promises, so as to make it possible to designate Jesus, on the basis of his birthplace, as the long-awaited shepherd of Israel (cf. Mic. 5:1–3; Matt. 2:6).

I do not see how a basis for this theory can be gleaned from the actual sources. As far as the birth of Jesus is concerned, the only sources we have are the infancy narratives of Matthew and Luke. The two evidently belong to quite distinct narrative traditions. They are marked by

82

different theological visions, just as their historical details are in some respects different.

Matthew apparently did not know that Joseph and Mary were both originally from Nazareth. Hence, on returning from Egypt, Joseph initially wants to go to Bethlehem, and it is only the news that a son of Herod is reigning in Judea that causes him to travel to Galilee instead. For Luke, on the other hand, it is clear from the outset that the holy family returned to Nazareth after the events surrounding the birth. The two different strands of tradition agree on the fact that Bethlehem was Jesus' birthplace. If we abide by the sources, it is clear that Jesus was born in Bethlehem and grew up in Nazareth.

The Birth of Jesus

"And while they were there [in Bethlehem], the time came for her to be delivered. And she gave birth to her first-born son and wrapped him in swaddling cloths, and laid him in a manger, because there was no room at the inn" (Luke 2:6f.).

Let us begin our exegesis with the concluding words of this passage: there was no room for them in the inn. Prayerful reflection over these words has highlighted an inner parallel between this saying and the profoundly moving verse from Saint John's Prologue: "He came to his own home, and his own people received him not" (John 1:11). For the Savior of the world, for him in whom all things were created (cf. Col. 1:16), there was no room. "Foxes have holes, and birds of the air have nests; but the Son of man has nowhere to lay his head" (Matt. 8:20). He who was crucified outside the city (cf. Heb. 13:12) also came into the world outside the city.

This should cause us to reflect—it points toward the reversal of values found in the figure of Jesus Christ and his message. From the moment of his birth, he belongs outside the realm of what is important and powerful in worldly terms. Yet it is this unimportant and powerless child that proves to be the truly powerful one, the one on whom ultimately everything depends. So one aspect of becoming a Christian is having to leave behind what everyone else thinks and wants, the prevailing standards, in order to enter the light of the truth of our being, and aided by that light to find the right path.

Mary laid her newborn child in a manger (cf. Luke 2:7). From this detail it has been correctly deduced that Jesus was born in a stable, in an inhospitable—one might even say unworthy—space, which nevertheless provided the necessary privacy for the sacred event.

CHAPTER 12

Jesus on the Cross

John's Gospel tells us that, "having loved his own who were in the world, [Jesus] loved them to the end" (John 13:1). In this excerpt, taken from his book *Jesus of Nazareth: Holy Week*, Ratzinger reflects on the love of the crucified Christ, which goes "to the very limit and even beyond that limit."

According to the account of the evangelists, Jesus died, praying, at the ninth hour, that is to say, around 3:00 P.M. Luke gives his final prayer as a line from Psalm 31: "Father, into your hands I commit my spirit" (Luke 23:46; Ps 31:5). In John's account, Jesus' last words are: "It is finished!" (19:30). In the Greek text, this word (*tetélestai*) points back to the very beginning of the Passion narrative, to the episode of the washing of the feet, which the evangelist introduces by observing that Jesus loved his own "to the end (*télos*)" (John 13:1). This "end," this *ne plus ultra* of loving, is now attained in the moment of death. He has truly gone right to the end, to the very limit and even beyond that limit. He has accomplished the utter fullness of love—he has given himself.

In our reflection on Jesus' prayer on the Mount of Olives . . . we encountered a further meaning of this same word (*teleioūn*) in connection with Hebrews 5:9: in the Torah it means consecration, bestowal of priestly dignity, in other words, total dedication to God. I think we may detect this same meaning here, on the basis of Jesus' high-priestly prayer. Jesus has accomplished the act of consecration—the priestly handing-over of himself and the world to God—right to the end (cf. John 17:19). So in this final word, the great mystery of the Cross shines forth. The new cosmic liturgy is accomplished. The Cross of Jesus replaces all other acts of worship as the one true glorification of God, in which God glorifies himself through him in whom he grants us his love, thereby drawing us to himself.

The Synoptic Gospels explicitly portray Jesus' death on the Cross as a cosmic and liturgical event: the sun is darkened, the veil of the Temple is torn in two, the earth quakes, the dead rise again.

Even more important than the cosmic sign is an act of faith: the Roman centurion—the commander of the execution squad—in his consternation over all that he sees taking place, acknowledges Jesus as God's Son: "Truly, this man was the Son of God" (Mark 15:39). At the foot of the Cross, the Church of the Gentiles comes into being. Through the Cross, the Lord gathers people together to form the new community of the worldwide Church. Through the suffering Son, they recognize the true God.

While the Romans, as a deterrent, deliberately left victims of crucifixion hanging on the cross after they had died, Jewish law required them to be taken down on the same day (cf. Deut. 21:22–23). Hence the execution squad had to hasten the victims' death by breaking their legs. This applied also in the case of the crucifixion on Golgotha. The legs of the two "thieves" are broken. But then the soldiers see that Jesus is already dead. So they do not break his legs. Instead, one of them pierces Jesus' right side—his heart—and "at once there came out blood and water" (John 19:34). It is the hour when the paschal lambs are being slaughtered. It was laid down that no bone of these lambs was to be broken (cf. Exod. 12:46). Jesus appears here as the true Paschal Lamb, pure and whole.

So in this passage we may detect a tacit reference to the very beginning of Jesus' story—to the hour when John the Baptist said: "Behold, the Lamb of God, who takes away the sin of the world!" (John 1:29). Those words, which were inevitably obscure at the time as a mysterious prophecy of things to come, are now a reality. Jesus is the Lamb chosen by God himself. On the Cross he takes upon himself the sins of the world, and he wipes them away.

Yet at the same time, there are echoes of Psalm 34, which says: "Many are the afflictions of the righteous, but the LORD delivers him out of them all. He keeps all his bones; not one of them is broken" (vv. 19–20).

The Lord, the just man, has suffered much, he has suffered everything, and yet God has kept guard over him: no bone of his has been broken.

Blood and water flowed from the pierced heart of Jesus. True to Zechariah's prophecy, the Church in every century has looked upon this pierced heart and recognized therein the source of the blessings that are symbolized in blood and water. The prophecy prompts a search for a deeper understanding of what really happened there.

An initial step toward this understanding can be found in the First Letter of Saint John, which emphatically takes up the theme of the blood and water flowing from Jesus' side: "This is he who came by water and blood, Jesus Christ, not with the water only but with the water and the blood. And the Spirit is the witness, because the Spirit is the truth. There are three witnesses, the Spirit, the water, and the blood; and these three agree" (5:6–8).

What does the author mean by this insistence that Jesus came not with water only but also with blood? We may assume that he is alluding to a tendency to place all the emphasis on Jesus' baptism while setting the Cross aside. And this probably also meant that only the word, the doctrine, the message was held to be important, but not "the flesh," the living body of Christ that bled on the Cross; it probably meant an attempt to create a Christianity of thoughts and ideas, divorced from the reality of the flesh—sacrifice and sacrament.

In this double outpouring of blood and water, the Fathers saw an image of the two fundamental sacraments—Eucharist and Baptism—which spring forth from the Lord's pierced side, from his heart. This is the new outpouring that creates the Church and renews mankind. Moreover, the opened side of the Lord asleep on the Cross prompted the Fathers to point to the creation of Eve from the side of the sleeping Adam, and so in this outpouring of the sacraments they also recognized the birth of the Church: the creation of the new woman from the side of the new Adam.

CHAPTER 13

The Resurrection

In *Jesus of Nazareth: Holy Week,* Ratzinger affirms the historical reality of the Resurrection of Jesus Christ, emphasizing that "the Christian faith stands or falls with the truth of the testimony that Christ is risen from the dead."

"If Christ has not been raised, then our preaching is in vain and your faith is in vain. We are even found to be misrepresenting God, because we testified of God that he raised Christ" (1 Cor. 15:14–15). With these words Saint Paul explains quite drastically what faith in the Resurrection of Jesus Christ means for the Christian message overall: it is its very foundation. The Christian faith stands or falls with the truth of the testimony that Christ is risen from the dead.

If this were taken away, it would still be possible to piece together from the Christian tradition a series of interesting ideas about God and men, about man's being and his obligations, a kind of religious world view: but the Christian faith itself would be dead. Jesus would be a failed religious leader, who despite his failure remains great and can cause us to reflect. But he would then remain purely human, and his authority would extend only so far as his message is of interest to us. He would no longer be a criterion; the only criterion left would be our own judgment in selecting from his heritage what strikes us as helpful. In other words, we would be alone. Our own judgment would be the highest instance.

Only if Jesus is risen has anything really new occurred that changes the world and the situation of mankind. Then he becomes the criterion on which we can rely. For then God has truly revealed himself.

To this extent, in our quest for the figure of Jesus, the Resurrection is the crucial point. Whether Jesus merely *was* or whether he also *is*—this depends on the Resurrection. In answering yes or no to this question, we are taking a stand not simply on one event among others, but on the figure of Jesus as such.

Therefore it is necessary to listen with particular attention as the New Testament bears witness to the Resurrection. Yet first we have to acknowledge that this testimony, considered from a historical point of view, is presented to us in a particularly complex form and gives rise to many questions.

What actually happened? Clearly, for the witnesses who encountered the risen Lord, it was not easy to say. They were confronted with what for them was an entirely new reality, far beyond the limits of their experience. Much as the reality of the event overwhelmed them and impelled them to bear witness, it was still utterly unlike anything they had previously known. Saint Mark tells us that the disciples on their way down from the mountain of the Transfiguration were puzzled by the saying of Jesus that the Son of Man would "rise from the dead." And they asked one another what "rising from the dead" could mean (9:9–10). And indeed, what does it mean? The disciples did not know, and they could find out only through encountering the reality itself.

Anyone approaching the Resurrection accounts in the belief that he knows what rising from the dead means will inevitably misunderstand those accounts and will then dismiss them as meaningless. Rudolf Bultmann raised an objection against Resurrection faith by arguing that even if Jesus had come back from the grave, we would have to say that "a miraculous natural event such as the resuscitation of a dead man" would not help us and would be existentially irrelevant (cf. *New Testament and Mythology*, p. 7).

Now it must be acknowledged that if in Jesus' Resurrection we were dealing simply with the miracle of a resuscitated corpse, it would ultimately be of no concern to us. For it would be no more important than the resuscitation of a clinically dead person through the art of doctors. For the world as such and for our human existence, nothing would have changed. The miracle of a resuscitated corpse would indicate that Jesus' Resurrection was equivalent to the raising of the son of the widow of Nain (Luke 7:11–17), the daughter of Jairus (Mark 5:22–24, 35–43 and parallel passages), and Lazarus (John 11:1–44). After a more or less short period, these individuals returned to their former lives, and then at a later point they died definitively.

The New Testament testimonies leave us in no doubt that what happened in the "Resurrection of the Son of Man" was utterly different. Jesus' Resurrection was about breaking out into an entirely new form of life, into a life that is no longer subject to the law of dying and becoming, but lies beyond it—a life that opens up a new dimension of human existence. Therefore the Resurrection of Jesus is not an isolated event that we could set aside as something limited to the past, but it constitutes an "evolutionary leap" (to draw an analogy, albeit one that is easily misunderstood). In Jesus' Resurrection a new possibility of human existence is attained that affects everyone and that opens up a future, a new kind of future, for mankind.

So Paul was absolutely right to link the resurrection of Christians and the Resurrection of Jesus inseparably together: "If the dead are not raised, then Christ has not been raised. . . . But in fact Christ has been raised from the dead, the first fruits of those who have fallen asleep" (1 Cor. 15:16, 20). Christ's Resurrection is either a universal event, or it is nothing, Paul tells us. And only if we understand it as a universal event, as the opening up of a new dimension of human existence, are we on the way toward any kind of correct understanding of the New Testament Resurrection testimony.

On this basis we can understand the unique character of this New Testament testimony. Jesus has not returned to a normal human life in this world like Lazarus and the others whom Jesus raised from the dead. He has entered upon a different life, a new life—he has entered the vast breadth of God himself, and it is from there that he reveals himself to his followers.

For the disciples, too, this was something utterly unexpected, to which they were only slowly able to adjust. Jewish faith did indeed know of a resurrection of the dead at the end of time. New life was linked to the inbreaking of a new world and thus made complete sense. If there is a new world, then there is also a new mode of life there. But a resurrection into definitive otherness in the midst of the continuing old world was not foreseen and therefore at first made no sense. So the promise of resurrection remained initially unintelligible to the disciples.

The process of coming to Resurrection faith is analogous to what we saw in the case of the Cross. Nobody had thought of a crucified Messiah. Now the "fact" was there, and it was necessary, on the basis of that fact, to take a fresh look at Scripture. We saw in the previous chapter how Scripture yielded new insights in the light of the unexpected turn of events and how the "fact" then began to make sense. Admittedly, the new reading of Scripture could begin only after the Resurrection, because it was only through the Resurrection that Jesus was accredited as the one sent by God. Now people had to search Scripture for both Cross and Resurrection, so as to understand them in a new way and thereby come to believe in Jesus as the Son of God.

This also presupposes that for the disciples the Resurrection was just as real as the Cross. It presupposes that they were simply overwhelmed by the reality, that, after their initial hesitation and astonishment, they could no longer ignore that reality. It is truly he. He is alive; he has spoken to us; he has allowed us to touch him, even if he no longer belongs to the realm of the tangible in the normal way.

The paradox was indescribable. He was quite different, no mere resuscitated corpse, but one living anew and forever in the power of God. And yet at the same time, while no longer belonging to our world, he was truly present there, he himself. It was an utterly unique experience, which burst open the normal boundaries of experience and yet for the disciples was quite beyond doubt. This explains the unique character of the Resurrection accounts: they speak of something paradoxical, of something that surpasses all experience and yet is utterly real and present.

But could it really be true? Can we—as men of the modern world—put our faith in such testimony? "Enlightened" thinking would say no.

For Gerd Lüdemann, for example, it seems clear that in consequence of the "revolution in the scientific image of the world . . . the traditional concepts of Jesus' Resurrection are to be considered outdated" (quoted in Wilckens, *Theologie des Neun Testaments* I/2, pp. 119–20). But what exactly is this "scientific image of the world"? How far can it be considered normative? Hartmut Gese in his important article "Die Frage des Weltbildes," to which I should like to draw attention, has painstakingly described the limits of this normativity.

Naturally there can be no contradiction of clear scientific data. The Resurrection accounts certainly speak of something outside our world of experience. They speak of something new, something unprecedented—a new dimension of reality that is revealed. What already exists is not called into question. Rather we are told that there is a further dimension, beyond what was previously known. Does that contradict science? Can there really only ever be what there has always been? Can there not be something unexpected, something unimaginable, something new? If there really is a God, is he not able to create a new dimension of human existence, a new dimension of reality altogether? Is not creation actually waiting for this last and highest "evolutionary leap," for the union of the finite with the infinite, for the union of man and God, for the conquest of death?

Throughout the history of the living, the origins of anything new have always been small, practically invisible, and easily overlooked. The Lord himself has told us that "heaven" in this world is like a mustard seed, the smallest of all the seeds (Matt. 13:31–32), yet contained within it are the infinite potentialities of God. In terms of world history, Jesus' Resurrection is improbable; it is the smallest mustard seed of history.

This reversal of proportions is one of God's mysteries. The great—the mighty—is ultimately the small. And the tiny mustard seed is something truly great. So it is that the Resurrection has entered the world only through certain mysterious appearances to the chosen few. And yet it was truly the new beginning for which the world was silently waiting. And for the few witnesses—precisely because they themselves could not fathom it—it was such an overwhelmingly real happening, confronting them so powerfully, that every doubt was dispelled, and they stepped forth before the world with an utterly new fearlessness in order to bear witness: Christ is truly risen.

CHAPTER 14

Eschatology: The True Shape
of Christian Hope

In his second encyclical, *Spe Salvi* (*Saved in Hope*), Benedict XVI offers an extended commentary on the nature of hope. In this section of the encyclical, he points out that hope, in order to be genuine, must be placed in God alone.

Let us ask once again: what may we hope? And what may we not hope? First of all, we must acknowledge that incremental progress is possible only in the material sphere. Here, amid our growing knowledge of the structure of matter and in the light of ever more advanced inventions, we clearly see continuous progress towards an ever greater mastery of nature. Yet in the field of ethical awareness and moral decision-making, there is no similar possibility of accumulation for the simple reason that man's freedom is always new and he must always make his decisions anew. These decisions can never simply be made for us in advance by others—if that were the case, we would no longer be free. Freedom presupposes that in fundamental decisions, every person and every generation is a new beginning. Naturally, new generations can build on the knowledge and experience of those who went before, and they can draw upon the moral treasury of the whole of humanity. But they can also reject it, because it can never be self-evident in the same way as material inventions. The moral treasury of humanity is not readily at hand like tools that we use; it is present as an appeal to freedom and a possibility for it. This, however, means that:

> a) The right state of human affairs, the moral well-being of the world can never be guaranteed simply through structures alone, however good they are. Such structures are not only import-

94

ant, but necessary; yet they cannot and must not marginalize human freedom. Even the best structures function only when the community is animated by convictions capable of motivating people to assent freely to the social order. Freedom requires conviction; conviction does not exist on its own, but must always be gained anew by the community.

b) Since man always remains free and since his freedom is always fragile, the kingdom of good will never be definitively established in this world. Anyone who promises the better world that is guaranteed to last forever is making a false promise; he is overlooking human freedom. Freedom must constantly be won over for the cause of good. Free assent to the good never exists simply by itself. If there were structures which could irrevocably guarantee a determined—good—state of the world, man's freedom would be denied, and hence they would not be good structures at all.

What this means is that every generation has the task of engaging anew in the arduous search for the right way to order human affairs; this task is never simply completed. Yet every generation must also make its own contribution to establishing convincing structures of freedom and of good, which can help the following generation as a guideline for the proper use of human freedom; hence, always within human limits, they provide a certain guarantee also for the future. In other words: good structures help, but of themselves they are not enough. Man can never be redeemed simply from outside. Francis Bacon and those who followed in the intellectual current of modernity that he inspired were wrong to believe that man would be redeemed through science. Such an expectation asks too much of science; this kind of hope is deceptive. Science can contribute greatly to making the world and mankind more human. Yet it can also destroy mankind and the world unless it is steered by forces that lie outside it. On the other hand, we must also acknowledge that modern Christianity, faced with the successes of science in progressively structuring the world, has to a large extent restricted its attention to the individual and his salvation. In so doing it has limited the horizon of its hope and has failed to recognize sufficiently the greatness of its task—even if it has continued to achieve great things in the formation of man and in care for the weak and the suffering.

It is not science that redeems man: man is redeemed by love. This applies even in terms of this present world. When someone has the experience of a great love in his life, this is a moment of "redemption" which gives a new meaning to his life. But soon he will also realize that the love bestowed upon him cannot by itself resolve the question of his life. It is a love that remains fragile. It can be destroyed by death. The human being needs unconditional love. He needs the certainty which makes him say: "neither death, nor life, nor angels, nor principalities, nor things present, nor things to come, nor powers, nor height, nor depth, nor anything else in all creation, will be able to separate us from the love of God in Christ Jesus our Lord" (Rom. 8:38–39). If this absolute love exists, with its absolute certainty, then—only then—is man "redeemed," whatever should happen to him in his particular circumstances. This is what it means to say: Jesus Christ has "redeemed" us. Through him we have become certain of God, a God who is not a remote "first cause" of the world, because his only-begotten Son has become man and of him everyone can say: "I live by faith in the Son of God, who loved me and gave himself for me" (Gal. 2:20).

In this sense it is true that anyone who does not know God, even though he may entertain all kinds of hopes, is ultimately without hope, without the great hope that sustains the whole of life (cf. Eph. 2:12). Man's great, true hope which holds firm in spite of all disappointments can only be God—God who has loved us and who continues to love us "to the end," until all "is accomplished" (cf. John 13:1 and 19:30). Whoever is moved by love begins to perceive what "life" really is. He begins to perceive the meaning of the word of hope that we encountered in the Baptismal Rite: from faith I await "eternal life"—the true life which, whole and unthreatened, in all its fullness, is simply life. Jesus, who said that he had come so that we might have life and have

96

it in its fullness, in abundance (cf. John 10:10), has also explained to us what "life" means: "this is eternal life, that they know you the only true God, and Jesus Christ whom you have sent" (John 17:3). Life in its true sense is not something we have exclusively in or from ourselves: it is a relationship. And life in its totality is a relationship with him who is the source of life. If we are in relation with him who does not die, who is Life itself and Love itself, then we are in life. Then we "live."

Yet now the question arises: are we not in this way falling back once again into an individualistic understanding of salvation, into hope for myself alone, which is not true hope since it forgets and overlooks others? Indeed we are not! Our relationship with God is established through communion with Jesus—we cannot achieve it alone or from our own resources alone. The relationship with Jesus, however, is a relationship with the one who gave himself as a ransom for all (cf. 1 Tim. 2:6). Being in communion with Jesus Christ draws us into his "being for all"; it makes it our own way of being. He commits us to live for others, but only through communion with him does it become possible truly to be there for others, for the whole. In this regard I would like to quote the great Greek Doctor of the Church, Maximus the Confessor († 662), who begins by exhorting us to prefer nothing to the knowledge and love of God, but then quickly moves on to practicalities: "The one who loves God cannot hold on to money but rather gives it out in God's fashion . . . in the same manner in accordance with the measure of justice."[1] Love of God leads to participation in the justice and generosity of God towards others. Loving God requires an interior freedom from all possessions and all material goods: the love of God is revealed in responsibility for others.[2] This same connection between love of God and responsibility for others can be seen in a striking way in the life of Saint Augustine. After his conversion to the Christian faith, he decided, together with some like-minded friends, to lead a life totally dedicated to the word of God and to things eternal. His intention was

1. *Chapters on charity*, Centuria 1, ch. 1: p. 90, 965.
2. Cf. ibid.: PG 90, 962–966.

to practice a Christian version of the ideal of the contemplative life expressed in the great tradition of Greek philosophy, choosing in this way the "better part" (cf. Luke 10:42). Things turned out differently, however. While attending the Sunday liturgy at the port city of Hippo, he was called out from the assembly by the Bishop and constrained to receive ordination for the exercise of the priestly ministry in that city. Looking back on that moment, he writes in his *Confessions*: "Terrified by my sins and the weight of my misery, I had resolved in my heart, and meditated flight into the wilderness; but you forbade me and gave me strength, by saying: 'Christ died for all, that those who live might live no longer for themselves but for him who for their sake died' (cf. 2 Cor. 5:15)."[3] Christ died for all. To live for him means allowing oneself to be drawn into his *being for others*.

For Augustine this meant a totally new life. He once described his daily life in the following terms: "The turbulent have to be corrected, the faint-hearted cheered up, the weak supported; the Gospel's opponents need to be refuted, its insidious enemies guarded against; the unlearned need to be taught, the indolent stirred up, the argumentative checked; the proud must be put in their place, the desperate set on their feet, those engaged in quarrels reconciled; the needy have to be helped, the oppressed to be liberated, the good to be encouraged, the bad to be tolerated; all must be loved."[4] "The Gospel terrifies me"[5]—producing that healthy fear which prevents us from living for ourselves alone and compels us to pass on the hope we hold in common. Amid the serious difficulties facing the Roman Empire—and also posing a serious threat to Roman Africa, which was actually destroyed at the end of Augustine's life—this was what he set out to do: to transmit hope, the hope which came to him from faith and which, in complete contrast with his introverted temperament, enabled him to take part decisively

---

3. *Conf.* X 43, 70: CSEL 33, 279.

4. *Sermo* 340, 3: PL 38, 1484; cf. F. Van der Meer, *Augustine the Bishop*, London and New York 1961, p.268.

5. *Sermo* 339, 4: PL 38, 1481.

and with all his strength in the task of building up the city. In the same chapter of the *Confessions* in which we have just noted the decisive reason for his commitment "for all," he says that Christ "intercedes for us, otherwise I should despair. My weaknesses are many and grave, many and grave indeed, but more abundant still is your medicine. We might have thought that your word was far distant from union with man, and so we might have despaired of ourselves, if this Word had not become flesh and dwelt among us."[6] On the strength of his hope, Augustine dedicated himself completely to the ordinary people and to his city—renouncing his spiritual nobility, he preached and acted in a simple way for simple people.

Let us summarize what has emerged so far in the course of our reflections. Day by day, man experiences many greater or lesser hopes, different in kind according to the different periods of his life. Sometimes one of these hopes may appear to be totally satisfying without any need for other hopes. Young people can have the hope of a great and fully satisfying love; the hope of a certain position in their profession, or of some success that will prove decisive for the rest of their lives. When these hopes are fulfilled, however, it becomes clear that they were not, in reality, the whole. It becomes evident that man has need of a hope that goes further. It becomes clear that only something infinite will suffice for him, something that will always be more than he can ever attain. In this regard our contemporary age has developed the hope of creating a perfect world that, thanks to scientific knowledge and to scientifically based politics, seemed to be achievable. Thus Biblical hope in the Kingdom of God has been displaced by hope in the kingdom of man, the hope of a better world which would be the real "Kingdom of God." This seemed at last to be the great and realistic hope that man needs. It was capable of galvanizing—for a time—all man's energies. The great objective seemed worthy of full commitment. In the course of time, however, it has become clear that this hope is constantly receding.

---

6. *Conf.* X 43, 69: CSEL 33, 279.

Above all it has become apparent that this may be a hope for a future generation, but not for me.

And however much "for all" may be part of the great hope—since I cannot be happy without others or in opposition to them—it remains true that a hope that does not concern me personally is not a real hope. It has also become clear that this hope is opposed to freedom, since human affairs depend in each generation on the free decisions of those concerned. If this freedom were to be taken away, as a result of certain conditions or structures, then ultimately this world would not be good, since a world without freedom can by no means be a good world. Hence, while we must always be committed to the improvement of the world, tomorrow's better world cannot be the proper and sufficient content of our hope. And in this regard the question always arises: when is the world "better"? What makes it good? By what standard are we to judge its goodness? What are the paths that lead to this "goodness"?

Let us say once again: we need the greater and lesser hopes that keep us going day by day. But these are not enough without the great hope, which must surpass everything else. This great hope can only be God, who encompasses the whole of reality and who can bestow upon us what we, by ourselves, cannot attain. The fact that it comes to us as a gift is actually part of hope. God is the foundation of hope: not any god, but the God who has a human face and who has loved us to the end, each one of us and humanity in its entirety. His Kingdom is not an imaginary hereafter, situated in a future that will never arrive; his Kingdom is present wherever he is loved and wherever his love reaches us. His love alone gives us the possibility of soberly persevering day by day, without ceasing to be spurred on by hope, in a world which by its very nature is imperfect. His love is at the same time our guarantee of the existence of what we only vaguely sense and which nevertheless, in our deepest self, we await: a life that is "truly" life.

PART IV

THE CHURCH

CHAPTER 15

The Holy, Catholic Church

Drawn from the final section of his book *Introduction to Christianity*, the following excerpt presents Ratzinger's comments on the two marks of the Church mentioned in the Apostles' Creed: holy and catholic.

Obviously it cannot be our aim here to develop a complete doctrine of the Church; leaving aside the individual, specialized theological questions, we shall simply make a brief attempt to discern the real nature of the stumbling block we encounter in pronouncing the formula about the "holy, catholic Church" and strive to understand the answer implied in the text of the Creed itself. What we have to say presupposes our earlier reflections about the spiritual location and inner coherence of these words, which, on the one hand, refer to the powerful operation of the Holy Spirit in history and, on the other, are explained in the phrases about the forgiveness of sins and the communion of saints, phrases in which baptism, penance, and Eucharist are declared to be the framework of the Church, her real content and her true mode of existence.

Perhaps much of what disturbs us about the profession of faith in the Church is removed by the mere consideration of this double context. Nevertheless, let us speak out and say plainly what worries us today at this point in the Creed. We are tempted to say, if we are honest with ourselves, that the Church is neither holy nor catholic: the Second Vatican Council itself ventured to the point of speaking no longer merely of the holy Church but of the sinful Church, and the only reproach it incurred was that of still being far too timorous; so deeply aware are we all of the sinfulness of the Church. This may well be partly due to the Lutheran theology of sin and also to an assumption arising out of dogmatic prejudgments. But what makes this "dogmatic theology" so reasonable is its harmony with our own experience. The centuries of the Church's history are so filled with all sorts of human failure that we can quite understand Dante's ghastly vision of the Babylonian whore sitting in the Church's chariot; and the dreadful words of William of Auvergne, Bishop of Paris in the thirteenth century, seem perfectly comprehensible. William said that the barbarism of the Church had to make everyone who saw it go rigid with horror: "We are no longer dealing with a bride but with a monster of terrible deformity and ferocity."

The catholicity of the Church seems just as questionable as her holiness. The one garment of the Lord is torn between the disputing parties, the one Church is divided up into many Churches, every one of which claims more or less insistently to be alone in the right. And so for many people today the Church has become the main obstacle to belief. They can no longer see in her anything but the human struggle for power, the petty spectacle of those who, with their claim to administer official Christianity, seem to stand most in the way of the true spirit of Christianity.

There is no theory in existence that could compellingly refute such ideas by mere reason, just as, conversely, these ideas themselves do not proceed from mere reason but from the bitterness of a heart that may perhaps have been disappointed in its high hopes and now, in the pain of wronged love, can see only the destruction of its hopes. How, then, are we to reply? Ultimately one can only acknowledge why one can still love this Church in faith, why one still dares to recognize in the distorted features the countenance of the holy Church. Nevertheless, let us start from the objective elements. As we have already seen, in all these statements of faith the word "holy" does not apply in the first place to the holiness of human persons but refers to the divine gift that bestows holiness in the midst of human unholiness. The Church is not called "holy" in the Creed because her members, collectively and individually, are holy, sinless men—this dream, which appears afresh in every century, has no place in the waking world of our text, however movingly it may express a human longing that man will never abandon until a new heaven and a new earth really grant him what this age will never give him. Even at this point we can say that the sharpest critics of the Church in our time secretly live on this dream and, when they find it disappointed, bang the door of the house shut again and denounce it as a deceit. But to return to our argument: The holiness of the Church consists in that power of sanctification which God exerts in her in spite of human sinfulness. We come up here against the real mark of the "New Covenant": in Christ, God has bound himself to men, has let himself be bound by them. The New Covenant no longer rests on the reciprocal keeping of the agreement; it is granted by God as grace that abides even in the face of man's faithlessness. It is the expression of God's love, which will not let itself be defeated by man's incapacity but always remains well disposed toward him, welcomes him again and again precisely because he is sinful, turns to him, sanctifies him, and loves him.

Because of the Lord's devotion, never more to be revoked, the Church is the institution sanctified by him forever, an institution in which the holiness of the *Lord* becomes present among men. But it is really and truly the holiness of the *Lord* that becomes present in her and that chooses again and again as the vessel of its presence—with a paradoxical love—the dirty hands of men. It is holiness that radiates as the holiness of Christ from the midst of the Church's sin. So the paradoxical figure of the Church, in which the divine so often presents itself in such unworthy hands, in which the divine is only ever present in the form of a "nevertheless," is to the faithful the sign of the "nevertheless" of the ever greater love shown by God. The thrilling interplay of God's loyalty and man's disloyalty that characterizes the structure of the Church is the dramatic form of grace, so to speak, through which the reality of grace as the pardoning of those who are in themselves unworthy continually becomes visibly present in history. One could actually say that precisely in her paradoxical combination of holiness and unholiness the Church is in fact the shape taken by grace in this world.

Let us go a step farther. In the human dream of a perfect world, holiness is always visualized as untouchability by sin and evil, as something unmixed with the latter; there always remains in some form or other a tendency to think in terms of black and white, a tendency to cut out and reject mercilessly the current form of the negative (which can be conceived in widely varying terms). In contemporary criticism of society and in the actions in which it vents itself, this relentless side always present in human ideals is once again only too evident. That is why the aspect of Christ's holiness that upset his contemporaries was the complete absence of this condemnatory note—fire did not fall on the unworthy, nor were the zealous allowed to pull up the weeds they saw growing luxuriantly on all sides. On the contrary, this holiness expressed itself precisely as mingling with the sinners whom Jesus drew into his vicinity; as mingling to the point where he himself was made "to be sin" and bore the curse of the law in execution as a criminal— complete community of fate with the lost (cf. 2 Cor. 5:21; Gal. 3:13). He has drawn sin to himself, made it his lot, and so revealed what true "holiness" is: not separation, but union; not judgment, but redeeming love. Is the Church not simply the continuation of God's deliberate plunge into human wretchedness; is she not simply the continuation of Jesus' habit of sitting at table with sinners, of his mingling with the misery of sin to the point where he actually seems to sink under its weight? Is there not revealed in the unholy holiness of the Church, as opposed to man's expectation of purity, God's true holiness, which is love, love that does not keep its distance in a sort of aristocratic, untouchable purity but mixes with the dirt of the world, in order thus to overcome it? Can, therefore, the holiness of the Church be anything else but the bearing with one another that comes, of course, from the fact that all of us are borne up by Christ?

I must admit that to me this unholy holiness of the Church has in itself something infinitely comforting about it. Would one not be bound to despair in face of a holiness that was spotless and could only operate on us by judging us and consuming us by fire? Who would dare to assert

106

of himself that he did not need to be tolerated by others, indeed borne up by them? And how can someone who lives on the forbearance of others himself renounce forbearing? Is it not the only gift he can offer in return, the only comfort remaining to him, that he endures just as he, too, is endured? Holiness in the Church begins with forbearance and leads to bearing up; where there is no more forbearing, there is no more bearing up either, and existence, lacking support, can only sink into the void. People may well say that such words express a sickly existence—but it is part of being a Christian to accept the impossibility of autonomy and the weakness of one's own resources. At bottom there is always hidden pride at work when criticism of the Church adopts that tone of rancorous bitterness which today is already beginning to become a fashionable habit. Unfortunately it is accompanied only too often by a spiritual emptiness in which the specific nature of the Church as a whole is no longer seen, in which she is only regarded as a political instrument whose organization is felt to be pitiable or brutal, as if the real function of the Church did not lie beyond organization, in the comfort of the Word and of the sacraments that she provides in good and bad days alike. Those who really believe do not attribute too much importance to the struggle for the reform of ecclesiastical structures. They live on what the Church always is; and if one wants to know what the Church really is one must go to them. For the Church is most present, not where organizing, reforming, and governing are going on, but in those who simply believe and receive from her the gift of faith that is life to them. Only someone who has experienced how, regardless of changes in her ministers and forms, the Church raises men up, gives them a home and a hope, a home that is hope—the path to eternal life—only someone who has experienced this knows what the Church is, both in days gone by and now.

This does not mean that everything must be left undisturbed and endured as it is. Endurance can also be a highly active process, a struggle to make the Church herself more and more that which supports and endures. After all, the Church does not live otherwise than in us; she lives from the struggle of the unholy to attain holiness, just as of course this struggle lives from the gift of God, without which it could not exist. But this effort only becomes fruitful and constructive if it is inspired by the spirit of forbearance, by real love. And here we have arrived at the criterion by which that critical struggle for better holiness must always be judged, a criterion that is not only not in contradiction with forbearance but is demanded by it. This criterion is constructiveness. A bitterness that only destroys stands self-condemned. A slammed door can, it is true, become a sign that shakes up those inside. But the idea that one can do more constructive work in isolation than in fellowship with others is just as much of an illusion as the notion of a Church of "holy people" instead of a "holy Church" that is holy because the Lord bestows holiness on her as a quite unmerited gift.

This brings us to the other word applied to the Church by the Creed: it calls her "catholic." The shades of meaning acquired by this word during the course of time are numerous, but one main idea can be shown to be decisive from the start. This word refers in a double way to the unity of the Church. It refers, first, to local unity—only the community united with the bishop is the "Catholic Church," not the sectional groups that have broken away from her, for whatever reasons. Second, the term describes the unity formed by the combination of the many local Churches, which are not entitled to encapsulate themselves in isolation; they can only remain the Church by being open to one another, by forming one Church in their common testimony to the Word and in the communion of the eucharistic table, which is open to everyone everywhere. In the old commentaries on the Creed, the "Catholic" Church is contrasted with those "Churches" that only exist "from time to time in their provinces" and thereby contradict the true nature of the Church.

Thus the word "catholic" expresses the episcopal structure of the Church and the necessity for the unity of all the bishops with one another; there is no allusion in the Creed to the crystallization of this unity in the bishopric of Rome. It would indubitably be a mistake to

THE HOLY, CATHOLIC CHURCH

conclude from this that such a focal point was only a secondary development. In Rome, where our Creed arose, this idea was taken for granted from the start. But it is true enough that it is not to be counted as one of the primary elements in the concept of "Church" and certainly cannot be regarded as the point around which the concept was constructed. Rather, the basic elements of the Church appear as forgiveness, conversion, penance, eucharistic communion, and hence plurality and unity: plurality of the local Churches that yet remain "the Church" only through incorporation in the unity of the one Church. This unity is first and foremost the unity of Word and sacrament: the Church is one through the one Word and the one bread. The episcopal organization appears in the background as a *means* to this unity. It is not there for its own sake but belongs to the category of means; its position is summed up by the phrase "in order to": it serves to turn the unity of the local Churches in themselves and among themselves into a reality. The function of the Bishop of Rome would thus be to form the next stage in the category of means.

One thing is clear: the Church is not to be deduced from her organization; the organization is to be understood from the Church. But at the same time it is clear that for the visible Church visible unity is more than "organization." The concrete unity of the common faith testifying to itself in the Word and of the common table of Jesus Christ is an essential part of the sign that the Church is to erect in the world. Only if she is "catholic," that is, visibly one in spite of all her variety, does she correspond to the demand of the Creed. In a world torn apart, she is to be the sign and means of unity; she is to bridge nations, races, and classes and unite them. How often she has failed in this, we know: even in antiquity it was infinitely difficult for her to be simultaneously the Church of the barbarians and that of the Romans; in modern times she was unable to prevent strife between the Christian nations; and today she is still not succeeding in so uniting rich and poor that the excess of the former becomes the satisfaction of the latter—the ideal of sitting at a common table remains largely unfulfilled. Yet even so one must not forget all the imperatives that have issued from the claim of catholicity; above all, instead of reckoning up the past, we should face the challenge of the present and try in it not only to profess catholicity in the Creed but to make it a reality in the life of our torn world.

CHAPTER 16

The Church in the Third Millennium

Pilgrim Fellowship of Faith, a collection of essays, lectures, letters, and presentations given by Ratzinger around the turn of the century, concluded with this piece on the witness of Christians needed in the world today.

I recently read in a newspaper of a German intellectual who said about himself that where the question of God was concerned, he was an agnostic: It was just not possible, he said, either to demonstrate the existence of God or absolutely to exclude it, so the matter would remain undecided. He said he was utterly convinced, on the other hand, of the existence of hell; a glance at the television was enough for him to see that it existed. While the first half of this confession corresponds entirely with modern consciousness, the second appears strange, indeed, incomprehensible—at least when you first hear it. For how can you believe in hell if there is no God? When you look closer at it, this statement turns out to be entirely logical: hell is, precisely, the situation in which God is absent. That is the definition of it: Where God is not there, where no glimmer of his presence can any longer penetrate, that place is hell. Perhaps it is not actually our daily look at the television that shows us that, but certainly a look at the history of the twentieth century, which has left us terms like Auschwitz and the Gulag Archipelago and names like Hitler, Stalin, and Pol Pot. Anyone who reads the witnesses' accounts of those anti-worlds will encounter visions that for atrocities and destruction in no way yield to Dante's descent into hell, are indeed even more frightful, because there appear dimensions of evil that Dante could have had no way of perceiving in advance. These hells were constructed in order to be able to bring about the future world of the man who was his own master, who was no longer supposed to need any God. Man was offered in sacrifice to the Moloch of that utopia of a God-free world, a world set free from God, for man was now wholly in control of his destiny and knew no limits to his ability to determine things, because there was no longer any God set over him, because no light of the image of God shone forth any more from man.

Wherever God is not, hell comes into existence: it consists simply in his absence. That may also come about in subtle forms and almost always does so under cover of the idea of something beneficial for people. If nowadays there is a traffic in human organs, if fetuses are being formed to provide a supply of such organs or in order to further research into health and sickness, it is for many the humanitarian content of these actions that is apparent; yet with the contempt for human beings that is inherent in them, with this way of using people, and even using them up, we are in fact, after all, again on our way down to hell. That does not imply that there cannot be—as in fact there are—atheists with high ethics. Yet I venture to maintain that these ethics are based on the lingering glimmer of the light that once came from Sinai—the light of God. Far-distant stars, now already dead, may still be shining upon us. Even when God seems to be dead, his light may still be around. Yet Nietzsche rightly pointed out that the moment when the news that God is dead has reached everywhere, the moment in which his light would finally be extinguished, can only be frightful.

Why am I saying all this in a meditation on the question of what we Christians have to do today, in this historic moment of ours at the beginning of the third millennium? I am saying it because it is on that very basis that our task as Christians becomes clear. It is both simple and very great: It is a matter of witnessing to God, of opening up the barred and darkened windows so that his light may shine among us, that there may be room for his presence. For it is true, conversely, that where God is, there is heaven: there, even in the tribulations of our daily living, life becomes bright. Christianity is not a complicated philosophy that has in the meanwhile also become obsolete, not a package of dogmas and rules beyond being grasped as a whole. **Christian faith is being touched by God and witnessing to him.** That is why Paul, on the Areopagus, described his task and his intention as wishing to make known to the Athenians, whom he addressed as representative of the peoples of the world, the unknown God—the God who had emerged from his hiddenness, who had made himself known, and who could therefore be proclaimed by him (Acts 17:16–34). The reference to the expression "the unknown god" presupposes that man, in not knowing, still does know about God in some way; it responds to the situation of the agnostic, who does not know God personally and yet cannot exclude him. It presupposes that man is in some sense waiting for God and yet cannot of his own resources reach him, so that he is in need of preaching, of the hand that helps him over into the sphere of his presence.

Thus we can say: **the Church is there so that God, the living God, may be made known—so that man may learn to live with God, live in his sight and in fellowship with him. The Church is there to prevent the advance of hell upon earth and to make the earth fit to live in through the light of God.** On the basis of God's presence, and only through him, is it humanized. We may also formulate this from the third petition of the Our Father: "Thy will be done on earth, as it is in heaven." Wherever God's will is carried out is heaven, and there earth can become heaven. That is why it is a matter of making it possible to discern God's will and of bringing man's will into harmony with God's will. For one cannot know God in a merely academic way; one cannot merely take note of his existence, as for instance I may note the existence of distant stars or that of the data of past history. Knowledge of God may be compared to the knowledge of someone in love: it concerns me as a whole; it also demands my will; and it comes to nothing if it does not attain this all-embracing assent.

But in saying this I have anticipated. For the moment, let us note that for the Church, it is never merely a matter of maintaining her membership or even of increasing or broadening her own membership.

The Church is not there for her own sake. She cannot be like an association that, in difficult circumstances, is simply trying to keep its head above water. She has a task to perform for the world, for mankind. The only reason she has to survive is because her disappearance would drag humanity into the whirlpool of the eclipse of God and, thus, into the eclipse, indeed the destruction, of all that is human. We are not fighting for our own survival; we know that we have been entrusted with a mission that lays upon us a responsibility for everyone. That is why the Church has to measure herself, and be measured by others, by the extent to which the presence of God, the knowledge of him, and the acceptance of his will are alive within her. A church that was merely an organization pursuing its own ends would be the caricature of a Church. To the extent to which she is revolving around herself and looks only to the aims necessary for maintaining herself, she is rendering herself redundant and is in decline, even if she disposes of considerable means and skillful management. She can live and be fruitful only if the primacy of God is alive within her.

The **Church** is there, not for her own sake, but **for mankind.** She is there **so that the world may become a sphere for God's presence, the sphere of the covenant between God and men.** Thus, that is what the creation story is saying (Gen. 1:1–2:4): the way that the text moves toward the Sabbath is trying to make clear that creation has an inner basis and purpose. It is there in order that the covenant may come to be in which God freely gives his love and receives the response of love. The idea that the Church is there for mankind has recently been appearing in a variant that makes sense to us but jeopardizes the essence of the matter. People are saying that in recent times the history of theology and of the Church's understanding of herself has passed through three stages: from ecclesially centered to being Christ-centered and, finally, God-centered. This, it is said, represents progress, but it has not yet reached its final stage. It is clear, people say, that ecclesially centered theology was wrong: the Church should not make herself the center of things; she is not there for her own sake. Therefore we moved on

114

to Christ-centered thinking; Christ was supposed to be at the heart. Then, however, it was recognized—they say—that Christ, too, points above and beyond himself to the Father, and thus we arrived at theo-centric, God-centered thinking, and this signified at the same time an opening up of the Church to the outside, to other religions: The Church divides people, but Christ also divides, so people say. And then people add: God, too, divides people, since people's images of God contradict one another, and there are religions without a personal God and ways of understanding the world without God. Thus, as a fourth stage, the centrality of the kingdom is postulated, and though this is apparently a development from the gospel, people call it, no longer the Kingdom of God, but just simply "the kingdom," as a cipher for the better world that is to be built up.

The centrality of the kingdom is supposed to mean that every-one, reaching beyond the boundaries of religions and ideologies, can now work together for the values of the kingdom, which are, to wit: peace, justice, and the conservation of creation. This trio of values has nowadays emerged as a substitute for the lost concept of God and, at the same time, as the unifying formula that could be the basis, beyond all distinctions and differences, for the worldwide community of men of goodwill (and who is not one of them?) and thus might really be able to lead to that better world. That sounds tempting. Who is there who does not feel bound to support the great aim of peace on earth? Who would not be bound to strive for justice to be done, so that finally the glaring differences between classes and races and continents might disappear? And who would not see the need today to defend creation against the modern forms of destruction it suffers? Has God become superfluous, then? Can this trio of values take his place? Yet, how do we know what will bring peace? Where do we find a standard for justice and a way of distinguishing paths that lead there from paths that turn aside? And how are we to know when technology is appropriate to the claims of creation and when it is becoming destructive? Anyone who sees how this trio of values is handled, worldwide, cannot hide the fact

115

that it is increasingly becoming a hotbed of ideologies and that without an all-embracing standard of what is consistent with existence, what is appropriate to creation, and what is humane, it cannot survive intact. Values cannot replace truth; they cannot replace God, for they are only a reflection of him, and without his light their outline becomes blurred.

Thus, we are left with this: **Without God, the world cannot be bright, and the Church is serving the world by the fact that God lives within her and that she is transparent for him and carries him to mankind**. And thereby we come at last to the quite practical question: How does that happen? How can we ourselves recognize God, and how can we bring him to other people? I think that for this purpose, several different ways must be interwoven. First there is the way that Paul adopted on the Areopagus—**the reference to the capacity to know God that is buried within men, appealing to reason**. "[God] is not far from each one of us," Paul says there. "In him we live and move and have our being" (Acts 17:27–28). In the Letter to the Romans, we meet the same idea, still more strongly expressed: "Ever since the creation of the world [God's] invisible nature, namely, his eternal power and deity, has been clearly perceived in the things that have been made" (1:20). Christian faith appeals to reason, to the transparency of creation in revealing the Creator. The Christian religion is a **logos-religion:** "In the beginning was the Word" is how we translate the first sentence of the Gospel of John, which is consciously referring, for its part, to the first sentence of the Bible as such, the account of the creation being carried out through the Word. Yet "word" (logos), in the biblical sense, also means reason, with its creative power.

CHAPTER 17

Remaining in the Church

This excerpt, which originally appeared in a book coauthored with Hans Urs von Balthasar in 1971, was translated into English and published in the collection *Credo for Today*. Ratzinger discusses why he has chosen to remain faithful to the Catholic Church.

But with that we have already given the fundamental answer to the question about which I was asked to speak: I am in the Church because I believe that now as ever "his Church" lives behind "our Church," that we cannot change this situation, and that I can stand by him only if I stand by and in his Church. I am in the Church because, despite everything, I believe that she is at the deepest level not our Church but precisely "his."

To put it quite concretely: It is the Church that, despite all the human foibles of the people in her, gives us Jesus Christ, and only through her can we receive him as a living, authoritative reality that summons and endows me here and now. Henri de Lubac formulated this state of affairs as follows: "Do they realize that if they still receive Christ, it is to the Church they owe it? . . . Jesus lives for us. But without the visible continuity of the Church, the desert sands would have long since swallowed up, if not perhaps his name and his memory, certainly the influence of his gospel and faith in his divinity. . . . 'Without the Church, Christ evaporates or is fragmented or cancels himself out.' And without Christ what would man be?" This elementary acknowledgment has to be made at the start: Whatever infidelity there is or may be in the Church, however true it is that she constantly needs to be measured anew by Jesus Christ, still there is ultimately no opposition between Christ and Church. It is through the Church that he remains alive despite the distance of history, that he speaks to us today, is with us today as master and Lord, as our brother who unites us all as brethren. And because the Church, and she alone, gives us Jesus Christ, causes him to be alive and present in the world, gives birth to him again in every age in the faith and prayer of the people, she gives mankind a light, a support, and a standard without which humanity would be unimaginable. Anyone who wants to find the presence of Jesus Christ in humanity cannot find it contrary to the Church but only in her.

With that we have already made the next point. I am in the Church for the same reasons that I am a Christian in the first place. For one cannot believe alone. One can believe only as a fellow believer. Faith is by its very nature a force for unification. Its primordial image is the story of Pentecost, the miracle of understanding among people who by their origins and history are foreign to one another. Faith is ecclesial or it is not faith. Furthermore, just as one cannot believe alone but only as a fellow believer, neither can one believe on the basis of one's own authority and ingenuity, but only when there is an authorization to believe that is not within my power and does not come from me but rather goes before me. A faith of one's own devising is an oxymoron. For a self-made faith would only vouch for and be able to say what I already am and know anyway; it could not go beyond the boundary of my ego. Hence a self-made Church, a congregation that creates itself, that exists by its own graces, is also an oxymoron. Although faith demands communion, it is the sort of communion that has authority and takes the lead, not the sort that is my own creation, the instrument of my own wishes.

The whole matter can also be formulated in terms of a more historical aspect: Either this Jesus was more than a man, so that he had an inherent authority that was more than the product of his own arbitrary will, or he was not. In other words, either an authority proceeded from him that extends and lasts through the ages, or else he left no such authority behind. In the latter case, I have to rely on my own reconstructions, and then he is nothing more than any other great founding figure that one makes present by reflection. But if he is more than that,

118

then he does not depend on my reconstructions; then the authority he left behind is valid even today.

Let us return to the crucial point: being Christian is possible only in Church. Not close by. And let us not hesitate to ask once more, quite soberly, the solemn-sounding question: Where would the world be without Christ? Without a God who speaks and knows man and whom man can therefore know? Nowadays the attempt to construct such a world is carried on with such grim obstinacy that we know very precisely what the answer is: an absurd experiment. An experiment without any standard. However much Christianity may have failed in practice during its history (and it has failed again and again appallingly), the standards of justice and love have nevertheless emanated from the good news preserved in the Church, even against her will, often in spite of her, and yet never without the quiet power of what has been deposited in her.

In other words: I remain in the Church because I view the faith—which can be practiced only in her and ultimately not against her—as a necessity for man, indeed, for the world, which lives on that faith even when it does not share it. For if there is no more God—and a silent God is no God—then there is no longer any truth that is accessible to the world and to man. In a world without truth, however, one cannot keep on living; even if we suppose that we can do without truth, we still feed on the quiet hope that it has not yet really disappeared, just as the light of the sun could remain for a while after the sun came to an end, momentarily disguising the worldwide night that had started.

We could express the same thing again differently from another perspective: I remain in the Church because only the Church's faith saves man. That sounds very traditional, dogmatic, and unreal, but it is meant quite soberly and realistically. In our world of compulsions and frustrations, the longing for salvation has reawakened with hurricane force. The efforts of Freud and C. G. Jung are just attempts to give redemption to the unredeemed. Marcuse, Adorno, and Habermas continue in their own way, from different starting points, to seek and proclaim salvation. In the background stands Marx, and his question, too, is the question of salvation. The more liberated, enlightened, and powerful man becomes, the more the longing for salvation gnaws at him, the less free he finds himself. The common element in the efforts of Marx, Freud, and Marcuse is that they look for salvation by striving for a world that is delivered from suffering, sickness, and need. A world free of dominion, suffering, and injustice has become the great slogan of our generation; the stormy protests of the young are aimed at this promise, and the resentments of the old rage against the fact that it has not yet been fulfilled, that there still is domination, injustice, and suffering. To fight against suffering and injustice in the world is indeed a thoroughly Christian impulse. But the notion that one can produce a world without suffering through social reform, through the abolition of government and the legal order, and the desire to achieve this here and now are symptoms of false doctrine, of a profound misunderstanding of human nature. Inequality of ownership and power, to tell the truth, are not the only causes of suffering in this world. And suffering is not just the burden that man should throw off: anyone who tries to do that must flee into the illusory world of drugs so as to destroy himself in earnest and come into conflict with reality. Only by suffering himself and by becoming free of the tyranny of egotism through suffering does man find himself, his truth, his joy, his happiness. We are led to believe that one can become a human being without conquering oneself, without the patience of renunciation and the toil of overcoming oneself; that there is no need to withstand the hardship of perseverance or to endure patiently the tension between what man ought to be and what he is in fact: this is the very essence of the crisis of the hour. If a man's hardship is taken away and he is led astray into the fool's paradise of his dreams, he loses what is distinctively his: himself. A human being in fact is saved in no other way but through the cross, through acceptance of his own passion and that of the world, which in God's Passion became the site of liberating meaning. Only in that way, in this acceptance, does a human being become free. All offers that promise it at less expense will fail and prove to be deceptive. The hope of Christianity, the prospect of faith is ultimately based quite simply on the fact that it tells the truth. The prospect of faith is the prospect of truth, which can be obscured and trampled upon, but cannot perish.

We come to our final point. A human being always sees only as much as he loves. Certainly, there is also the clear-sightedness of denial and hatred. But they can see only what is suited to them: the negative. They can thereby preserve love from a blindness in which it overlooks its own limitations and risks. But they cannot build up. Without a certain measure of love, one finds nothing. Someone who does not get involved at least for a while in the experiment of faith, in the experiment of becoming affirmatively involved with the Church, who does not take the risk of looking with the eyes of love, only vexes himself. The venture of love is the prerequisite for faith. If it is ventured, then one does not have to hide from the dark areas in the Church. But one discovers that they are not the only thing after all. One discovers that alongside the Church history of scandals there is another Church history that has proved to be fruitful throughout the centuries in great figures such as Augustine, Francis of Assisi, the Dominican priest Las Casas, who fought passionately for the Indians, Vincent de Paul, and John XXIII. He finds that the Church has brought forth in history a gleaming path that cannot be ignored. And the beauty that has sprung up in response to her message and is still manifest to us today in incomparable works of art becomes for him a witness to the truth: something that could express itself in that way cannot be mere darkness. The beauty of the great cathedrals, the beauty of the music that has developed within the context of the faith, the dignity of the Church's liturgy, and in general the reality of the festival, which one cannot make for oneself but can only receive, the elaboration of the seasons in the liturgical year, in which then and now, time and eternity interpenetrate—all that is in my view no insignificant accident. Beauty is the radiance of truth, Thomas Aquinas once said, and one might add that the distortion of the beautiful is the self-irony of lost truth. The lasting impression that

Christianity was able to make upon history testifies to the faith, to the truth that stands behind it.

There is another point that I do not want to omit, even though it seems to lead us into the realm of subjectivity. Even today, if you keep your eyes open, you can still meet people who are a living witness to the liberating power of the Christian faith. And there is nothing wrong with being and remaining a Christian, too, on account of the people who exemplified Christianity for us and through their lives made it worth believing and loving. After all, it is an illusion when a human being tries to make himself into a sort of transcendental subject in whom only that which is not accidental has any validity. Certainly there is a duty then to reflect on such experiences, to test their reliability, to purify them and comply with them anew. But even then, in this necessary process of making them objective, is it not a respectable proof of Christianity that it has made human beings human by uniting them with God? Is not the most subjective element here at the same time something completely objective for which we do not have to apologize to anyone?

One more remark at the conclusion. When we speak, as we have done here, about the fact one cannot see anything without love, that one must therefore also learn to love the Church in order to recognize her, many people today become uneasy: Is not love the opposite of criticism? And in the final analysis, is not it the subterfuge of the ruling powers that are trying to divert criticism and maintain the status quo for their own benefit? Do we serve mankind by reassuring it and putting a good face on the present situation, or do we serve them by standing up for them constantly against entrenched injustice and oppressive social structures? Those are very far-reaching questions that cannot be examined here in detail. But one thing ought to be clear: Real love is neither static nor uncritical. If there is any possibility at all of changing another human being for the better, then it is only by loving him and by slowly helping him to change from what he is into what he can be. Should it be any different with the Church? Just look at recent history: in the liturgical and theological renewal during the first half of the twentieth century, a real reform developed that brought about positive change; that was possible only because there were watchful individuals who, with the gift of discernment, loved the Church "critically" and were willing to suffer for her. If nothing succeeds any more today, maybe it is because all of us are all too intent on merely proving ourselves right. Staying in a Church that we actually have to make first in order for her to be worth staying in is just not worthwhile; it is self-contradictory. Remaining in the Church because she is worthy of remaining; because she is worth loving and transforming ever anew through love so that she transcends herself and becomes more fully herself—that is the path that the responsibility of faith shows us even today.

CHAPTER 18

Christianity and the World Religions

Ratzinger has long had a great interest in interreligious dialogue. In this excerpt, drawn from his book *Many Religions—One Covenant*, he offers some principles for effective dialogue with those of other faiths.

The Christian Faith and the Mystical Religions

So we come to the question we have so far deferred. What, in concrete terms, is Christianity's position in the dialogue of religions? Is theistic, dogmatic, and hierarchically ordered religion necessarily intolerant? Does belief in the truth formulated by dogma make us incapable of dialogue? Does readiness for peace imply the jettisoning of truth?

The mystical dimension of the Christian faith

I would like to answer this question in two stages. First we must once more remember that the Christian faith has within it a mystical and an apophatic side. One of the reasons why the modern encounter with the religions of Asia will be significant for Christians is that they will be reminded once again of this side of their faith; one-sided and hardened positions in statements of Christian faith are broken down.

An objection may be raised here: What about the doctrines of the Trinity and the Incarnation? Are they not radical forms of this hardened positivity, suggesting that God is formally graspable and can be held in concepts and that the mystery of God can be trapped in fixed forms and a historically datable figure?

At this point one should remember the dispute between Gregory of Nyssa and Eunomius: Eunomius had asserted that God was fully understandable on the basis of the given revelation, whereas Gregory opposed him by interpreting trinitarian theology and Christology as *mystical* theology, inviting us to an infinite journey to a God who is always infinitely greater.

The cloud of mystery

In fact, trinitarian theology is apophatic insofar as it cancels the simple idea of the human person acquired from human experience; while it does acknowledge the God who speaks, the God-Logos, it simultaneously preserves the greater silence that comes from the Logos and bids us enter it.

Something similar can be said of the Incarnation. Yes, God becomes concrete, tangible in history. He approaches men in bodily form. But this very God, become graspable, is utterly mysterious. The humiliation he himself has chosen, his "kenosis," is in a new way, so to speak, the cloud of mystery in which he both conceals and reveals himself. For what greater paradox could there be than this, that God is vulnerable and can be killed? The Word, which the Incarnate and Crucified One is, always far surpasses all human words; thus God's kenosis is the place where the religions can meet without claims of sovereignty.

Plato's Socrates, particularly in the *Apology* and *Crito*, points to the connection between truth and defenselessness, between truth and poverty. Socrates is credible because his commitment to "God" brings him neither position nor possessions; on the contrary, it consigns him to poverty and ultimately to the role of an accused criminal. Poverty is the truly divine manifestation of truth: thus it can demand obedience without involving alienation.

Concluding Points

The question remains: What does this mean in concrete terms? What can be expected from Christianity, thus understood, in the dialogue of religions? Does the theistic, incarnational model bring us farther than the mystical and the pragmatic?

Let me speak plainly: Anyone who expects the dialogue between religions to result in their unification is bound for disappointment. This is hardly possible within our historical time, and perhaps it is not even desirable.

What then? I would like to say three things.

No renunciation of truth

First, the encounter of the religions is not possible by renouncing truth but only by a deeper entering into it. Skepticism does not unite people. Nor does mere pragmatism. Both only make way for ideologies that become all the more self-confident as a result.

The renunciation of truth and conviction does not elevate man but hands him over to the calculations of utility and robs him of his greatness.

What we need, however, is respect for the beliefs of others and the readiness to look for the truth in what strikes us as strange or foreign; for such truth concerns us and can correct us and lead us farther along the path. What we need is the willingness to look behind the alien appearances and look for the deeper truth hidden there.

Furthermore, I need to be willing to allow my narrow understanding of truth to be broken down. I shall learn my own truth better if I understand the other person and allow myself to be moved along the road to the God who is ever greater, certain that I never hold the whole truth about God in my own hands but am always a learner, on pilgrimage toward it, on a path that has no end.

Criticism of one's own religion

Second, if this is the case, if I must always look for what is positive in the other's beliefs—and in this way he becomes a help to me in searching for the truth—the critical element can and may not be missing; in fact, it is needed. Religion contains the precious pearl of truth, so to speak, but it is always hiding it, and it is continually in danger of losing sight of its own essence. Religion can fall sick, it can become something destructive. It can and should lead us to truth, but it can also cut men off from truth. The criticism of religion found in the Old Testament is still very relevant today. We may find it relatively easy to criticize the religion of others, but we must be ready to accept criticism of ourselves and of our own religion.

Karl Barth distinguished in Christianity between religion and faith. He was wrong if he was intending to make a complete separation between them, seeing only faith as positive and religion as negative. Faith without religion is unreal; religion belongs to it, and Christian faith, of its very nature, must live as a religion. But he was right insofar as the religion of the Christian can succumb to sickness and become superstition: the concrete religion in which faith is lived out must continually be purified on the basis of truth, that truth which shows itself, on the one hand, in faith and, on the other hand, reveals itself anew through dialogue, allowing us to acknowledge its mystery and infinity.

Proclamation of the gospel as a dialogical process

Third: Does this mean that missionary activity should cease and be replaced by dialogue, where it is not a question of truth but of making one another better Christians, Jews, Moslems, Hindus, or Buddhists? My answer is No. For this would be nothing other than total lack of conviction; under the pretext of affirming one another in our best points, we would in fact be failing to take ourselves (or others) seriously; we would be finally renouncing truth. Rather, the answer must be that mission and dialogue should no longer be opposites but should mutually interpenetrate.

Dialogue is not aimless conversation: it aims at conviction, at finding the truth; otherwise it is worthless. Conversely, missionary activity in the future cannot proceed as if it were simply a case of communicating to someone who has no knowledge at all of God what he has to believe.

There can be this kind of communication, of course, and perhaps it will become more widespread in certain places in a world that is

127

becoming increasingly atheistic. But in the world of the religions we meet people who have heard of God through their religion and try to live in relationship with him.

In this way, proclamation of the gospel must be necessarily a dialogical process. We are not telling the other person something that is entirely unknown to him; rather, we are opening up the hidden depth of something with which, in his own religion, he is already in touch.

The reverse is also the case: the one who proclaims is not only the giver; he is also the receiver. In this sense, what Cusanus saw in his vision of the heavenly council, which he expressed as both a wish and a hope, should come true in the dialogue of religions: the dialogue of religions should become more and more a listening to the Logos, who is pointing out to us, in the midst of our separation and our contradictory affirmations, the unity we already share.

PART V

THE SECOND VATICAN COUNCIL

CHAPTER 19

A Council to Be Rediscovered

In 1985, four years after he was appointed Prefect of the Congregation for the Doctrine of the Faith by Pope John Paul II, Ratzinger sat down for an interview with Vittorio Messori on the state of the Church, which was published as *The Ratzinger Report*. In the following excerpt, drawn from chapter 2 of the book, Ratzinger discusses the proper way of interpreting and implementing the Second Vatican Council. Rather than a question-and-answer format, Messori weaves Ratzinger's answers in with his own commentary; Ratzinger's words appear in the quotation marks.

In order to get to the heart of the matter we must, almost of necessity, begin with the extraordinary event of Vatican Council II, the twentieth anniversary of whose close will be celebrated in 1985. Twenty years which by far have brought about more changes in the Catholic Church than were wrought over the span of two centuries.

Today no one who is and wishes to remain Catholic nourishes any doubts—nor can he nourish them—that the great documents of Vatican Council II are important, rich, opportune, and indispensable. Least of all, naturally, the Prefect of the Congregation for the Doctrine of the Faith. To remind him of this would not only be superfluous but ridiculous. Oddly enough, nevertheless, some commentators have obviously considered it necessary to advance doubts on this matter.

Yet, not only were the statements in which Cardinal Ratzinger defended Vatican II and its decisions eminently clear, but he repeatedly corroborated them at every opportunity. Among countless examples, I shall cite an article he wrote in 1975 on the occasion of the tenth anniversary of the close of the Council. I reread the text of that article to him in Brixen, and he confirmed to me that he still wholly recognized himself therein.

Thus ten years before our conversation, he had already written: "Vatican II today stands in a twilight. For a long time it has been regarded by the so-called progressive wing as completely surpassed and, consequently, as a thing of the past, no longer relevant to the present. By the opposite side, the 'conservative' wing, it is, conversely, viewed as the cause of the present decadence of the Catholic Church and even judged as an apostasy from Vatican I and from the Council of Trent. Consequently demands have been made for its retraction or for a revision that would be tantamount to a retraction." Thereupon he continued: "Over against both tendencies, before all else, it must be stated that Vatican II is upheld by the same authority as Vatican I and the Council of Trent, namely, the Pope and the College of Bishops in communion with him, and that also with regard to its contents, Vatican II is in the strictest continuity with both previous councils and incorporates their texts word for word in decisive points."

From this Ratzinger drew two conclusions. First: "It is impossible ('for a Catholic') to take a position for Vatican II but against Trent or Vatican I. Whoever accepts Vatican II, as it has clearly expressed and understood itself, at the same time accepts the whole binding tradition of the Catholic Church, particularly also the two previous councils. And that also applies to the so-called 'progressivism,' at least in its extreme forms." Second: "It is likewise impossible to decide in favor of Trent and Vatican I, but against Vatican II. Whoever denies Vatican II denies the authority that upholds the other two councils and thereby detaches them from their foundation. And this also applies to the so-called 'traditionalism,' also in its extreme forms." "Every partisan choice destroys the whole (the very history of the Church) which can exist only as an indivisible unity."

Let us rediscover the true Vatican II

Hence it is not Vatican II and its documents (it is hardly necessary to recall this) that are problematic. At all events, many see the problem— and Joseph Ratzinger is among them, and not just since yesterday—to lie in the manifold interpretations of those documents which have led to many abuses in the post-conciliar period.

Ratzinger's judgment on this period has been clearly formulated for a long time: "It is incontestable that the last ten years have been decidedly unfavorable for the Catholic Church." "Developments since the Council seem to be in striking contrast to the expectations of all, beginning with those of John XXIII and Paul VI. Christians are once again a minority, more than they have ever been since the end of antiquity."

He explains his stark judgment (which he also repeated during the interview—but that should not cause any surprise, whatever judgment we might make of it, for he confirmed it many times) as follows: "What the Popes and the Council Fathers were expecting was a new Catholic unity, and instead one has encountered a dissension which—to use the words of Paul VI—seems to have passed over from self-criticism to self-destruction. There had been the expectation of a new enthusiasm, and instead too often it has ended in boredom and discouragement. There had been the expectation of a step forward, and instead one found oneself facing a progressive process of decadence that to a large measure has been unfolding under the sign of a summons to a presumed 'spirit of the Council' and by so doing has actually and increasingly discredited it."

Thus, already ten years ago, he had arrived at the following conclusion: "It must be clearly stated that a real reform of the Church presupposes an unequivocal turning away from the erroneous paths whose catastrophic consequences are already incontestable."

On one occasion he also wrote: "Cardinal Julius Dopfner once remarked that the Church of the post-conciliar period is a huge construction site. But a critical spirit later added that it was a construction site where the blueprint had been lost and everyone continues to build according to his taste. The result is evident."

Nevertheless the Cardinal constantly takes pains to repeat, with equal clarity, that "Vatican II in its official promulgations, in its authentic documents, cannot be held responsible for this development which, on the contrary, radically contradicts both the letter and the spirit of the Council Fathers."

He says: "I am convinced that the damage that we have incurred in these twenty years is due, not to the 'true' Council, but to the unleashing within the Church of latent polemical and centrifugal forces; and outside the Church it is due to the confrontation with a cultural revolution in the West: the success of the upper middle class, the new 'tertiary bourgeoisie,' with its liberal-radical ideology of individualistic, rationalistic and hedonistic stamp."

Hence his message, his exhortation to all Catholics who wish to remain such, is certainly not to "turn back" but, rather, *"to return to the authentic texts of the original Vatican II."*

For him, he repeats to me, "to defend the true tradition of the Church today means to defend the Council. It is also our fault if we have at times provided a pretext (to the 'right' and 'left' alike) to view Vatican II as a 'break' and an abandonment of the tradition. There is, instead, a continuity that allows neither a return to the past nor a flight forward, neither anachronistic longings nor unjustified impatience. We must remain faithful to the today of the Church, not the yesterday or tomorrow. And this today of the Church is the documents of Vatican II, without reservations that amputate them and without arbitrariness that distorts them."

A prescription against anachronism

Although critical of the "left," Ratzinger also exhibits an unmistakable severity toward the "right," toward that integralist traditionalism quintessentially symbolized by the old Archbishop Marcel Lefebvre. In a reference to it, he told me: "I see no future for a position that, out of principle, stubbornly renounces Vatican II. In fact in itself it is an illogical position. The point of departure for this tendency is, in fact, the strictest fidelity to the teaching particularly of Pius IX and Pius X and, still more fundamentally, of Vatican I and its definition of papal primacy. But why only the popes up to Pius XII and not beyond? Is perhaps obedience to the Holy See divisible according to years or according to the nearness of a teaching to one's own already-established convictions?"

The fact remains, I observe, that if Rome has intervened with respect to the "left," it has not yet intervened with respect to the "right" with the same vigor.

In reply, he states: "The followers of Msgr. Lefebvre assert the very opposite. They contend that whereas there was an immediate intervention in the case of the respected retired archbishop with the harsh punishment of suspension, there is an incomprehensible toleration of every kind of deviation from the other side. I don't wish to get involved in a polemic on the greater or lesser severity toward the one or the other side. Besides, both types of opposition present entirely different features. The deviation toward the 'left' no doubt represents a broad current of the contemporary thought and action of the Church, but hardly anywhere have they found a juridically definable common form. On the other hand, Archbishop Lefebvre's movement is probably much less broad numerically, but it has a well-defined juridical organization, seminaries, religious houses, etc. Clearly everything possible must be done to prevent this movement from giving rise to a schism peculiar to it that would come into being whenever Msgr. Lefebvre should decide to consecrate a bishop which, thank God, in the hope of a reconciliation, he has not yet done. In the ecumenical sphere today one deplores that not enough was done in the past to prevent incipient divisions through a greater openness to reconciliation and to an understanding of the different groups. Well, that should apply as a behavioral maxim for us too in the present time. We must commit ourselves to reconciliation, so long and so far as it is possible, and we must utilize all the opportunities granted to us for this purpose."

But Lefebvre, I object, has ordained priests and continues to do so.

"Canon law speaks of ordinations that are illicit but not invalid. We must also consider the human aspect of these young men who, in the eyes of the Church, are 'true' priests, albeit in an irregular situation. The point of departure and the orientation of individuals are certainly different. Some are strongly influenced by their family situations and have accepted the latter's decision. In others, disillusionment with the present-day Church has driven them to bitterness and to negation. Others still would like to collaborate fully in the normal pastoral activity of the Church. Nevertheless they have let themselves be driven to their choice by the unsatisfactory situation that has arisen in the seminaries in many countries. So just as there are some who in some way have put up with the division, there are also many who hope for reconciliation and remain in Msgr. Lefebvre's priestly community only in this hope."

His prescription for cutting the ground from under the Lefebvre case and other anachronistic resistances seems to re-echo that of the last popes, from Paul VI to today: "Similar absurd situations have been able to endure up to now precisely by nourishing themselves on the arbitrariness and thoughtlessness of many post-conciliar interpretations. This places a further obligation upon us to show the true face of the Council: thus one will be able to cut the ground from under these false protests."

Spirit and anti-spirit

But, I say, opinions differ as regard the "true" Council. Apart from the cases of that irresponsible "neo-triumphalism" to which you referred and which refuses to look at reality, there is general agreement that the present situation of the Church is a difficult one. But opinions come to a parting of the ways with respect to diagnosis as well as well as therapy. The *diagnosis* of some is that the appearances of crisis are only the salutary fevers of a period of growth. For others, instead, they are symptoms of a grave illness. As regards the therapy, some demand a greater application of Vatican II, even beyond the texts. Others propose a minor dose of reforms and changes. How to choose? Who is to be declared right?

He answers: "As I shall explain in great detail, my diagnosis is that we are dealing with an authentic crisis and that it must be treated and cured. Thus, I confirm that even for this healing process, Vatican II is a reality that must be fully accepted. On condition, however, that it must not be viewed as merely a point of departure from which one gets further away by running forward, but as a base on which to build solidly. Today, in fact, we are discovering its 'prophetic' function: some texts of Vatican II at the moment of their proclamation seemed really to be ahead of the times. Then came the cultural revolutions and the social convulsions that the Fathers in no way could have foreseen but which have shown how their answers—at that time anticipatory—were those that were needed in the future. Hence it is obvious that return to the documents is of special importance at the present time: they give us the right instrument with which to face the problems of our day. We are summoned to reconstruct the Church, not despite, but thanks to the true Council."

Continuing his diagnosis, he recalls that this "true" Council, "already during its sessions and then increasingly in the subsequent period, was opposed by a self-styled 'spirit of the Council,' which in reality is a true 'anti-spirit' of the Council. According to this pernicious anti-spirit [*Konzils-Ungeist* in German], everything that is 'new' (or presumed such: how many old heresies have surfaced again in recent years that have been presented as something new!) is always and in every case better than what has been or what is. It is the anti-spirit according to which the history of the Church would first begin with Vatican II, viewed as a kind of point zero."

"Not rupture but continuity"

On this point, he insists, he wants to be very precise. "This schematism of a before and after in the history of the Church, wholly unjustified by the documents of Vatican II, which do nothing but reaffirm the continuity of Catholicism, must be decidedly opposed. There is no 'pre-' or 'post-' conciliar Church: there is but one, unique Church that walks the path toward the Lord, ever deepening and ever better understanding the treasure of faith that he himself has entrusted to her. There are no leaps in this history, there are no fractures, and there is no break in continuity. In no wise did the Council intend to introduce a temporal dichotomy in the Church."

Continuing his analysis, he recalls that "in no way was it the intention of the pope who took the initiative for Vatican II, John XXIII, and of the pope who continued it faithfully, Paul VI, to bring up for discussion a *depositum fidei* which was viewed by them as undisputed and already assured."

Do you wish, perhaps, as some do, to stress the primarily *pastoral* concerns of Vatican II?

"I should like to say that Vatican II surely did not want 'to change' the faith, but to represent it in a more effective way. Further, I should say that dialogue is possible only on the foundation of a clear identity. One can, one must be 'open,' but only when one has something to say and has acquired one's own identity. This is how the Popes and the Council Fathers understood it. Some of them no doubt harbored an optimism that from our present-day perspective we would judge as not critical or realistic enough. But if they thought that they could open themselves with confidence to what is positive in the modern world, it was precisely because they were sure of their identity, of their faith. Whereas on the part of many Catholics in recent years there has been an unrestrained and unfiltered opening to the world, that is to say, to the dominant modern mentality, which at the same time brings up for discussion the very foundations of the *depositum fidei* which for many were no longer clear."

He continues: "Vatican II was right in its desire for a revision of the relations between the Church and the world. There are in fact values, which, even though they originated outside the Church, can find their place—provided they are clarified and corrected—in her perspective. This task has been accomplished in these years. But whoever thinks that these two realities can meet each other without conflict or even be identical would betray that he understands neither the Church nor the world."

138

Are you proposing, perhaps, a return to the old spirit of "opposition to the world"?

"It is not Christians who oppose the world, but rather the world which opposes itself to them when the truth about God, about Christ and about man is proclaimed. The world waxes indignant when sin and grace are called by their names. After the phase of indiscriminate 'openness' it is time that the Christian reacquire the consciousness of belonging to a minority and of often being in opposition to what is obvious, plausible, and natural for that mentality which the New Testament calls—and certainly not in a positive sense—the 'spirit of the world.' It is time to find again the courage of nonconformism, the capacity to oppose many of the trends of the surrounding culture, renouncing a certain euphoric post-conciliar solidarity."

Restoration

At this point—here, too, as during the whole interview, the tape recorder whirred in the silence of the room overlooking the seminary garden—I posed to Cardinal Ratzinger the question whose answer aroused the liveliest reactions. Reactions which were also due to the incomplete ways in which it has often been reported, as well as to the emotion-laden content of the word involved ("restoration"), which hearkens back to times long past and which are certainly neither repeatable nor—at least in our view—even desirable.

Accordingly I asked the Prefect of the Congregation for the Faith: "Considering what you are saying, it would seem that those who assert that the Church hierarchy intends to close the first phase of the post-conciliar period are not wrong. And that (even though it certainly would not be a return to the pre-conciliar period but to the 'authentic' documents of Vatican II) the same hierarchy intends to set a kind of 'restoration' in motion."

This is the Cardinal's reply, in his own words: "If by 'restoration' is meant a turning back, no restoration of such kind is possible. The Church moves forward toward the consummation of history, she looks ahead to the Lord who is coming. No, there is no going back, nor is it possible to go back. Hence there is no 'restoration' whatsoever in this sense. But if by *restoration* we understand the search for a new balance after all the exaggerations of an indiscriminate opening to the world, after the overly positive interpretations of an agnostic and atheistic world, well, then a *restoration* understood in this sense (a newly found balance of orientations and values within the Catholic totality) is altogether desirable and, for that matter, is already in operation in the Church. In this sense it can be said that the first phase after Vatican II has come to a close."

Unforeseen effects

In his view, as he explains to me, "the situation has changed, the climate has changed for the worse with respect to that which sustained a euphoria whose fruits now lie before us as a warning. The Christian is held to that realism which is nothing but complete attention to the signs of the times. Therefore I exclude the possibility that any thought can be given (unrealistically) to go back along the road as if Vatican II had never been. Many of the concrete effects, as we see them now, do not correspond to the intentions of the Council Fathers, but we certainly cannot say: 'It would have been better if it had not been.' John Henry Cardinal Newman, the historian of the councils, the great scholar who was converted to Catholicism from Anglicanism, said that a council was always a risk for the Church and that, consequently, it should only be called to discuss a limited number of issues and not be overly protracted. True, reforms require time, patience, and a readiness to take risks, but it is still not permissible to say: 'Let's not convoke councils because they are dangerous.' I believe, rather, that the true time of Vatican II has not yet come, that its authentic reception has not yet begun: its documents were quickly buried under a pile of superficial or frankly inexact publications. The reading of the letter of the documents will enable us to discover their true spirit. If thus rediscovered in their truth, those great texts will make it possible for us to understand just what happened and to react with a new vigor. I repeat: the Catholic who clearly and, consequently, painfully perceives the damage that has been wrought in his Church by the misinterpretations of Vatican II must find the possibility of revival in Vatican II itself. The Council is his, it does not belong to those who want to continue along a road whose results have been catastrophic. It does not belong to those, who, not by chance, don't know just what to make of Vatican II, which they look upon as a 'fossil of the clerical era.'"

CHAPTER 20

The Meaning of *Subsistit In*

In *Lumen Gentium*, the Second Vatican Council's Dogmatic Constitution on the Church, we read that "the one Church of Christ . . . subsists in [*subsistit in*] the Catholic Church." Following the council, this passage became a point of controversy, as a number of individuals sought to interpret it in a way not in accord with the intended meaning of the council fathers. In this excerpt, taken from a presentation given at a 2000 symposium in Rome on the council (later published in English in the book *Pilgrim Fellowship of Faith*), Ratzinger reaffirms the proper reading of this phrase.

At this point I should like to . . . briefly say how I stand in relation to perhaps the most controversial point in *Lumen gentium*: the meaning of that sentence already referred to, in *Lumen gentium*, number 8—that the one Church of Christ, which we confess in the Creed as being one, holy, catholic, and apostolic, **"subsists"** in the Catholic Church, which is led by Peter and by the bishops in communion with him. The Congregation for the Doctrine of the Faith found itself, in 1985, needing to declare its position in relation to this much-discussed text; this was occasioned by a book by Leonardo Boff in which the author propounded the thesis that just as the one Church of Christ subsists in the Roman Catholic Church, so it does also in other Christian churches. Needless to say, what the Congregation for the Doctrine of the Faith said was overwhelmed with sharp criticisms and then set aside. If we are trying to think about where we are today in the reception of the Council's ecclesiology, then the question of the interpretation of this *subsistit* is unavoidable, and in that case the only official pronouncement of the Magisterium concerning this expression since the Council, the *notificatio* to which we just referred, cannot be ignored. At a distance of fifteen years, it becomes clearer than it was at the time that this was not just a matter of a single theological writer; rather, it is a view of the Church current in a number of different variations and is just as much current today.

The 1985 clarification portrayed the context of Boff's thesis, which we have just briefly repeated, in some detail. We do not need to enter into all these particularities again here, as we are concerned with a more fundamental issue. The thesis of which Boff was at that time the representative might be characterized as ecclesiological relativism. It is justified by its adherents with the view that the "historical Jesus" himself did not think about a Church at all, still less found one. The concrete structure of the Church is said not to have developed until after the Resurrection, in the process of ridding Christianity of eschatology, through the more immediate sociological requirements of institution-alization; and it is said that at the beginning there was certainly no "catholic" Church, but merely various distinct local Churches with varying theologies, with offices that differed, and so on. No institutional Church therefore, it is said, can maintain that she is the one Church of Jesus Christ in accordance with God's will; for then all institutional structures have arisen through various sociological requirements and, hence, are all, as such, human constructions that in new situations may also be radically altered, perhaps indeed must be. They differ from one another in theological quality at a secondary level at most, it is said, and that is why one can say that the "one Church of Christ" subsists in them all, or at any rate in many of them—but the question here, of course, is what right anyone has, taking such a view of things, to talk about the Church of Christ at all.

The Catholic tradition, in contrast to that, has chosen a different starting point: it trusts the evangelists; it believes what they say. Then it is clear that Jesus, who was proclaiming the coming of the Kingdom of God, gathered disciples around himself for realizing that Kingdom in practice; that he not only imparted to them his message as a new inter-pretation of the Old Testament, but also gave them in the Sacrament of the Lord's Supper a new and unifying heart, through which everyone who confessed his name could become one with him in an entirely new way—so much so, that Paul could describe this fellowship as "being one body with Christ," as a spiritual union in the body. It is likewise then clear that the promise of the Holy Spirit was, not just a vague proclamation, but referred to the reality of Pentecost—and, thus, to the fact that the Church was not devised and built up by men but was created by the Holy Spirit and is and remains the creation of the Holy Spirit.

In that case, however, institution and spirit stand in a somewhat different relationship to one another in the Church than the representatives of those tendencies we have mentioned would like to persuade us. The institution is not then a structure we can rebuild or demolish just as we like, which has (allegedly) nothing at all to do with the business of believing. This kind of embodiment is then inherent in the Church herself. The Church of Christ is not hidden behind the multitude of human constructions, intangible and unattainable; she exists in reality as a corporal Church that shows her identity in the Creed, in the sacraments, and in the apostolic succession.

With the *subsistit* formula, Vatican II intended—in line with the Catholic tradition—to say something the exact opposite of "ecclesiological relativism": there is a Church of Jesus Christ. He himself willed her existence, and ever since Pentecost the Holy Spirit is constantly creating her, despite all human failures, and preserves her in her substantial identity. The institution is not an unavoidable—although theologically irrelevant or even damaging—external phenomenon; it is, in its essential core, a part of the concrete character of the Incarnation. The Lord is keeping his word: "The gates of hell shall not prevail against it."

At this point it becomes necessary to trace the term *subsistit* somewhat more carefully. With this expression the Council changed Pius XII's formulation, when he said in his encyclical *Mystici Corporis Christi*: The Catholic Church "is" (*est*) the one Mystical Body of Christ. The distinction between *subsistit* and *est* contains and conceals the entire difficulty of ecumenism. The term *subsistit* derives from classical philosophy, as it was further developed in Scholasticism. The Greek word corresponding to it is *hypostasis*, which plays a central role in

144

Christology, for describing the unity between divine nature and human in the Person of Christ. *Subsistere* is a special variant of *esse*. It is "being" in the form of an independent agent. That is exactly what is concerned here. The Council is trying to tell us that the Church of Jesus Christ may be encountered in this world as **a concrete agent** in the Catholic Church. That can happen only once, and the view that *subsistit* should be multiplied fails to do justice to the particular point intended. With the term *subsistit*, the Council was trying to express the particular quality of the Catholic Church and the fact that this quality cannot be multiplied: the Church exists as an active agent within historical reality.

The distinction between *subsistit* and *est* does, however, imply the drama of the schism of the Church: although the Church is only one, and does really exist, there is being that is derived from the being of the Church, an ecclesiastical entity, even outside the one Church. Because sin is a contradiction, this distinction between *subsistit* and *est* is, in the end, something that cannot be entirely explained logically. Reflected in the paradox of the distinction between the uniqueness and the concrete existence of the Church, on the one hand, and, on the other, the continuing existence of a concrete ecclesiastical entity outside of the one active agent is the contradictory element of human sin, the contradictory element of schism. Such schism is quite different from the relativistic dialectic described above, in which the divisions between Christians are divested of their pain and are not really schisms at all but merely a representation of the multitudinous variations upon a theme, in which all the variations are in some sense right, and all in some sense wrong. There is not in that case actually any inner requirement to seek for unity, because even without it the Church is everywhere and nowhere. Christianity can then only exist at all in variations that are dialectically opposed to one another. Ecumenism then consists of everyone granting each other mutual recognition in some sense, because they are all merely fragments of what Christianity is. Ecumenism then consists in coming to terms with a relativistic dialectical process, because the historical Jesus belongs to the past, and truth in any case remains hidden.

The Council's view is quite different: The fact that in the Catholic Church the *subsistit* of the one active agent, the Church, is present is in absolutely no way the achievement of Catholics but solely the work of God, which he maintains despite the persistent demerits of the human officeholders. They cannot take any credit for this; rather, they can simply marvel at it, with shame at their own sins, at the same time being filled with thanksgiving for the faithfulness of God. Yet the work of their own sins can be seen: the whole world is aware of that drama, in which divided Christian communities stand in opposition to one another, advance their opposing claims to truth, and thus apparently thwart what Christ was praying for on the night before his Passion. While schism is a historical reality anyone can grasp, it is only in faith that one can be aware of the continuing existence, as such, of the one Church in the concrete form of the Catholic Church.

It is because the Second Vatican Council comprehended this paradox that it declared that ecumenism, as a search for true unity, is a duty and handed this on to the Church of the future to be taken with her on the way.

CHAPTER 21

The Hermeneutic of Continuity

During his Christmas address to the Roman Curia in 2005, his first year as pope, Benedict XVI offered an extended reflection on the proper interpretation of the Second Vatican Council, speaking of the need to read the council with a "hermeneutic of reform" and "continuity" rather than a "hermeneutic of discontinuity and rupture."

The last event of this year on which I wish to reflect here is the celebration of the conclusion of the Second Vatican Council 40 years ago. This memory prompts the question: What has been the result of the Council? Was it well received? What, in the acceptance of the Council, was good and what was inadequate or mistaken? What still remains to be done? No one can deny that in vast areas of the Church the implementation of the Council has been somewhat difficult, even without wishing to apply to what occurred in these years the description that St. Basil, the great Doctor of the Church, made of the Church's situation after the Council of Nicaea: he compares her situation to a naval battle in the darkness of the storm, saying among other things: "The raucous shouting of those who through disagreement rise up against one another, the incomprehensible chatter, the confused din of uninterrupted clamoring, has now filled almost the whole of the Church, falsifying through excess or failure the right doctrine of the faith . . ." (*De Spiritu Sancto*, XXX, 77; PG 32, 213 A; SCh 17 ff., p. 524).

We do not want to apply precisely this dramatic description to the situation of the post-conciliar period, yet something from all that occurred is nevertheless reflected in it. The question arises: Why has the implementation of the Council, in large parts of the Church, thus far been so difficult?

Well, it all depends on the correct interpretation of the Council or—as we would say today—on its proper hermeneutics, the correct key to its interpretation and application. The problems in its implementation arose from the fact that two contrary hermeneutics came face to face and quarreled with each other. One caused confusion, the other, silently but more and more visibly, bore and is bearing fruit.

On the one hand, there is an interpretation that I would call "a hermeneutic of discontinuity and rupture"; it has frequently availed itself of the sympathies of the mass media, and also one trend of modern theology. On the other, there is the "hermeneutic of reform," of renewal in the continuity of the one subject-Church which the Lord has given to us. She is a subject which increases in time and develops, yet always remaining the same, the one subject of the journeying People of God.

The hermeneutic of discontinuity risks ending in a split between the pre-conciliar Church and the post-conciliar Church. It asserts that the texts of the Council as such do not yet express the true spirit of the Council. It claims that they are the result of compromises in which, to reach unanimity, it was found necessary to keep and reconfirm many old things that are now pointless. However, the true spirit of the Council is not to be found in these compromises but instead in the impulses toward the new that are contained in the texts.

These innovations alone were supposed to represent the true spirit of the Council, and starting from and in conformity with them, it would be possible to move ahead. Precisely because the texts would only imperfectly reflect the true spirit of the Council and its newness, it would be necessary to go courageously beyond the texts and make room for the newness in which the Council's deepest intention would be expressed, even if it were still vague.

In a word: it would be necessary not to follow the texts of the Council but its spirit. In this way, obviously, a vast margin was left open for the question on how this spirit should subsequently be defined and room was consequently made for every whim.

The nature of a Council as such is therefore basically misunderstood. In this way, it is considered as a sort of constituent that eliminates an old constitution and creates a new one. However, the Constituent Assembly needs a mandator and then confirmation by the mandator, in other words, the people the constitution must serve. The Fathers had no such mandate and no one had ever given them one; nor could anyone have given them one because the essential constitution of the Church comes from the Lord and was given to us so that we might attain eternal life and, starting from this perspective, be able to illuminate life in time and time itself.

Through the Sacrament they have received, Bishops are stewards of the Lord's gift. They are "stewards of the mysteries of God" (1 Cor. 4:1); as such, they must be found to be "faithful" and "wise" (cf. Luke 12:41–48). This requires them to administer the Lord's gift in the right way, so that it is not left concealed in some hiding place but bears fruit, and the Lord may end by saying to the administrator: "Since you were dependable in a small matter I will put you in charge of larger affairs" (cf. Matt. 25:14–30; Luke 19:11–27).

These Gospel parables express the dynamic of fidelity required in the Lord's service; and through them it becomes clear that, as in a Council, the dynamic and fidelity must converge.

The hermeneutic of discontinuity is countered by the hermeneutic of reform, as it was presented first by Pope John XXIII in his Speech inaugurating the Council on October 11, 1962 and later by Pope Paul VI in his Discourse for the Council's conclusion on December 7, 1965.

Here I shall cite only John XXIII's well-known words, which unequivocally express this hermeneutic when he says that the Council wishes "to transmit the doctrine, pure and integral, without any attenuation or distortion." And he continues: "Our duty is not only to guard this precious treasure, as if we were concerned only with antiquity, but to dedicate ourselves with an earnest will and without fear to that work which our era demands of us . . ." It is necessary that "adherence to all the teaching of the Church in its entirety and preciseness . . ."

be presented in "faithful and perfect conformity to the authentic doctrine, which, however, should be studied and expounded through the methods of research and through the literary forms of modern thought. The substance of the ancient doctrine of the deposit of faith is one thing, and the way in which it is presented is another . . . ," retaining the same meaning and message (*The Documents of Vatican II*, Walter M. Abbott, S.J., p. 715).

It is clear that this commitment to expressing a specific truth in a new way demands new thinking on this truth and a new and vital relationship with it; it is also clear that new words can only develop if they come from an informed understanding of the truth expressed, and on the other hand, that a reflection on faith also requires that this faith be lived. In this regard, the program that Pope John XXIII proposed was extremely demanding, indeed, just as the synthesis of fidelity and dynamic is demanding.

However, wherever this interpretation guided the implementation of the Council, new life developed and new fruit ripened. Forty years after the Council, we can show that the positive is far greater and livelier than it appeared to be in the turbulent years around 1968. Today, we see that although the good seed developed slowly, it is nonetheless growing; and our deep gratitude for the work done by the Council is likewise growing.

In his Discourse closing the Council, Paul VI pointed out a further specific reason why a hermeneutic of discontinuity can seem convincing.

In the great dispute about man which marks the modern epoch, the Council had to focus in particular on the theme of anthropology. It had to question the relationship between the Church and her faith on the one hand, and man and the contemporary world on the other (cf. ibid.). The question becomes even clearer if, instead of the generic term "contemporary world," we opt for another that is more precise: the Council had to determine in a new way the relationship between the Church and the modern era.

This relationship had a somewhat stormy beginning with the Galileo case. It was then totally interrupted when Kant described "religion within pure reason" and when, in the radical phase of the French Revolution, an image of the State and the human being that practically no longer wanted to allow the Church any room was disseminated.

In the 19th century under Pius IX, the clash between the Church's faith and a radical liberalism and the natural sciences, which also claimed to embrace with their knowledge the whole of reality to its limit, stubbornly proposing to make the "hypothesis of God" superfluous, had elicited from the Church a bitter and radical condemnation of this spirit of the modern age. Thus, it seemed that there was no longer any milieu open to a positive and fruitful understanding, and the rejection by those who felt they were the representatives of the modern era was also drastic.

In the meantime, however, the modern age had also experienced developments. People came to realize that the American Revolution was offering a model of a modern State that differed from the theoretical model with radical tendencies that had emerged during the second phase of the French Revolution.

The natural sciences were beginning to reflect more and more clearly their own limitations imposed by their own method, which, despite achieving great things, was nevertheless unable to grasp the global nature of reality.

So it was that both parties were gradually beginning to open up to each other. In the period between the two World Wars and especially after the Second World War, Catholic statesmen demonstrated that a modern secular State could exist that was not neutral regarding values but alive, drawing from the great ethical sources opened by Christianity.

Catholic social doctrine, as it gradually developed, became an important model between radical liberalism and the Marxist theory of the State. The natural sciences, which without reservation professed a method of their own to which God was barred access, realized ever more

151

clearly that this method did not include the whole of reality. Hence, they once again opened their doors to God, knowing that reality is greater than the naturalistic method and all that it can encompass.

It might be said that three circles of questions had formed which then, at the time of the Second Vatican Council, were expecting an answer. First of all, the relationship between faith and modern science had to be redefined. Furthermore, this did not only concern the natural sciences but also historical science for, in a certain school, the historical-critical method claimed to have the last word on the interpretation of the Bible and, demanding total exclusivity for its interpretation of Sacred Scripture, was opposed to important points in the interpretation elaborated by the faith of the Church.

Secondly, it was necessary to give a new definition to the relationship between the Church and the modern State that would make room impartially for citizens of various religions and ideologies, merely assuming responsibility for an orderly and tolerant coexistence among them and for the freedom to practice their own religion.

Thirdly, linked more generally to this was the problem of religious tolerance—a question that required a new definition of the relationship between the Christian faith and the world religions. In particular, before the recent crimes of the Nazi regime and, in general, with a retrospective look at a long and difficult history, it was necessary to evaluate and define in a new way the relationship between the Church and the faith of Israel.

These are all subjects of great importance—they were the great themes of the second part of the Council—on which it is impossible to reflect more broadly in this context. It is clear that in all these sectors, which all together form a single problem, some kind of discontinuity might emerge. Indeed, a discontinuity had been revealed but in which, after the various distinctions between concrete historical situations and their requirements had been made, the continuity of principles proved not to have been abandoned. It is easy to miss this fact at a first glance.

It is precisely in this combination of continuity and discontinuity at different levels that the very nature of true reform consists. In this process of innovation in continuity we must learn to understand more practically than before that the Church's decisions on contingent matters—for example, certain practical forms of liberalism or a free interpretation of the Bible—should necessarily be contingent themselves, precisely because they refer to a specific reality that is changeable in itself. It was necessary to learn to recognize that in these decisions it is only the principles that express the permanent aspect, since they remain as an undercurrent, motivating decisions from within. On the other hand, not so permanent are the practical forms that depend on the historical situation and are therefore subject to change.

Basic decisions, therefore, continue to be well-grounded, whereas the way they are applied to new contexts can change. Thus, for example, if religious freedom were to be considered an expression of the human inability to discover the truth and thus become a canonization of relativism, then this social and historical necessity is raised inappropriately to the metaphysical level and thus stripped of its true meaning. Consequently, it cannot be accepted by those who believe that the human person is capable of knowing the truth about God and, on the basis of the inner dignity of the truth, is bound to this knowledge.

It is quite different, on the other hand, to perceive religious freedom as a need that derives from human coexistence, or indeed, as an intrinsic consequence of the truth that cannot be externally imposed but that the person must adopt only through the process of conviction.

The Second Vatican Council, recognizing and making its own an essential principle of the modern State with the Decree on Religious Freedom, has recovered the deepest patrimony of the Church. By so doing she can be conscious of being in full harmony with the teaching of Jesus himself (cf. Matt. 22:21), as well as with the Church of the martyrs of all time. The ancient Church naturally prayed for the emperors and political leaders out of duty (cf. 1 Tim. 2:2); but while she prayed for the emperors, she refused to worship them and thereby clearly rejected the religion of the State.

The martyrs of the early Church died for their faith in that God who was revealed in Jesus Christ, and for this very reason they also died for freedom of conscience and the freedom to profess one's own faith—a profession that no State can impose but which, instead, can only be claimed with God's grace in freedom of conscience. A missionary Church known for proclaiming her message to all peoples must necessarily work for the freedom of the faith. She desires to transmit the gift of the truth that exists for one and all.

At the same time, she assures peoples and their Governments that she does not wish to destroy their identity and culture by doing so, but to give them, on the contrary, a response which, in their innermost depths, they are waiting for—a response with which the multiplicity of cultures is not lost but instead unity between men and women increases and thus also peace between peoples.

The Second Vatican Council, with its new definition of the relationship between the faith of the Church and certain essential elements of modern thought, has reviewed or even corrected certain historical decisions, but in this apparent discontinuity it has actually preserved and deepened her inmost nature and true identity.

The Church, both before and after the Council, was and is the same Church, one, holy, catholic, and apostolic, journeying on through time; she continues "her pilgrimage amid the persecutions of the world and the consolations of God," proclaiming the death of the Lord until he comes (cf. *Lumen Gentium*, no. 8).

Those who expected that with this fundamental "yes" to the modern era all tensions would be dispelled and that the "openness towards the world" accordingly achieved would transform everything into pure harmony, had underestimated the inner tensions as well as the contradictions inherent in the modern epoch.

They had underestimated the perilous frailty of human nature which has been a threat to human progress in all the periods of history and in every historical constellation. These dangers, with the new possibilities and new power of man over matter and over himself, did not disappear but instead acquired new dimensions: a look at the history of the present day shows this clearly.

In our time too, the Church remains a "sign that will be opposed" (Luke 2:34)—not without reason did Pope John Paul II, then still a Cardinal, give this title to the theme for the Spiritual Exercises he preached in 1976 to Pope Paul VI and the Roman Curia. The Council could not have intended to abolish the Gospel's opposition to human dangers and errors.

On the contrary, it was certainly the Council's intention to overcome erroneous or superfluous contradictions in order to present to our world the requirement of the Gospel in its full greatness and purity.

The steps the Council took towards the modern era which had rather vaguely been presented as "openness to the world," belong in short to the perennial problem of the relationship between faith and reason that is re-emerging in ever new forms. The situation that the Council had to face can certainly be compared to events of previous epochs.

In his First Letter, St Peter urged Christians always to be ready to give an answer (apo-logia) to anyone who asked them for the logos, the reason for their faith (cf. 3:15).

This meant that biblical faith had to be discussed and come into contact with Greek culture and learn to recognize through interpretation the separating line but also the convergence and the affinity between them in the one reason, given by God.

When, in the 13th century through the Jewish and Arab philosophers, Aristotelian thought came into contact with Medieval Christianity formed in the Platonic tradition and faith and reason risked entering an irreconcilable contradiction, it was above all St Thomas Aquinas who mediated the new encounter between faith and Aristotelian philosophy, thereby setting faith in a positive relationship with the form of reason prevalent in his time. There is no doubt that the wearing dispute between modern reason and the Christian faith, which had begun negatively with the Galileo case, went through many phases, but with the Second Vatican Council the time came when broad new thinking was required.

Its content was certainly only roughly traced in the conciliar texts, but this determined its essential direction, so that the dialogue between reason and faith, particularly important today, found its bearings on the basis of the Second Vatican Council.

This dialogue must now be developed with great open-mindedness but also with that clear discernment that the world rightly expects of us in this very moment. Thus, today we can look with gratitude at the Second Vatican Council: if we interpret and implement it guided by a right hermeneutic, it can be and can become increasingly powerful for the ever necessary renewal of the Church.

PART VI

THE BIBLE

CHAPTER 22

The Limits of the
Historical-Critical Method

In the introduction to the first of his three Jesus of Nazareth *books, Ratzinger explains his approach to reading and interpreting the Gospel accounts of the life of Christ. While recognizing the historical-critical method as an "indispensable tool," he notes that it does not exhaust the interpretation of Scripture, and must be supplemented by a more holistic reading shaped by the faith of the Church.*

The historical-critical method—specifically because of the intrinsic nature of theology and faith—is and remains an indispensable dimension of exegetical work. For it is of the very essence of biblical faith to be about real historical events. It does not tell stories symbolizing supra-historical truths, but is based on history, history that took place here on this earth. The *factum historicum* (historical fact) is not an interchangeable symbolic cipher for biblical faith, but the foundation on which it stands: *Et incarnatus est*—when we say these words, we acknowledge God's actual entry into real history.

If we push this history aside, Christian faith as such disappears and is recast as some other religion. So if history, if facticity in this sense, is an essential dimension of Christian faith, then faith must expose itself to the historical method—indeed, faith itself demands this. I have already mentioned the conciliar Constitution on Divine Revelation; it makes the same point quite explicitly in paragraph 12 and goes on to list some concrete elements of method that have to be kept in mind when interpreting Scripture. The Pontifical Biblical Commission's document on the interpretation of Holy Scripture develops the same idea much more amply in the chapter entitled "Methods and Approaches for Interpretation."

The historical-critical method—let me repeat—is an indispensable tool, given the structure of Christian faith. But we need to add two points. This method is a fundamental dimension of exegesis, but it does not exhaust the interpretive task for someone who sees the biblical writings as a single corpus of Holy Scripture inspired by God. We will have to return to this point at greater length in a moment.

For the time being, it is important—and this is a second point—to recognize the limits of the historical-critical method itself. For someone who considers himself directly addressed by the Bible today, the method's first limit is that by its very nature it has to leave the biblical word in the past. It is a *historical* method, and that means that it investigates the then-current context of events in which the texts originated. It attempts to identify and to understand the past—as it was in itself—with the greatest possible precision, in order then to find out what the author could have said and intended to say in the context of the mentality and events of the time. To the extent that it remains true to itself, the historical method not only has to investigate the biblical word as a thing of the past, but also has to let it remain in the past. It can glimpse points of contact with the present and it can try to apply the biblical word to the present; the one thing it cannot do is make it into something present *today*—that would be overstepping its bounds. Its very precision in interpreting the reality of the past is both its strength and its limit.

This is connected with a further point. Because it is a historical method, it presupposes the uniformity of the context within which the events of history unfold. It must therefore treat the biblical words it investigates as human words. On painstaking reflection, it can intuit something of the "deeper value" the word contains. It can in some sense catch the sounds of a higher dimension through the human word. But its specific object is the human word as human.

Ultimately, it considers the individual books of Scripture in the context of their historical period, and then analyzes them further according to their sources. The unity of all of these writings as one "Bible," however, is not something it can recognize as an immediate historical datum. Of course it can examine the lines of development, the growth of traditions, and in that sense can look beyond the individual books to see how they come together to form the one "Scripture." Nevertheless, it always has to begin by going back to the origin of the individual texts, which means placing them in their past context, even if it goes on to complement this move back in time by following up the process through which the texts were later brought together.

We have to keep in mind the limit of all efforts to know the past: We can never go beyond the domain of hypothesis, because we simply cannot bring the past into the present. To be sure, some hypotheses enjoy a high degree of certainty, but overall we need to remain conscious of the limit of our certainties—indeed, the history of modern exegesis makes this limit perfectly evident.

So far, then, we have said something about the importance of the historical-critical method, on one hand, and we have described its limit, on the other. Something more than just the limit has come into view, though, I hope: the fact that the inner nature of the method points beyond itself and contains within itself an openness to complementary methods. In these words from the past, we can discern the question concerning their meaning for today; a voice greater than man's echoes in Scripture's human words; the individual writings [Schrifte] of the Bible point somehow to the living process that shapes the one Scripture [Schrift].

Indeed, the realization of this last point some thirty years ago led American scholars to develop the project of "canonical exegesis." The aim of this exegesis is to read individual texts within the totality of the one Scripture, which then sheds new light on all the individual texts. Paragraph 12 of the Second Vatican Council's Constitution on Divine Revelation had already dearly underscored this as a fundamental principle of theological exegesis: If you want to understand the Scripture in the spirit in which it is written, you have to attend to the content and to the unity of Scripture as a whole. The Council goes on to stress the need for taking account of the living tradition of the whole Church and of the analogy of faith (the intrinsic correspondences within the faith).

Let us dwell for the time being on the unity of Scripture. It is a theological datum. But it is not simply imposed from the outside on what is in itself a heterogeneous ensemble of writings. Modern exegesis has brought to light the process of constant rereading that forged the words transmitted in the Bible into Scripture: Older texts are reappropriated, reinterpreted, and read with new eyes in new contexts. They become Scripture by being read anew, evolving in continuity with their original sense, tacitly corrected and given added depth and breadth of meaning. This is a process in which the word gradually unfolds its inner potentialities, already somehow present like seeds, but needing the challenge of new situations, new experiences and new sufferings, in order to open up.

This process is certainly not linear, and it is often dramatic, but when you watch it unfold in light of Jesus Christ, you can see it moving in a single overall direction; you can see that the Old and New Testaments belong together. This Christological hermeneutic, which sees Jesus Christ as the key to the whole and learns from him how to understand the Bible as a unity, presupposes a prior act of faith. It cannot be the conclusion of a purely historical method. But this act of faith is based upon reason—historical reason—and so makes it possible to see the internal unity of Scripture. By the same token, it enables us to understand anew the individual elements that have shaped it, without robbing them of their historical originality.

"Canonical exegesis"—reading the individual texts of the Bible in the context of the whole—is an essential dimension of exegesis. It does not contradict historical-critical interpretation, but carries it forward in an organic way toward becoming theology in the proper sense. There are two further aspects of theological exegesis that I would like to underscore. Historical-critical interpretation of a text seeks to discover the precise sense the words were intended to convey at their time and place of origin. That is good and important. But—aside from the fact that such reconstructions can claim only a relative certainty—it is necessary to keep in mind that any human utterance of a certain weight contains more than the author may have been immediately aware of at the time. When a word transcends the moment in which it is spoken, it carries within itself a "deeper value." This "deeper value" pertains most of all to words that have matured in the course of faith-history. For in this case the author is not simply speaking for himself on his own authority. He is speaking from the perspective of a common history that sustains him and that already implicitly contains the possibilities of its future, of the further stages of its journey. The process of continually rereading and drawing out new meanings from words would not have been possible unless the words themselves were already open to it from within.

At this point we get a glimmer, even on the historical level, of what inspiration means: The author does not speak as a private, self-contained subject. He speaks in a living community, that is to say, in a living historical movement not created by him, nor even by the collective, but which is led forward by a greater power that is at work. There are dimensions of the word that the old doctrine of the fourfold sense of Scripture pinpointed with remarkable accuracy. The four senses of Scripture are not individual meanings arrayed side by side, but dimensions of the one word that reaches beyond the moment.

This already suggests the second aspect I wanted to speak about. Neither the individual books of Holy Scripture nor the Scripture as a whole are simply a piece of literature. The Scripture emerged from within the heart of a living subject—the pilgrim People of God—and lives within this same subject. One could say that the books of Scripture involve three interacting subjects. First of all, there is the individual author or group of authors to whom we owe a particular scriptural text. But these authors are not autonomous writers in the modern sense; they form part of a collective subject, the "People of God," from within whose heart and to whom they speak. Hence, this subject is actually the deeper "author" of the Scriptures. And yet likewise, this people does not exist alone; rather, it knows that it is led, and spoken to, by God himself,

163

who—through men and their humanity—is at the deepest level the one speaking.

The connection with the subject we call "People of God" is vital for Scripture. On one hand, this book—Scripture—is the measure that comes from God, the power directing the people. On the other hand, though, Scripture lives precisely within this people, even as this people transcends itself in Scripture. Through their self-transcendence (a fruit, at the deepest level, of the incarnate Word) they become the people of God. The People of God—the Church—is the living subject of Scripture; it is in the Church that the words of the Bible are always in the present. This also means, of course, that the People has to receive its very self from God, ultimately from the incarnate Christ; it has to let itself be ordered, guided, and led by him.

CHAPTER 23

The Senses of Scripture

In his 2010 apostolic exhortation *Verbum Domini* (*The Word of the Lord*), Benedict XVI offers some key insights into the literal and spiritual senses of Scripture, which allow Christians to understand the "intrinsic unity" of the Bible as a whole.

Literal sense and spiritual sense

A significant contribution to the recovery of an adequate scriptural hermeneutic, as the synodal assembly stated, can also come from renewed attention to the Fathers of the Church and their exegetical approach.[1] The Church Fathers present a theology that still has great value today because at its heart is the study of sacred Scripture as a whole. Indeed, the Fathers are primarily and essentially "commentators on sacred Scripture."[2] Their example can "teach modern exegetes a truly religious approach to sacred Scripture, and likewise an interpretation that is constantly attuned to the criterion of communion with the experience of the Church, which journeys through history under the guidance of the Holy Spirit."[3]

While obviously lacking the philological and historical resources at the disposal of modern exegesis, the patristic and mediaeval tradition could recognize the different senses of Scripture, beginning with the literal sense, namely, "the meaning conveyed by the words of Scripture and discovered by exegesis, following the rules of sound interpretation."[4] Saint Thomas Aquinas, for example, states that "all the senses of sacred

---

1. Cf. *Propositio* 6.

2. Cf. Saint Augustine, *De libero arbitrio*, III, XXI, 59: PL 32, 1300; *De Trinitate*, II, I, 2: PL 42, 845.

3. Congregation for Catholic Education, Instruction *Inspectis Dierum* (November 10, 1989), 26: AAS 82 (1990), 618.

4. *Catechism of the Catholic Church*, 116.

Scripture are based on the literal sense."[5] It is necessary, however, to remember that in patristic and medieval times every form of exegesis, including the literal form, was carried out on the basis of faith, without there necessarily being any distinction between the *literal sense* and the *spiritual sense*. One may mention in this regard the medieval couplet which expresses the relationship between the different senses of Scripture:

> "*Littera gesta docet, quid credas allegoria,*
> *Moralis quid agas, quo tendas anagogia.*

> The letter speaks of deeds; allegory about the faith;
> The moral about our actions; anagogy about our destiny."[6]

Here we can note the unity and interrelation between the *literal sense* and the *spiritual sense*, which for its part is subdivided into three senses which deal with the contents of the faith, with the moral life and with our eschatological aspiration.

In a word, while acknowledging the validity and necessity, as well as the limits, of the historical-critical method, we learn from the Fathers that exegesis "is truly faithful to the proper intention of biblical texts when it goes not only to the heart of their formulation to find the reality of faith there expressed, but also seeks to link this reality to the experience of faith in our present world."[7] Only against this horizon can we recognize that the word of God is living and addressed to each of us in the here and now of our lives. In this sense, the Pontifical Biblical Commission's definition of the spiritual sense, as understood by Christian faith, remains fully valid: it is "the meaning expressed by the biblical texts when read, under the influence of the Holy Spirit, in the context of the paschal mystery of Christ and of the new life which flows from it. This context truly exists. In it the New Testament

---

5. *Summa Theologiae*, I, q. 1, art. 10, ad 1.

6. *Catechism of the Catholic Church*, 118.

7. Pontifical Biblical Commission, *The Interpretation of the Bible in the Church* (April 15, 1993), II, A, 2: *Enchiridion Vaticanum* 13, No. 2987.

recognizes the fulfilment of the Scriptures. It is therefore quite accept-able to re-read the Scriptures in the light of this new context, which is that of life in the Spirit."[8]

The need to transcend the "letter"

In rediscovering the interplay between the different senses of Scripture it thus becomes essential to grasp the *passage from letter to spirit.* This is not an automatic, spontaneous passage; rather, the letter needs to be transcended: "the word of God can never simply be equated with the letter of the text. To attain to it involves a progression and a process of understanding guided by the inner movement of the whole corpus, and hence it also has to become a vital process."[9] Here we see the reason why an authentic process of interpretation is never purely an intellec-tual process but also a lived one, demanding full engagement in the life of the Church, which is life "according to the Spirit" (Gal. 5:16). The criteria set forth in Number 12 of the Dogmatic Constitution *Dei Verbum* thus become clearer: this progression cannot take place with regard to an individual literary fragment unless it is seen in relation to the whole of Scripture. Indeed, the goal to which we are necessarily progressing is the one Word. There is an inner drama in this process, since the passage that takes place in the power of the Spirit inevita-bly engages each person's freedom. Saint Paul lived this passage to the full in his own life. In his words: *"the letter kills, but the Spirit gives life"* (2 Cor. 3:6), he expressed in radical terms the significance of this pro-cess of transcending the letter and coming to understand it only in terms of the whole. Paul discovered that "the Spirit of freedom has a name, and hence that freedom has an inner criterion: 'The Lord is the Spirit and where the Spirit of the Lord is, there is freedom' (2 Cor. 3:17). The Spirit of freedom is not simply the exegete's own idea, the exegete's own vision. The Spirit is Christ, and Christ is the Lord who shows

8. Ibid., II, B, 2: *Enchiridion Vaticanum* 13, No. 3003.

9. Benedict XVI, *Address to Representatives of the World of Culture at the "Collège des Bernardins" in Paris* (September 12, 2008): AAS 100 (2008), 726.

us the way."[10] We know that for Saint Augustine too this passage was at once dramatic and liberating; he came to believe the Scriptures—which at first sight struck him as so disjointed in themselves and in places so coarse—through the very process of transcending the letter which he learned from Saint Ambrose in typological interpretation, wherein the entire Old Testament is a path to Jesus Christ. For Saint Augustine, transcending the literal sense made the letter itself credible, and enabled him to find at last the answer to his deep inner restlessness and his thirst for truth.[11]

The Bible's intrinsic unity

In the passage from letter to spirit, we also learn, within the Church's great tradition, to see the unity of all Scripture, grounded in the unity of God's word, which challenges our life and constantly calls us to conversion.[12] Here the words of Hugh of Saint Victor remain a sure guide: "All divine Scripture is one book, and this one book is Christ, speaks of Christ and finds its fulfilment in Christ."[13] Viewed in purely historical or literary terms, of course, the Bible is not a single book, but a collection of literary texts composed over the course of a thousand years or more, and its individual books are not easily seen to possess an interior unity; instead, we see clear inconsistencies between them. This was already the case with the Bible of Israel, which we Christians call the Old Testament. It is all the more so when, as Christians, we relate the New Testament and its writings as a kind of hermeneutical key to Israel's Bible, thus interpreting the latter as a path to Christ. The New Testament generally does not employ the term "Scripture" (cf. Rom. 4:3; 1 Pet. 2:6), but rather "the Scriptures" (cf. Matt. 21:43; John 5:39; Rom. 1:2; 2 Pet. 3:16), which nonetheless are seen in their entirety as the one word of God addressed

---

10. Ibid.
11. Cf. Id., *General Audience* (January 9, 2008): *Insegnamenti* IV, 1 (2008), 41–45.
12. Cf. *Propositio* 29.
13. *De Arca Noe*, 2, 8: PL 176, 642C–D.

to us.[14] This makes it clear that the person of Christ gives unity to all the "Scriptures" in relation to the one "Word." In this way we can understand the words of Number 12 of the Dogmatic Constitution *Dei Verbum*, which point to the internal unity of the entire Bible as a decisive criterion for a correct hermeneutic of faith.

The relationship between the Old and the New Testaments

Against this backdrop of the unity of the Scriptures in Christ, theologians and pastors alike need to be conscious of the relationship between Old and the New Testaments. First of all, it is evident that *the New Testament itself acknowledges the Old Testament as the word of God* and thus accepts the authority of the sacred Scriptures of the Jewish people.[15] It implicitly acknowledges them by using the same language and by frequently referring to passages from these Scriptures. It explicitly acknowledges them by citing many parts of them as a basis for argument. In the New Testament, an argument based on texts from the Old Testament thus has a definitive quality, superior to that of mere human argumentation. In the Fourth Gospel, Jesus states that "Scripture cannot be rejected" (John 10:35) and Saint Paul specifically makes clear that the Old Testament revelation remains valid for us Christians (cf. Rom. 15:4; 1 Cor. 10:11).[16] We also affirm that "Jesus of Nazareth was a Jew and the Holy Land is the motherland of the Church":[17] the roots of Christianity are found in the Old Testament, and Christianity continually draws nourishment from these roots. Consequently, sound Christian doctrine has always resisted all new forms of Marcionism, which tend, in different ways, to set the Old Testament in opposition to the New.[18]

---

14. Cf. Benedict XVI, *Address to Representatives of the World of Culture at the "Collège des Bernardins" in Paris* (September 12, 2008): AAS 100 (2008), 725.

15. Cf. *Propositio* 10; Pontifical Biblical Commission, *The Jewish People and their Sacred Scriptures in the Christian Bible* (May 24, 2001): Enchiridion Vaticanum 20, Nos. 748–755.

16. Cf. *Catechism of the Catholic Church*, 121–122.

17. *Propositio* 52.

18. Cf. Pontifical Biblical Commission, *The Jewish People and their Sacred Scriptures in the Christian Bible* (May 24, 2001), 19: Enchiridion Vaticanum 20, Nos. 799–801; Origen, Homily on Numbers 9, 4: SC 415, 238–242.

Moreover, the New Testament itself claims to be consistent with the Old and proclaims that in the mystery of the life, death, and resurrection of Christ the sacred Scriptures of the Jewish people have found their perfect fulfilment. It must be observed, however, that the concept of the fulfilment of the Scriptures is a complex one, since it has three dimensions: a basic aspect of *continuity* with the Old Testament revelation, an aspect of *discontinuity* and an aspect of *fulfilment and transcendence.* The mystery of Christ stands in continuity of intent with the sacrificial cult of the Old Testament, but it came to pass in a very different way, corresponding to a number of prophetic statements and thus reaching a perfection never previously obtained. The Old Testament is itself replete with tensions between its institutional and its prophetic aspects. The paschal mystery of Christ is in complete conformity—albeit in a way that could not have been anticipated—with the prophecies and the foreshadowings of the Scriptures; yet it presents clear aspects of discontinuity with regard to the institutions of the Old Testament.

These considerations show the unique importance of the Old Testament for Christians, while at the same time bringing out the *newness of Christological interpretation.* From apostolic times and in her living Tradition, the Church has stressed the unity of God's plan in the two Testaments through the use of typology; this procedure is in no way arbitrary, but is intrinsic to the events related in the sacred text and thus involves the whole of Scripture. Typology "discerns in God's works of the Old Covenant prefigurations of what he accomplished in the fullness of time in the person of his incarnate Son."[19] Christians, then, read the Old Testament in the light of Christ crucified and risen. While typological interpretation manifests the inexhaustible content of the Old Testament from the standpoint of the New, we must not forget that the Old Testament retains its own inherent value as revelation, as our Lord himself reaffirmed (cf. Mark 12:29–31). Consequently, "the New Testament has to be read in the light of the Old. Early Christian

---

19. *Catechism of the Catholic Church*, 128.

catechesis made constant use of the Old Testament (cf. 1 Cor. 5:6–8; 1 Cor. 10:1–11)."[20] For this reason the Synod Fathers stated that "the Jewish understanding of the Bible can prove helpful to Christians for their own understanding and study of the Scriptures."[21]

"The New Testament is hidden in the Old and the Old is made manifest in the New,"[22] as Saint Augustine perceptively noted. It is important, therefore, that in both pastoral and academic settings the close relationship between the two Testaments be clearly brought out, in keeping with the dictum of Saint Gregory the Great that "what the Old Testament promised, the New Testament made visible; what the former announces in a hidden way, the latter openly proclaims as present. Therefore the Old Testament is a prophecy of the New Testament; and the best commentary on the Old Testament is the New Testament."[23]

20. Ibid., 129.

21. *Propositio* 52.

22. *Quaestiones in Heptateuchum*, 2, 73: PL 34, 623.

23. *Homiliae in Ezechielem* I, VI, 15: PL 76, 836B.

CHAPTER 24

Lectio Divina

Latin for "holy reading," *lectio divina* refers to the practice of prayerfully reading Scripture as a way to listen to the voice of God in our lives. In this excerpt, taken from his 2010 apostolic exhortation *Verbum Domini*, Benedict XVI outlines the basic steps of this method of prayer.

The Synod frequently insisted on the need for a prayerful approach to the sacred text as a fundamental element in the spiritual life of every believer, in the various ministries and states in life, with particular reference to *lectio divina*.[1] The word of God is at the basis of all authentic Christian spirituality. The Synod Fathers thus took up the words of the Dogmatic Constitution *Dei Verbum*: "Let the faithful go gladly to the sacred text itself, whether in the sacred liturgy, which is full of the divine words, or in devout reading, or in such suitable exercises and various other helps which, with the approval and guidance of the pastors of the Church, are happily spreading everywhere in our day. Let them remember, however, that prayer should accompany the reading of sacred Scripture."[2] The Council thus sought to reappropriate the great patristic tradition which had always recommended approaching the Scripture in dialogue with God. As Saint Augustine puts it: "Your prayer is the word you speak to God. When you read the Bible, God speaks to you; when you pray, you speak to God."[3] Origen, one of the great masters of this way of reading the Bible, maintains that understanding Scripture demands, even more than study, closeness to Christ and prayer. Origen was convinced, in fact, that the best way to know God is through love,

---

1. *Propositiones* 9 and 22.
2. No. 25.
3. *Enarrationes in Psalmos,* 85, 7: PL 37, 1086.

and that there can be no authentic *scientia Christi* apart from growth in his love. In his *Letter to Gregory*, the great Alexandrian theologian gave this advice: "Devote yourself to the *lectio* of the divine Scriptures; apply yourself to this with perseverance. Do your reading with the intent of believing in and pleasing God. If during the *lectio* you encounter a closed door, knock and it will be opened to you by that guardian of whom Jesus said, 'The gatekeeper will open it for him.' By applying your-self in this way to *lectio divina*, search diligently and with unshakable trust in God for the meaning of the divine Scriptures, which is hidden in great fullness within. You ought not, however, to be satisfied merely with knocking and seeking: to understand the things of God, what is absolutely necessary is *oratio*. For this reason, the Savior told us not only: 'Seek and you will find,' and 'Knock and it shall be opened to you,' but also added, 'Ask and you shall receive.'"[4]

In this regard, however, one must *avoid the risk of an individualistic approach*, and remember that God's word is given to us precisely to build communion, to unite us in the Truth along our path to God. While it is a word addressed to each of us personally, it is also a word which builds community, which builds the Church. Consequently, *the sacred text must always be approached in the communion of the Church*. In effect, "a communal reading of Scripture is extremely important, because the living subject in the sacred Scriptures is the People of God, it is the Church. . . . Scripture does not belong to the past, because its subject, the People of God inspired by God himself, is always the same, and therefore the word is always alive in the living subject. As such, it is important to read and experience sacred Scripture in communion with the Church, that is, with all the great witnesses to this word, beginning with the earliest Fathers up to the saints of our own day, up to the pres-ent-day magisterium."[5]

---

4. Origen, *Epistola ad Gregorium*, 3: PG 11, 92.

5. Benedict XVI, *Address to the Students of the Roman Major Seminary* (February 19, 2007): AAS 99 (2007), 253–254.

For this reason, *the privileged place* for the prayerful reading of sacred Scripture *is the liturgy*, and particularly *the Eucharist*, in which, as we celebrate the Body and Blood of Christ in the sacrament, the word itself is present and at work in our midst. In some sense the prayerful reading of the Bible, personal and communal, must always be related to the Eucharistic celebration. Just as the adoration of the Eucharist prepares for, accompanies, and follows the liturgy of the Eucharist,[6] so too prayerful reading, personal and communal, prepares for, accompanies and deepens what the Church celebrates when she proclaims the word in a liturgical setting. By so closely relating *lectio* and liturgy, we can better grasp the criteria which should guide this practice in the area of pastoral care and in the spiritual life of the People of God.

The documents produced before and during the Synod mentioned a number of methods for a faith-filled and fruitful approach to sacred Scripture. Yet the greatest attention was paid to *lectio divina*, which is truly "capable of opening up to the faithful the treasures of God's word, but also of bringing about an encounter with Christ, the living word of God."[7] I would like here to review the basic steps of this procedure. It opens with the reading (*lectio*) of a text, which leads to a desire to understand its true content: *what does the biblical text say in itself?* Without this, there is always a risk that the text will become a pretext for never moving beyond our own ideas. Next comes meditation (*meditatio*), which asks: *what does the biblical text say to us?* Here, each person, individually but also as a member of the community, must let himself or herself be moved and challenged. Following this comes prayer (*oratio*), which asks the question: *what do we say to the Lord in response to his word?* Prayer, as petition, intercession, thanksgiving and praise, is the primary way by which the word transforms us. Finally, *lectio divina* concludes with contemplation (*contemplatio*), during which we take up, as a gift from God, his own way of seeing and judging reality, and ask

---

6. Cf. Id., Post-Synodal Apostolic Exhortation *Sacramentum Caritatis* (February 22, 2007), 66; AAS 99 (2007), 155–156.

7. *Final Message*, III, 9.

ourselves *what conversion of mind, heart, and life is the Lord asking of us?* In the *Letter to the Romans*, Saint Paul tells us: "Do not be conformed to this world, but be transformed by the renewal of your mind, that you may prove what is the will of God, what is good and acceptable and perfect" (12:2). Contemplation aims at creating within us a truly wise and discerning vision of reality, as God sees it, and at forming within us "the mind of Christ" (1 Cor. 2:16). The word of God appears here as a criterion for discernment: it is "living and active, sharper than any two-edged sword, piercing to the division of soul and spirit, of joints and marrow, and discerning the thoughts and intentions of the heart" (Heb. 4:12). We do well also to remember that the process of *lectio divina* is not concluded until it arrives at action (*actio*), which moves the believer to make his or her life a gift for others in charity.

We find the supreme synthesis and fulfilment of this process in the Mother of God. For every member of the faithful Mary is the model of docile acceptance of God's word, for she "kept all these things, pondering them in her heart" (Luke 2:19; cf. 2:51); she discovered the profound bond which unites, in God's great plan, apparently disparate events, actions, and things.[8]

I would also like to echo what the Synod proposed about the importance of the personal reading of Scripture, also as a practice allowing for the possibility, in accordance with the Church's usual conditions, of gaining an indulgence either for oneself or for the faithful departed.[9] The practice of indulgences[10] implies the doctrine of the infinite merits of Christ—which the Church, as the minister of the redemption, dispenses and applies, but it also implies that of the communion of saints, and it teaches us that "to whatever degree we are united in Christ, we are united to one another, and the supernatural life of each one can be

---

8. Ibid.

9. "*Plenaria indulgentia* conceditur christifideli qui Sacram Scripturam, iuxta textum a competenti auctoritate adprobatum, cum veneratione divino eloquio debita et ad modum lectionis spiritalis, per dimidiam saltem horam legerit; si per minus tempus id egerit *indulgentia* erit partialis": apostolic penitentiary, *Enchiridion Indulgentiarum. Normae et Concessiones* (July 16, 1999), 30, §1.

10. Cf. *Catechism of the Catholic Church*, 1471–1479.

useful for the others."[11] From this standpoint, the reading of the word of God sustains us on our journey of penance and conversion, enables us to deepen our sense of belonging to the Church, and helps us to grow in familiarity with God. As Saint Ambrose puts it, "When we take up the sacred Scriptures in faith and read them with the Church, we walk once more with God in the Garden."[12]

---

11. Paul VI, Apostolic Constitution *Indulgentiarum Doctrina* (January 1, 1967): AAS 59 (1967), 18–19.

12. Cf. *Epistula* 49, 3: PL 16, 1204A.

PART VII

LITURGY, THE SACRAMENTS, AND THE PRIESTHOOD

CHAPTER 25

Liturgy and Life: The Place of the Liturgy in Reality

Taken from chapter 1 of his book *The Spirit of the Liturgy*, published in 2000, this selection offers Ratzinger's reflections on the true nature of liturgy, a topic of central importance throughout his life and writings.

What *is* the liturgy? What happens during the liturgy? What kind of reality do we encounter here? In the 1920s the suggestion was made that we should understand the liturgy in terms of "play." The point of the analogy was that a game has its own rules, sets up its own world, which is in force from the start of play but then, of course, is suspended at the close of play. A further point of similarity was that play, though it has a meaning, does not have a purpose and that for this very reason there is something healing, even liberating, about it. Play takes us out of the world of daily goals and their pressures and into a sphere free of purpose and achievement, releasing us for a time from all the burdens of our daily world of work. Play is a kind of other world, an oasis of freedom, where for a moment we can let life flow freely. We need such moments of retreat from the pressure of daily life if its burden is to be bearable. Now there is some truth in this way of thinking, but it is insufficient. It all depends on what we are playing. Everything we have said can be applied to any game, and the trouble is that serious commitment to the rules needed for playing the game soon develops its own burdens and leads to new kinds of purposefulness. Whether we look at modern sport or at chess championships or, indeed, at any game, we find that play, when it does not degenerate into mere fooling about, quickly turns from being another world, a counter-world or non-world, to being a bit of the normal world with its own laws.

We should mention another aspect of this theory of play, something that brings us closer to the essence of the liturgy. Children's play seems in many ways a kind of anticipation of life, a rehearsal for later life, without its burdens and gravity. On this analogy, the liturgy would be a reminder that we are all children, or should be children, in relation to that true life toward which we yearn to go. Liturgy would be a kind of anticipation, a rehearsal, a prelude for the life to come, for eternal life, which St. Augustine describes, by contrast with life in this world, as a fabric woven, no longer of exigency and need, but of the freedom of generosity and gift. Seen thus, liturgy would be the rediscovery within us of true childhood, of openness to a greatness still to come, which is still unfulfilled in adult life. Here, then, would be the concrete form of hope, which lives in advance the life to come, the only true life, which initiates us into authentic life—the life of freedom, of intimate union with God, of pure openness to our fellowman. Thus it would imprint on the seemingly real life of daily existence the mark of future freedom, break open the walls that confine us, and let the light of heaven shine down upon earth.

This application of play-theory distinguishes the liturgy by its essence from the ordinary kinds of play, which doubtless always contain a longing for the real "game," for a wholly different world in which order and freedom are at one. By contrast with the superficial, utilitarian, or humanly vacuous aspects of ordinary play, the play-theory of liturgy brings out what is special and different about that "play" of Wisdom of which the Bible speaks, the play that can be compared to the liturgy. But this analogy still lacks something, something essential. The idea of a life to come appears only as a vague postulate. The reference to God, without whom the "life to come" would only be a wasteland, remains quite indeterminate. I should like to suggest, therefore, a new approach, this time starting from specific biblical texts.

In the accounts of the events leading up to Israel's flight from Egypt, as well as in those that describe the flight itself, the Exodus appears to have two distinct goals. The first, which is familiar to us all, is the reaching of the Promised Land, in which Israel will at last live on its own soil and territory, with secure borders, as a people with the freedom and independence proper to it. But we also hear repeatedly of another goal. God's original command to Pharaoh runs as follows: "Let my people go, that they may serve me in the wilderness" (Exod. 7:16). These words—"Let my people go, that they may serve me"—are repeated four times, with slight variations, in all the meetings of Pharaoh with Moses and Aaron (cf. Exod. 8:1; 9:1; 9:13; 10:3). In the course of the negotiations with Pharaoh, the goal becomes more concrete. Pharaoh shows he is willing to compromise. For him the issue is the Israelites' freedom of worship, which he first of all concedes in the following form: "Go, sacrifice to your God within the land" (Exod. 8:25). But Moses insists—in obedience to God's command—that they must go out in order to worship. The proper place of worship is the wilderness: "We must go three days' journey into the wilderness and sacrifice to the LORD our God as he will command us" (Exod. 8:27). After the plagues that follow, Pharaoh extends his compromise. He now concedes that worship according to the will of the Deity should take place in the wilderness, but he wants only the men to leave: the women and children, together with the cattle, must stay in Egypt. He is assuming the current religious practice, according to which only men are active participants in worship. But Moses cannot negotiate about the liturgy with a foreign potentate, nor can he subject worship to any form of political compromise. The manner in which God is to be worshipped is not a question of political feasibility. It contains its measure within itself, that is, it can only be ordered by the measure of revelation, in dependency upon God. That is why the third and most far-reaching compromise suggested by the earthly ruler is also rejected. Pharaoh now offers women and children the permission to leave with the men: "Only let your flocks and your herds remain" (Exod. 10:24). Moses objects: All the livestock must

181

go too, for "we do not know with what we must serve the LORD until we arrive there" (10:26). In all this, the issue is not the Promised Land: the only goal of the Exodus is shown to be worship, which can only take place according to God's measure and therefore eludes the rules of the game of political compromise.

Israel departs, not in order to be a people like all the others; it departs in order to serve God. The goal of the departure is the still unknown mountain of God, the service of God. Now the objection could be made that focusing on worship in the negotiations with Pharaoh was purely tactical. The real goal of the Exodus, ultimately its only goal, was not worship but land—this, after all, was the real content of the promise to Abraham. I do not think that this does justice to the seriousness that pervades the texts. To oppose land and worship makes no sense. The land is given to the people to be a place for the worship of the true God. Mere possession of the land, mere national autonomy, would reduce Israel to the level of all the other nations. The pursuit of such a goal would be a misunderstanding of what is distinctive about Israel's election. The whole history recounted in the books of the Judges and Kings, which is taken up afresh and given a new interpretation in the Chronicles, is intended to show precisely this, that the land, considered just in itself, is an indeterminate good. It only becomes a true good, a real gift, a promise fulfilled, when it is the place where God reigns. Then it will not be just some independent state or other, but the realm of obedience, where God's will is done and the right kind of human existence developed. Looking at the biblical texts enables us to define more exactly the relationship of the two goals of the Exodus. In its wanderings, Israel discovers the kind of sacrifice God wants, not after three days (as suggested in the conversation with Pharaoh), but after three months, on the day they come "into the wilderness of Sinai" (Exod. 19:1). On the third day God comes down onto the top of the mountain (cf. 19:16, 20). Now he speaks to the people. He makes known his will to them in the Ten Commandments (cf. 20:1–17) and, through the mediation of Moses, makes a covenant with them (cf. Exod. 24), a covenant concretized in a minutely regulated form of worship. In this way, the purpose of the wandering in the wilderness, as explained to Pharaoh, is fulfilled. Israel learns how to worship God in the way he himself desires. Cult, liturgy in the proper sense, is part of this worship, but so too is life according to the will of God; such a life is an indispensable part of true worship. "The glory of God is the living man, but the life of man is the vision of God," says St. Irenaeus (cf. *Adv. Haer.* 4, 20, 7), getting to the heart of what happens when man meets God on the mountain in the wilderness. Ultimately, it is the very life of man, man himself as living righteously, that is the true worship of God, but life only becomes real life when it receives its form from looking toward God. Cult exists in order to communicate this vision and to give life in such a way that glory is given to God.

Three things are important for the question we are considering. First of all, on Sinai the people receive not only instructions about worship, but also an all-embracing rule of law and life. Only thus can it become a people. A people without a common rule of law cannot live. It destroys itself in anarchy, which is a parody of freedom, its exaltation to the point of abolition. When every man lives without law, every man lives without freedom. This brings me to my second point. In the ordering of the covenant on Sinai, the three aspects of worship, law, and ethics are inseparably interwoven. This is the greatness of the Sinai covenant but also its limitation, as is shown in the transition from Israel to the Church of the Gentiles, where the interweaving was to unravel, to make room for a diversity of legal forms and political structures. In the modern age this necessary unravelling has led finally to the total secularization of the law and the exclusion of any God-ward perspective from the fashioning of the law. But we must not forget that there is an essential connection between the three orders of worship, law, and ethics. Law without a foundation in morality becomes injustice. When morality and law do not originate in a God-ward perspective, they degrade man, because they rob him of his highest measure and his highest capacity, deprive him of any vision of the infinite and eternal.

This seeming liberation subjects him to the dictatorship of the ruling majority, to shifting human standards, which inevitably end up doing him violence. Thus we come to a third point, which takes us back to where we started, to the question of the nature of worship and liturgy. When human affairs are so ordered that there is no recognition of God, there is a belittling of man. That is why, in the final analysis, worship and law cannot be completely separated from each other. God has a right to a response from man, to man himself, and where that right of God totally disappears, the order of law among men is dissolved, because there is no cornerstone to keep the whole structure together.

What does this mean for the question we have been considering? We were looking at the two goals of the Exodus, and we saw that the issue was ultimately about the nature of the liturgy. Now it becomes clear that what took place on Sinai, in the period of rest after the wandering through the wilderness, is what gives meaning to the taking of the land. Sinai is not a halfway house, a kind of stop for refreshment on the road to what really matters. No, Sinai gives Israel, so to speak, its interior land without which the exterior one would be a cheerless prospect. Israel is constituted as a people through the covenant and the divine law it contains. It has received a common rule for righteous living. This and this alone is what makes the land a real gift. Sinai remains present in the Promised Land. When the reality of Sinai is lost, the Land, too, is inwardly lost, until finally the people are thrust into exile. Whenever Israel falls away from the right worship of God, when she turns away from God to the false gods (the powers and values of this world), her freedom, too, collapses. It is possible for her to live in her own land and yet still be as she was in Egypt. Mere possession of your own land and state does not give you freedom; in fact, it can be the grossest kind of slavery. And when the loss of law becomes total, it ends in the loss even of the land. The "service of God," the freedom to give right worship to God, appears, in the encounter with Pharaoh, to be the sole purpose of the Exodus, indeed, its very essence. This fact is evident throughout the Pentateuch. This real "canon in the canon," the very

184

heart of Israel's Bible, is set entirely outside of the Holy Land. It ends on the edge of the wilderness, "beyond the Jordan," where Moses once more sums up and repeats the message of Sinai. Thus we can see what the foundation of existence in the Promised Land must be, the necessary condition for life in community and freedom. It is this: steadfast adherence to the law of God, which orders human affairs rightly, that is, by organizing them as realities that come from God and are meant to return to God.

But, once again, what does all this mean for our problem? First, it becomes clear that "cult," seen in its true breadth and depth, goes beyond the action of the liturgy. Ultimately, it embraces the ordering of the whole of human life in Irenaeus' sense. Man becomes glory for God, puts God, so to speak, into the light (and that is what worship is), when he lives by looking toward God. On the other hand, it is also true that law and ethics do not hold together when they are not anchored in the liturgical center and inspired by it. What kind of reality, then, do we find in the liturgy? As a first answer we can now say this: The man who puts to one side any consideration of the reality of God is a realist only in appearance. He is abstracting himself from the One in whom we "live and move and have our being" (Acts 17:28). It is only, therefore, when man's relationship with God is right that all of his other relationships—his relationships with his fellowmen, his dealings with the rest of creation—can be in good order. As we have seen, law is essential for freedom and community; worship—that is, the right way to relate to God—is, for its part, essential for law. We can now broaden the insight by taking a further step. Worship, that is, the right kind of cult, of relationship with God, is essential for the right kind of human existence in the world. It is so precisely because it reaches beyond everyday life. Worship gives us a share in heaven's mode of existence, in the world of God, and allows light to fall from that divine world into ours. In this sense, worship—as we said when we were discussing play—has the character of anticipation. It lays hold in advance of a more perfect life and, in so doing, gives our present life its proper measure. A life

185

without such anticipation, a life no longer opened up to heaven, would be empty, a leaden life. That is why there are in reality no societies altogether lacking in cult. Even the decidedly atheistic, materialistic systems create their own forms of cult, though, of course, they can only be an illusion and strive in vain, by bombastic trumpeting, to conceal their nothingness.

And so we come to a final reflection. Man himself cannot simply "make" worship. If God does not reveal himself, man is clutching empty space. Moses says to Pharaoh: "[W]e do not know with what we must serve the LORD" (Exod. 10:26). These words display a fundamental law of all liturgy. When God does not reveal himself, man can, of course, from the sense of God within him, build altars "to the unknown god" (cf. Acts 17:23). He can reach out toward God in his thinking and try to feel his way toward him. But real liturgy implies that God responds and reveals how we can worship him. In any form, liturgy includes some kind of "institution." It cannot spring from imagination, our own creativity—then it would remain just a cry in the dark or mere self-affirmation. Liturgy implies a real relationship with Another, who reveals himself to us and gives our existence a new direction.

CHAPTER 26

The Eucharist and the Sacraments of Mission

Written at the conclusion of the 2005 Synod on the Eucharist, Benedict XVI's apostolic exhortation *Sacramentum Caritatis* (*The Sacrament of Charity*) discusses the central place of the Eucharist in the life of the Church. In the following excerpt, Benedict XVI explains the relationship of the Eucharist to the two sacraments of mission: Holy Orders and Matrimony.

The Eucharist and the Sacrament of Holy Orders

In persona Christi capitis

The intrinsic relationship between the Eucharist and the sacrament of Holy Orders clearly emerges from Jesus' own words in the Upper Room: "Do this in memory of me" (Luke 22:19). On the night before he died, Jesus instituted the Eucharist and at the same time established the *priesthood of the New Covenant*. He is priest, victim, and altar: the mediator between God the Father and his people (cf. Heb. 5:5–10), the victim of atonement (cf. 1 John 2:2, 4:10) who offers himself on the altar of the Cross. No one can say "this is my body" and "this is the cup of my blood" except in the name and in the person of Christ, the one high priest of the new and eternal Covenant (cf. Heb. 8–9). Earlier meetings of the Synod of Bishops had considered the question of the ordained priesthood, both with regard to the nature of the ministry[1] and the formation of candidates.[2] Here, in the light of the discussion that took place during the last Synod, I consider it important to recall several

---

1. Cf. Synod of Bishops, Second General Assembly, Document on the Ministerial Priesthood *Ultimis Temporibus* (November 30, 1971): AAS 63 (1971), 898–942.

2. Cf. John Paul II, Post-Synodal Apostolic Exhortation *Pastores Dabo Vobis* (March 25, 1992), 42–69: AAS 84 (1992), 729–778.

important points about the relationship between the sacrament of the Eucharist and Holy Orders. First of all, we need to stress once again that the connection between *Holy Orders and the Eucharist* is seen most clearly at Mass, when the Bishop or priest presides *in the person of Christ the Head.*

The Church teaches that priestly ordination is the indispensable condition for the valid celebration of the Eucharist.[3] Indeed, "in the ecclesial service of the ordained minister, it is Christ himself who is present to his Church as Head of his Body, Shepherd of his flock, High Priest of the redemptive sacrifice."[4] Certainly the ordained minister also acts "in the name of the whole Church, when presenting to God the prayer of the Church, and above all when offering the eucharistic sacrifice."[5] As a result, priests should be conscious of the fact that in their ministry they must never put themselves or their personal opinions in first place, but Jesus Christ. Any attempt to make themselves the center of the liturgical action contradicts their very identity as priests. The priest is above all a servant of others, and he must continually work at being a sign pointing to Christ, a docile instrument in the Lord's hands. This is seen particularly in his humility in leading the liturgical assembly, in obedience to the rite, uniting himself to it in mind and heart, and avoiding anything that might give the impression of an inordinate emphasis on his own personality. I encourage the clergy always to see their eucharistic ministry as a humble service offered to Christ and his Church. The priesthood, as Saint Augustine said, is *amoris officium,*[6] it is the office of the good shepherd, who offers his life for his sheep (cf. John 10:14–15).

---

3. Cf. Second Vatican Ecumenical Council, Dogmatic Constitution on the Church *Lumen Gentium,* 10; Congregation for the Doctrine of the Faith, Letter on Certain Questions Concerning the Minister of the Eucharist *Sacerdotium Ministeriale* (August 6, 1983): AAS 75 (1983), 1001–1009.

4. *Catechism of the Catholic Church,* 1548.

5. Ibid., 1552.

6. Cf. *In Iohannis Evangelium Tractatus,* 123, 5: PL 35, 1967.

The Eucharist and priestly celibacy

The Synod Fathers wished to emphasize that the ministerial priesthood, through ordination, calls for complete configuration to Christ. While respecting the different practice and tradition of the Eastern Churches, there is a need to reaffirm the profound meaning of priestly celibacy, which is rightly considered a priceless treasure, and is also confirmed by the Eastern practice of choosing Bishops only from the ranks of the celibate. These Churches also greatly esteem the decision of many priests to embrace celibacy. This choice on the part of the priest expresses in a special way the dedication which conforms him to Christ and his exclusive offering of himself for the Kingdom of God.[7] The fact that Christ himself, the eternal priest, lived his mission even to the sacrifice of the Cross in the state of virginity constitutes the sure point of reference for understanding the meaning of the tradition of the Latin Church. It is not sufficient to understand priestly celibacy in purely functional terms. Celibacy is really a special way of conforming oneself to Christ's own way of life. This choice has first and foremost a nuptial meaning; it is a profound identification with the heart of Christ the Bridegroom who gives his life for his Bride. In continuity with the great ecclesial tradition, with the Second Vatican Council[8] and with my predecessors in the papacy,[9] I reaffirm the beauty and the importance of a priestly life lived in celibacy as a sign expressing total and exclusive devotion to Christ, to the Church and to the Kingdom of God, and I therefore confirm that it remains obligatory in the Latin tradition. Priestly celibacy lived with maturity, joy, and dedication is an immense blessing for the Church and for society itself.

---

7. Cf. *In Iohannis Evangelium Tractatus*, 123, 5: PL 35, 1967.

8. Cf. Decree on the Ministry and Life of Priests *Presbyterorum Ordinis*, 16.

9. Cf. John XXIII, Encyclical Letter *Sacerdotii Nostri Primordia* (August 1, 1959): AAS 51 (1959), 545–579; Paul VI, Encyclical Letter *Sacerdotalis Coelibatus* (June 24, 1967): AAS 59 (1967), 657–697; John Paul II, Post-Synodal Apostolic Exhortation *Pastores Dabo Vobis* (March 25, 1992), 29: AAS 84 (1992), 703–705; Benedict XVI, Address to the Roman Curia (December 22, 2006): *L'Osservatore Romano*, December 23, 2006, p. 6.

The clergy shortage and the pastoral care of vocations

In the light of the connection between the sacrament of Holy Orders and the Eucharist, the Synod considered the difficult situation that has arisen in various Dioceses which face a shortage of priests. This happens not only in some areas of first evangelization, but also in many countries of long-standing Christian tradition. Certainly a more equitable distribution of clergy would help to solve the problem. Efforts need to be made to encourage a greater awareness of this situation at every level. Bishops should involve Institutes of Consecrated Life and the new ecclesial groups in their pastoral needs, while respecting their particular charisms, and they should invite the clergy to become more open to serving the Church wherever there is need, even if this calls for sacrifice.[10] The Synod also discussed pastoral initiatives aimed at promoting, especially among the young, an attitude of interior openness to a priestly calling. The situation cannot be resolved by purely practical decisions. On no account should Bishops react to real and understandable concerns about the shortage of priests by failing to carry out adequate vocational discernment, or by admitting to seminary formation and ordination candidates who lack the necessary qualities for priestly ministry.[11] An insufficiently formed clergy, admitted to ordination without the necessary discernment, will not easily be able to offer a witness capable of evoking in others the desire to respond generously to Christ's call. The pastoral care of vocations needs to involve the entire Christian community in every area of its life.[12] Obviously, this pastoral work on all levels also includes exploring the matter with families,

10. Cf. *Propositio* 11.

11. Cf. Second Vatican Ecumenical Council, Decree on Priestly Formation *Optatam Totius*, 6; Code of Canon Law, can. 241, § 1 and can. 1029; Code of Canons of the Eastern Churches, can. 342 § 1 and can. 758; John Paul II, Post-Synodal Apostolic Exhortation *Pastores Dabo Vobis* (March 25, 1992), 11, 34, 50: AAS 84 (1992), 673–675; 712–714; 746–748; Congregation for the Clergy, Directory for the Ministry and Life of Priests *Dives Ecclesiae* (March 31, 1994), 58; Congregation for Catholic Education, Instruction Concerning the Criteria for the Discernment of Vocations with regard to Persons with Homosexual Tendencies in view of their Admission to the Seminary and to Holy Orders (November 4, 2005): AAS 97 (2005), 1007–1013.

12. Cf. *Propositio* 12; John Paul II, Post-Synodal Apostolic Exhortation *Pastores Dabo Vobis* (March 25, 1992), 41: AAS 84 (1992), 726–729.

which are often indifferent or even opposed to the idea of a priestly vocation. Families should generously embrace the gift of life and bring up their children to be open to doing God's will. In a word, they must have the courage to set before young people the radical decision to follow Christ, showing them how deeply rewarding it is.

Gratitude and hope

Finally, we need to have ever greater faith and hope in God's providence. Even if there is a shortage of priests in some areas, we must never lose confidence that Christ continues to inspire men to leave everything behind and to dedicate themselves totally to celebrating the sacred mysteries, preaching the Gospel and ministering to the flock. In this regard, I wish to express the gratitude of the whole Church for all those Bishops and priests who carry out their respective missions with fidelity, devotion and zeal. Naturally, the Church's gratitude also goes to deacons, who receive the laying on of hands "not for priesthood but for service."[13] As the Synod Assembly recommended, I offer a special word of thanks to those *Fidei Donum* priests who work faithfully and generously at building up the community by proclaiming the word of God and breaking the Bread of Life, devoting all their energy to serving the mission of the Church.[14] Let us thank God for all those priests who have suffered even to the sacrifice of their lives in order to serve Christ. The eloquence of their example shows what it means to be a priest to the end. Theirs is a moving witness that can inspire many young people to follow Christ and to expend their lives for others, and thus to discover true life.

The Eucharist and Matrimony

The Eucharist, a nuptial sacrament

The Eucharist, as the sacrament of charity, has a particular relationship with the love of man and woman united in marriage. A deeper

---

13. Second Vatican Ecumenical Council, Dogmatic Constitution on the Church *Lumen Gentium*, 29.

14. Cf. *Propositio* 38.

understanding of this relationship is needed at the present time.[15] Pope John Paul II frequently spoke of the nuptial character of the Eucharist and its special relationship with the sacrament of Matrimony: "The Eucharist is the sacrament of our redemption. It is the sacrament of the Bridegroom and of the Bride."[16] Moreover, "the entire Christian life bears the mark of the spousal love of Christ and the Church. Already Baptism, the entry into the People of God, is a nuptial mystery; it is so to speak the nuptial bath which precedes the wedding feast, the Eucharist."[17] The Eucharist inexhaustibly strengthens the indissoluble unity and love of every Christian marriage. By the power of the sacrament, the marriage bond is intrinsically linked to the eucharistic unity of Christ the Bridegroom and his Bride, the Church (cf. Eph. 5:31–32). The mutual consent that husband and wife exchange in Christ, which establishes them as a community of life and love, also has a eucharistic dimension. Indeed, in the theology of Saint Paul, conjugal love is a sacramental sign of Christ's love for his Church, a love culminating in the Cross, the expression of his "marriage" with humanity and at the same time the origin and heart of the Eucharist. For this reason the Church manifests her particular spiritual closeness to all those who have built their family on the sacrament of Matrimony.[18] The family—the domestic Church[19]—is a primary sphere of the Church's life, especially because of its decisive role in the Christian education of children.[20] In this context, the Synod also called for an acknowledgment of the unique mission of women in the family and in society, a mission that needs to be defended,

---

15. Cf. John Paul II, Post-Synodal Apostolic Exhortation *Familiaris Consortio* (November 22, 1981), 57: AAS 74 (1982), 149–150.

16. Apostolic Letter *Mulieris Dignitatem* (August 15, 1988), 26: AAS 80 (1988), 1715–1716.

17. *Catechism of the Catholic Church*, 1617.

18. Cf. *Propositio* 8.

19. Cf. Second Vatican Ecumenical Council, Dogmatic Constitution on the Church *Lumen Gentium*, 11.

20. Cf. *Propositio* 8.

protected, and promoted.[21] Marriage and motherhood represent essential realities which must never be denigrated.

The Eucharist and the unicity of marriage

In the light of this intrinsic relationship between marriage, the family, and the Eucharist, we can turn to several pastoral problems. The indissoluble, exclusive, and faithful bond uniting Christ and the Church, which finds sacramental expression in the Eucharist, corresponds to the basic anthropological fact that man is meant to be definitively united to one woman and vice versa (cf. Gen. 2:24, Matt. 19:5). With this in mind, the Synod of Bishops addressed the question of pastoral practice regarding people who come to the Gospel from cultures in which polygamy is practiced. Those living in this situation who open themselves to Christian faith need to be helped to integrate their life-plan into the radical newness of Christ. During the catechumenate, Christ encounters them in their specific circumstances and calls them to embrace the full truth of love, making whatever sacrifices are necessary in order to arrive at perfect ecclesial communion. The Church accompanies them with a pastoral care that is gentle yet firm,[22] above all by showing them the light shed by the Christian mysteries on nature and on human affections.

The Eucharist and the indissolubility of marriage

If the Eucharist expresses the irrevocable nature of God's love in Christ for his Church, we can then understand why it implies, with regard to the sacrament of Matrimony, that indissolubility to which all true love necessarily aspires.[23] There was good reason for the pastoral attention that the Synod gave to the painful situations experienced by some of

---

21. Cf. John Paul II, Apostolic Letter *Mulieris Dignitatem* (August 15, 1988): AAS 80 (1988), 1653–1729; Congregation for the Doctrine of the Faith, *Letter to the Bishops of the Catholic Church on the Collaboration of Men and Women in the Church and in the World* (May 31, 2004): AAS 96 (2004), 671–687.

22. Cf. *Propositio 9*.

23. Cf. *Catechism of the Catholic Church*, 1640.

the faithful who, having celebrated the sacrament of Matrimony, then divorced and remarried. This represents a complex and troubling pastoral problem, a real scourge for contemporary society, and one which increasingly affects the Catholic community as well. The Church's pastors, out of love for the truth, are obliged to discern different situations carefully, in order to be able to offer appropriate spiritual guidance to the faithful involved.[24] The Synod of Bishops confirmed the Church's practice, based on Sacred Scripture (cf. Mark 10:2–12), of not admitting the divorced and remarried to the sacraments, since their state and their condition of life objectively contradict the loving union of Christ and the Church signified and made present in the Eucharist. Yet the divorced and remarried continue to belong to the Church, which accompanies them with special concern and encourages them to live as fully as possible the Christian life through regular participation at Mass, albeit without receiving communion, listening to the word of God, eucharistic adoration, prayer, participation in the life of the community, honest dialogue with a priest or spiritual director, dedication to the life of charity, works of penance, and commitment to the education of their children.

---

24. Cf. John Paul II, Post-Synodal Apostolic Exhortation *Familiaris Consortio* (November 22, 1981), 84: AAS 74 (1982), 184–186; Congregation for the Doctrine of the Faith, Letter to the Bishops of the Catholic Church concerning the Reception of Holy Communion by Divorced and Remarried Members of the Faithful *Annus Internationalis Familiae* (September 14, 1994): AAS 86 (1994), 974–979.

CHAPTER 27

On Being a Priest

In 2009, Benedict XVI released the following letter proclaiming a "Year for Priests." 2009 was the 150th anniversary of the death of St. John Vianney, the patron saint of parish priests, so Benedict XVI uses him as a model for this beautiful meditation on the nature of the priesthood.

On the forthcoming Solemnity of the Most Sacred Heart of Jesus, Friday June 19, 2009—a day traditionally devoted to prayer for the sanctification of the clergy—I have decided to inaugurate a "Year for Priests" in celebration of the 150th anniversary of the *"dies natalis"* of John Mary Vianney, the patron saint of parish priests worldwide.[1] This Year, meant to deepen the commitment of all priests to interior renewal for the sake of a stronger and more incisive witness to the Gospel in today's world, will conclude on the same Solemnity in 2010. *"The priesthood is the love of the heart of Jesus,"* the saintly Curé of Ars would often say. This touching expression makes us reflect, first of all, with heartfelt gratitude on the immense gift which priests represent, not only for the Church, but also for humanity itself. I think of all those priests who quietly present Christ's words and actions each day to the faithful and to the whole world, striving to be one with the Lord in their thoughts and their will, their sentiments and their style of life. How can I not pay tribute to their apostolic labors, their tireless and hidden service, their universal charity? And how can I not praise the courageous fidelity of so many priests who, even amid difficulties and incomprehension, remain faithful to their vocation as "friends of Christ," whom he has called by name, chosen, and sent?

---

1. He was proclaimed as such by Pope Pius XI in 1929.

I still treasure the memory of the first parish priest at whose side I exercised my ministry as a young priest: he left me an example of unreserved devotion to his pastoral duties, even to meeting his own death in the act of bringing viaticum to a gravely ill person. I also recall the countless confreres whom I have met and continue to meet, not least in my pastoral visits to different countries: men generously dedicated to the daily exercise of their priestly ministry. Yet the expression of Saint John Mary also makes us think of Christ's pierced Heart and the crown of thorns which surrounds it. I also think, therefore, of the countless situations of suffering endured by many priests, either because they themselves share in the manifold human experience of pain or because they encounter misunderstanding from the very persons to whom they minister. How can we not also think of all those priests who are offended in their dignity, obstructed in their mission and persecuted, even at times to offering the supreme testimony of their own blood? There are also, sad to say, situations which can never be sufficiently deplored where the Church herself suffers as a consequence of infidelity on the part of some of her ministers. Then it is the world which finds grounds for scandal and rejection. What is most helpful to the Church in such cases is not only a frank and complete acknowledgment of the weaknesses of her ministers, but also a joyful and renewed realization of the greatness of God's gift, embodied in the splendid example of generous pastors, religious afire with love for God and for souls, and insightful, patient spiritual guides. Here the teaching and example of Saint John Mary Vianney can serve as a significant point of reference for us all. The Curé of Ars was very humble, yet as a priest he was conscious of being an immense gift to his people: "A good shepherd, a pastor after God's heart, is the greatest treasure which the good Lord can grant to a parish, and one of the most precious gifts of divine mercy." He spoke of the priesthood as if incapable of fathoming the grandeur of the *gift* and *task* entrusted to a human creature: "O, how great is the priest! . . . If he realized what he is, he would die. . . . God obeys him: he utters a few words and the Lord descends from heaven at his voice, to be contained within a small host . . ." Explaining to his parishioners the importance of the sacraments, he would say: "Without the Sacrament of Holy Orders, we would not have the Lord. Who put him there in that tabernacle? The priest. Who welcomed your soul at the beginning of your life? The priest. Who feeds your soul and gives it strength for its journey? The priest. Who will prepare it to appear before God, bathing it one last time in the blood of Jesus Christ? The priest, always the priest. And if this soul should happen to die [as a result of sin], who will raise it up, who will restore its calm and peace? Again, the priest. . . . After God, the priest is everything! . . . Only in heaven will he fully realize what he is." These words, welling up from the priestly heart of the holy pastor, might sound excessive. Yet they reveal the high esteem in which he held the sacrament of the priesthood. He seemed overwhelmed by a boundless sense of responsibility: "Were we to fully realize what a priest is on earth, we would die: not of fright, but of love. . . . Without the priest, the passion and death of our Lord would be of no avail. It is the priest who continues the work of redemption on earth. . . . What use would be a house filled with gold, were there no one to open its door? The priest holds the key to the treasures of heaven: it is he who opens the door: he is the steward of the good Lord; the adminis-trator of his goods. . . . Leave a parish for twenty years without a priest, and they will end by worshiping the beasts there. . . . The priest is not a priest for himself, he is a priest for you."

He arrived in Ars, a village of 230 souls, warned by his Bishop beforehand that there he would find religious practice in a sorry state: "There is little love of God in that parish; you will be the one to put it there." As a result, he was deeply aware that he needed to go there to embody Christ's presence and to bear witness to his saving mercy: "[Lord,] grant me the conversion of my parish; I am willing to suffer whatever you wish, for my entire life!": with this prayer he entered upon his mission. The Curé devoted himself completely to his parish's con-version, setting before all else the Christian education of the people in his care. Dear brother priests, let us ask the Lord Jesus for the grace to

197

learn for ourselves something of the pastoral plan of Saint John Mary Vianney! The first thing we need to learn is the complete identification of the man with his ministry. In Jesus, person and mission tend to coincide: all Christ's saving activity was, and is, an expression of his "filial consciousness" which from all eternity stands before the Father in an attitude of loving submission to his will. In a humble yet genuine way, every priest must aim for a similar identification. Certainly this is not to forget that the efficacy of the ministry is independent of the holiness of the minister; but neither can we overlook the extraordinary fruitfulness of the encounter between the ministry's objective holiness and the subjective holiness of the minister. The Curé of Ars immediately set about this patient and humble task of harmonizing his life as a minister with the holiness of the ministry he had received, by deciding to "*live,*" physically, in his parish church: As his first biographer tells us: "Upon his arrival, he chose the church as his home. He entered the church before dawn and did not leave it until after the evening Angelus. There he was to be sought whenever needed."

The pious excess of his devout biographer should not blind us to the fact that the Curé also knew how to "live" actively within the entire territory of his parish: he regularly visited the sick and families, organized popular missions and patronal feasts, collected and managed funds for charitable and missionary works, embellished and furnished his parish church, cared for the orphans and teachers of the "*Providence*" (an institute he founded); provided for the education of children; founded confraternities and enlisted lay persons to work at his side.

His example naturally leads me to point out that there are sectors of cooperation which need to be opened ever more fully to the lay faithful. Priests and laity together make up the one priestly people and in virtue of their ministry priests live in the midst of the lay faithful, "that they may lead everyone to the unity of charity, 'loving one another with mutual affection; and outdoing one another in sharing honor'(Rom. 12:10)."[2] Here we ought to recall the Second Vatican

---

2. *Presbyterorum Ordinis*, 9.

Council's hearty encouragement to priests "to be sincere in their appreciation and promotion of the dignity of the laity and of the special role they have to play in the Church's mission. . . . They should be willing to listen to lay people, give brotherly consideration to their wishes, and acknowledge their experience and competence in the different fields of human activity. In this way they will be able together with them to discern the signs of the times."[3]

Saint John Mary Vianney taught his parishioners primarily by the witness of his life. It was from his example that they learned to pray, halting frequently before the tabernacle for a visit to Jesus in the Blessed Sacrament.[4] "One need not say much to pray well"—the Curé explained to them—"We know that Jesus is there in the tabernacle: let us open our hearts to him, let us rejoice in his sacred presence. That is the best prayer." And he would urge them: "Come to communion, my brothers and sisters, come to Jesus. Come to live from him in order to live with him . . . Of course you are not worthy of him, but *you need him!*" This way of educating the faithful *to the Eucharistic presence and to communion* proved most effective when they saw him celebrate the Holy Sacrifice of the Mass. Those present said that "it was not possible to find a finer example of worship. . . . He gazed upon the Host with immense love." "All good works, taken together, do not equal the sacrifice of the Mass"—he would say—"since they are human works, while the Holy Mass is the work of God." He was convinced that the fervor of a priest's life depended entirely upon the Mass: "The reason why a priest is lax is that he does not pay attention to the Mass! My God, how we ought to pity a priest who celebrates as if he were engaged in something routine!" He was accustomed, when celebrating, also to offer his own life in sacrifice: "What a good thing it is for a priest each morning to offer himself to God in sacrifice!"

This deep personal identification with the Sacrifice of the Cross led him—by a sole inward movement—from the altar to the confessional. Priests ought never to be resigned to empty confessionals or the

---

3. Ibid.

apparent indifference of the faithful to this sacrament. In France, at the time of the Curé of Ars, confession was no more easy or frequent than in our own day, since the upheaval caused by the revolution had long inhibited the practice of religion. Yet he sought in every way, by his preaching and his powers of persuasion, to help his parishioners to redis-cover the meaning and beauty of the sacrament of Penance, presenting it as an inherent demand of the Eucharistic presence. He thus created a *"virtuous" circle*. By spending long hours in church before the taberna-cle, he inspired the faithful to imitate him by coming to visit Jesus with the knowledge that their parish priest would be there, ready to listen and offer forgiveness. Later, the growing numbers of penitents from all over France would keep him in the confessional for up to sixteen hours a day. It was said that Ars had become "a great hospital of souls." His first biographer relates that "the grace he obtained [for the conversion of sinners] was so powerful that it would pursue them, not leaving them a moment of peace!" The saintly Curé reflected something of the same idea when he said: "It is not the sinner who returns to God to beg his forgiveness, but God himself who runs after the sinner and makes him return to him." "This good Savior is so filled with love that he seeks us everywhere."

We priests should feel that the following words, which he put on the lips of Christ, are meant for each of us personally: "I will charge my ministers to proclaim to sinners that I am ever ready to welcome them, that my mercy is infinite." From Saint John Mary Vianney we can learn to put our unfailing trust in the sacrament of Penance, to set it once more at the center of our pastoral concerns, and to take up the "dialogue of salvation" which it entails. The Curé of Ars dealt with different penitents in different ways. Those who came to his confes-sional drawn by a deep and humble longing for God's forgiveness found in him the encouragement to plunge into the "flood of divine mercy" which sweeps everything away by its vehemence. If someone was trou-bled by the thought of his own frailty and inconstancy, and fearful of sinning again, the Curé would unveil the mystery of God's love in these beautiful and touching words: "The good Lord knows everything. Even before you confess, he already knows that you will sin again, yet he still forgives you. How great is the love of our God: he *even forces himself to forget the future*, so that he can grant us his forgiveness!" But to those who made a lukewarm and rather indifferent confession of sin, he clearly demonstrated by his own tears of pain how "abominable" this attitude was: "I weep because you don't weep," he would say. "If only the Lord were not so good! *But he is so good!* One would have to be a brute to treat so good a Father this way!" He awakened repentance in the hearts of the lukewarm by forcing them to see God's own pain at their sins reflected in the face of the priest who was their confessor. To those who, on the other hand, came to him already desirous of and suited to a deeper spiritual life, he flung open the abyss of God's love, explaining the untold beauty of living in union with him and dwelling in his presence: "Everything in God's sight, everything with God, everything to please God. . . . How beautiful it is!" And he taught them to pray: "My God, grant me the grace to love you as much as I possibly can."

In his time the Curé of Ars was able to transform the hearts and the lives of so many people because he enabled them to experience the Lord's merciful love. Our own time urgently needs a similar proclamation and witness to the truth of Love: *Deus caritas est* (1 John 4:8). Thanks to the word and the sacraments of Jesus, John Mary Vianney built up his flock, although he often trembled from a conviction of his personal inadequacy, and desired more than once to withdraw from the responsibilities of the parish ministry out of a sense of his unworthiness. Nonetheless, with exemplary obedience he never abandoned his post, consumed as he was by apostolic zeal for the salvation of souls. He sought to remain completely faithful to his own vocation and mission through the practice of an austere asceticism: "The great misfortune for us parish priests"—he lamented—"is that our souls grow tepid"; meaning by this that a pastor can grow dangerously inured to the state of sin or of indifference in which so many of his flock are living. He himself kept a tight rein on his body, with vigils and fasts, lest it rebel against his priestly soul. Nor did he avoid self-mortification for the good of the souls in his care and as a help to expiating the many sins he heard in confession. To a priestly confrere he explained: "I will tell you my recipe: I give sinners a small penance and the rest I do in their place." Aside from the actual penances which the Curé of Ars practiced, the core of his teaching remains valid for each of us: souls have been won at the price of Jesus' own blood, and a priest cannot devote himself to their salvation if he refuses to share personally in the "precious cost" of redemption.

In today's world, as in the troubled times of the Curé of Ars, the lives and activity of priests need to be distinguished by *a determined witness to the Gospel*. As Pope Paul VI rightly noted, "modern man listens more willingly to witnesses than to teachers, and if he does listen to teachers, it is because they are witnesses."[5] Lest we experience existential emptiness and the effectiveness of our ministry be compromised, we need to ask ourselves ever anew: "Are we truly pervaded by the word of God? Is that word truly the nourishment we live by, even more than bread and the things of this world? Do we really know that word? Do we love it? Are we deeply engaged with this word to the point that it really leaves a mark on our lives and shapes our thinking?"[6] Just as Jesus called the Twelve to be with him (cf. Mark 3:14), and only later sent them forth to preach, so too in our days priests are called to assimilate that "new style of life" which was inaugurated by the Lord Jesus and taken up by the Apostles.[7]

It was complete commitment to this "new style of life" which marked the priestly ministry of the Curé of Ars. Pope John XXIII, in his Encyclical Letter *Sacerdotii nostri primordia*, published in 1959 on the first centenary of the death of Saint John Mary Vianney, presented his asceticism with special reference to the "three evangelical counsels" which the Pope considered necessary also for diocesan priests: "even

---

5. *Evangelii Nuntiandi*, 41.

6. Benedict XVI, Homily at the Chrism Mass, April 9, 2009.

7. Cf. Benedict XVI, Address to the Plenary Assembly of the Congregation for the Clergy, March 16, 2009.

though priests are not bound to embrace these evangelical counsels by virtue of the clerical state, these counsels nonetheless offer them, as they do all the faithful, the surest road to the desired goal of Christian perfection."[8] The Curé of Ars lived the "evangelical counsels" in a way suited to his priestly state. His *poverty* was not the poverty of a religious or a monk, but that proper to a priest: while managing much money (since well-to-do pilgrims naturally took an interest in his charitable works), he realized that everything had been donated to his church, his poor, his orphans, the girls of his "*Providence*,"[9] his families of modest means. Consequently, he "was rich in giving to others and very poor for himself." As he would explain: "My secret is simple: give everything away; hold nothing back." When he lacked money, he would say amiably to the poor who knocked at his door: "Today I'm poor just like you, I'm one of you." At the end of his life, he could say with absolute tranquility: "I no longer have anything. The good Lord can call me whenever he wants!" His *chastity*, too, was that demanded of a priest for his ministry. It could be said that it was a chastity suited to one who must daily touch the Eucharist, who contemplates it blissfully and with that same bliss offers it to his flock. It was said of him that "he radiated chastity"; the faithful would see this when he turned and gazed at the tabernacle with loving eyes. Finally, Saint John Mary Vianney's *obedience* found full embodiment in his conscientious fidelity to the daily demands of his ministry. We know how he was tormented by the thought of his inadequacy for parish ministry and by a desire to flee "in order to bewail his poor life, in solitude." Only obedience and a thirst for souls convinced him to remain at his post. As he explained to himself and his flock: "There are no two good ways of serving God. There is only one: serve him as he desires to be served." He considered this the golden rule for a life of obedience: "Do only what can be offered to the good Lord."

---

8. John XXIII, Encyclical Letter *Sacerdotii nostri primordia*, P. I.

9. The name given to the house where more than sixty abandoned girls were taken in and educated. To maintain this house he would do anything: "*J'ai fait tous les commerces imaginables*," he would say with a smile (Nodet, p. 214).

In this context of a spirituality nourished by the practice of the evangelical counsels, I would like to invite all priests, during this Year dedicated to them, to welcome the new springtime which the Spirit is now bringing about in the Church, not least through the ecclesial movements and the new communities. "In his gifts the Spirit is multifaceted. . . . He breathes where he wills. He does so unexpectedly, in unexpected places, and in ways previously unheard of . . . but he also shows us that he works with a view to the one body and in the unity of the one body."[10] In this regard, the statement of the Decree *Presbyterorum Ordinis* continues to be timely: "While testing the spirits to discover if they be of God, priests must discover with faith, recognize with joy, and foster diligently the many and varied charismatic gifts of the laity, whether these be of a humble or more exalted kind."[11] These gifts, which awaken in many people the desire for a deeper spiritual life, can benefit not only the lay faithful but the clergy as well. The communion between ordained and charismatic ministries can provide "a helpful impulse to a renewed commitment by the Church in proclaiming and bearing witness to the Gospel of hope and charity in every corner of the world."[12] I would also like to add, echoing the Apostolic Exhortation *Pastores Dabo Vobis* of Pope John Paul II, that the ordained ministry has a radical "*communitarian form*" and can be exercised only in the communion of priests with their Bishop.[13] This communion between priests and their Bishop, grounded in the sacrament of Holy Orders and made manifest in Eucharistic concelebration, needs to be translated into various concrete expressions of an effective and affective priestly fraternity.[14] Only thus will priests be able to live fully the gift of celibacy and build thriving Christian communities in which the miracles which accompanied the first preaching of the Gospel can be repeated.

---

10. Benedict XVI, Homily for the Vigil of Pentecost, June 3, 2006.

11. No. 9.

12. Benedict XVI, Address to Bishop-Friends of the Focolare Movement and the Sant'Egidio Community, February 8, 2007.

13. Cf. No. 17.

14. Cf. John Paul II, Apostolic Exhortation *Pastores Dabo Vobis*, 74.

The Pauline Year now coming to its close invites us also to look to the Apostle of the Gentiles, who represents a splendid example of a priest entirely devoted to his ministry. "The love of Christ urges us on"—he wrote—"because we are convinced that one has died for all; therefore all have died" (2 Cor. 5:14). And he adds: "He died for all, so that those who live might live no longer for themselves, but for him who died and was raised for them" (2 Cor. 5:15). Could a finer program be proposed to any priest resolved to advance along the path of Christian perfection?

Dear brother priests, the celebration of the 150th anniversary of the death of Saint John Mary Vianney (1859) follows upon the celebration of the 150th anniversary of the apparitions of Lourdes (1858). In 1959 Blessed Pope John XXIII noted that "shortly before the Curé of Ars completed his long and admirable life, the Immaculate Virgin appeared in another part of France to an innocent and humble girl, and entrusted to her a message of prayer and penance which continues, even a century later, to yield immense spiritual fruits. The life of this holy priest whose centenary we are commemorating in a real way anticipated the great supernatural truths taught to the seer of Massabielle. He was greatly devoted to the Immaculate Conception of the Blessed Virgin; in 1836 he had dedicated his parish church to Our Lady Conceived without Sin and he greeted the dogmatic definition of this truth in 1854 with deep faith and great joy."[15] The Curé would always remind his faithful that "after giving us all he could, Jesus Christ wishes in addition to bequeath us his most precious possession, his Blessed Mother."

To the Most Holy Virgin I entrust this Year for Priests. I ask her to awaken in the heart of every priest a generous and renewed commitment to the ideal of complete self-oblation to Christ and the Church which inspired the thoughts and actions of the saintly Curé of Ars. It was his fervent prayer life and his impassioned love of Christ Crucified that enabled John Mary Vianney to grow daily in his total self-oblation to God and the Church. May his example lead all priests to offer that

---

15. Encyclical Letter *Sacerdotii nostri primordia*, P. III.

witness of unity with their Bishop, with one another and with the lay faithful, which today, as ever, is so necessary. Despite all the evil present in our world, the words which Christ spoke to his Apostles in the Upper Room continue to inspire us: "In the world you have tribulation; but take courage, I have overcome the world" (John 16:33). Our faith in the Divine Master gives us the strength to look to the future with confidence. Dear priests, Christ is counting on you. In the footsteps of the Curé of Ars, let yourselves be enthralled by him. In this way you too will be, for the world in our time, heralds of hope, reconciliation, and peace!

PART VIII

MARY

CHAPTER 28

The Place of Mariology
in the Bible

From his book *Daughter Zion: Meditations on the Church's Marian Belief*, first published in English in 1983, this excerpt presents Ratzinger's argument that a correct understanding of Mary is key to a proper reading of Scripture.

But let us attempt, at long last, to get down to details. By tracing back into the Old Testament those elements by means of which the New Testament theologically interprets the figure of Mary, we have already hit upon three strands of a theology of woman.

1. In the first place we have to mention the figure of Eve. She is depicted as the necessary opposite pole of man, Adam. His being without her would be "not good" (Gen. 2:18). She comes, not from the earth, but from himself: in the "myth" or "legend" of the rib is expressed the most intimate reference of man and woman to each other. In that mutual reference the wholeness of humanity is first realized. The necessary condition for the creation of mankind, to be fulfilled in the oneness of man and woman, becomes apparent here, just as previously Genesis 1:27 had portrayed mankind from the very beginning as masculine and feminine in its likeness to God, and had mysteriously, cryptically, linked its likeness to God with the mutual reference of the sexes to each other. Admittedly the text also allows the ambivalence of this reference to become evident: woman can become a temptation for man, but simultaneously she is the mother of all life, whence she receives her name. In my opinion it is significant that her name is bestowed in Genesis 3:20 *after* the fall, *after* God's words of judgment. In this way the undestroyed dignity and majesty of woman are expressed. She preserves the mystery

of life, the power opposed to death; for death is like the power of nothingness, the antithesis of Yahweh, who is the creator of life and the God of the living. She, who offers the fruit which leads to death, whose task manifests a mysterious kinship with death, is nonetheless from now on the keeper of the seal of life and the antithesis of death. The woman, who bears the key of life, thus touches directly the mystery of being, the living God, from whom in the last analysis all life originates and who, for that reason, is called "life," the "living one." We shall see how precisely these relationships are taken up again in the dogma of the Assumption.

2. In the Old Testament's history of promises, it is true that the patriarchs stand in the foreground as the true bearers of that history. Yet the mothers also played a specific role. In the history of the patriarchs, Sarah-Hagar, Rachel-Leah, and Hannah-Penina are those pairs of women in whom the extraordinary element in the path of the promises stands out. In each case the fertile and the infertile stand opposite each other, and in the process a remarkable reversal in values is reached. In archaic modes of thought, fertility is a blessing, infertility is a curse. Yet here all is reversed: the infertile one ultimately turns out to be the truly blessed, while the fertile one recedes into the ordinary or even has to struggle against the curse of repudiation, of being unloved. The theological implication of this overthrow of values becomes clear only gradually; from it Paul developed his theology of spiritual birth: the true son of Abraham is not the one who traces his physical origin to him, but the one who, in a new way beyond mere physical birth, has been conceived through the creative power of God's word of promise. Physical life as such is not really wealth; this promise, which endures beyond life, is what first makes life fully itself (cf. Rom. 4; Gal. 3:1–14; 4:21–31).

At an earlier stage of the Old Testament's evolution, a theology of grace was developed from this reversal of values in the song of Hannah, which is echoed in Mary's Magnificat: the Lord raises the humble from the dust, he lifts the poor from the ashes (1 Sam. 2:8). God bends down to the humble, the powerless, the rejected, and in this condescension

210

the love of God, which truly saves, shines forth both for Hannah and for Mary, in the remarkable phenomenon of unblessed-blessed women. The mystery of the last place (Luke 14:10), the exchange between the first and the last place (Mark 10:31), the reversal of values in the Sermon on the Mount, the reversal of earthly values founded upon *hybris*, all of this is intimated. Here also the theology of virginity finds its first, still hidden formulation: earthly infertility becomes true fertility. . . .

3. Near the end of the Old Testament canon, in its late writings, a new and, again, entirely original type of theology of woman is developed. The great salvific figures of Esther and Judith appear, taking up again the most ancient tradition as it was embodied, for example, in the figure of the judge Deborah. Both women have an essential characteristic in common with the great mothers: one is a widow, the other is a harem-wife at the Persian court, and thus both find themselves—in different ways—in an oppressed state. Both embody the defeated Israel: Israel who has become a widow and wastes away in sorrow, Israel who has been abducted and dishonored among the nations, enslaved within their arbitrary desires. Yet both personify at the same time Israel's unconquered spiritual strength, which cannot boast as do the worldly powers and for that very reason knows how to scorn and overcome the mighty. The woman as savior, the embodiment of Israel's hope, thereby takes her place alongside the unblessed-blessed mothers. It is significant that the woman always figures in Israel's thought and belief, not as a priestess, but as prophetess and judge-savior. What is specifically hers, the place assigned to her, emerges from this. The essence of what has previously been seen is repeated and strengthened: the infertile one, the powerless one becomes the savior because it is there that the locus for the revelation of God's power is found. After every fall into sin, the woman remains "mother of life."

4. In the theological short-story type of the woman-savior, one finds already presupposed and newly expressed what the prophetic preaching had developed with theological profundity from the image of the great maternal women and what is considered to be the proper center of the

211

Old Testament's theology of woman: Israel herself, the chosen people, is interpreted simultaneously as woman, virgin, beloved, wife, and mother. The great women of Israel represent what this people itself is. The history of these women becomes the theology of God's people and, at the same time, the theology of the covenant. By making the category of covenant comprehensible and by giving it meaning and spiritual orientation, the figure of the woman enters into the most intimate reaches of Old Testament piety, of the Old Testament relationship with God. Probably the notion of covenant was at first largely patterned after the model of ancient Eastern vassal indentures, in which the sovereign king assigns rights and duties. This political and legal notion of the covenant, however, is continually deepened and surpassed in the theology of the prophets: the covenant relation of Yahweh to Israel is a covenant of marital love, which—as in Hosea's magnificent vision—moves and stirs Yahweh himself to his heart. He has loved the young maiden Israel with a love that has proved to be indestructible, eternal. He can be angry with the wife of his youth on account of her adultery. He can punish her, but all this is simultaneously directed against himself and pains him, the lover, whose "bowels churn." He cannot repudiate her without rendering judgment against himself. It is on this, on his personal, innermost bewilderment as lover, that the covenant's eternal and irrevocable character is based. "How could I betray you, Ephraim, or hand you over, Israel . . .? My heart turns against me, my mercy catches fire all at once. I do not act according to the fire of my anger, I no longer annihilate Ephraim, for I am God and not man, the Holy One in your midst. I do not come to destroy all in flames" (Hos. 11:8–9). God's divinity is no longer revealed in his ability to punish but in the indestructibility and constancy of his love.

This means that the relationship between God and Israel includes not only God but also Israel as woman, who in this relationship with God is at once virgin and mother. For this reason the covenant, which forms the very basis of the existence of Israel as a nation and the existence of each individual as Israelite, is expressed interpersonally in the fidelity of the marriage covenant and in no other way. Marriage is the form of the mutual relationship between husband and wife that results from the covenant, the fundamental human relationship upon which all human history is based. It bears a theology within itself, and indeed it is possible and intelligible only theologically. But above all, this also means that to God, the One, is joined, not a goddess, but, as in his historical revelation, the chosen creature, Israel, the daughter Zion, the woman. To leave woman out of the whole of theology would be to deny creation and election (salvation history) and thereby to nullify revelation. In the women of Israel, the mothers and the saviors, in their fruitful infertility is expressed most purely and most profoundly what creation is and what election is, what "Israel" is as God's people. And because election and revelation are one, what ultimately becomes apparent in this for the first time is who and what God is.

Of course this line of development in the Old Testament remains just as incomplete and open as all the other lines of the Old Testament. It acquires its definitive meaning for the first time in the New Testament: in the woman who is herself described as the true holy remnant, as the authentic daughter Zion, and who is thereby the mother of the savior, yes, the mother of God. In passing, one might mention that the acceptance of the Canticle of Canticles into the canon of Scripture would have been impossible if this theology of love and woman had not existed. The Canticle is certainly, on technical grounds, a collection of profane love songs with a heavily erotic coloring. But once the songs have entered the canon, they serve as an expression of God's dialogue with Israel, and to that extent such an interpretation of them is anything but mere allegory.

5. In the last layers of the Old Testament, a further, remarkable line of development comes to light, which likewise does not lend itself to interpretation within the context of the Old Testament alone. The figure of wisdom (Sophia) attains central significance. She was probably taken over from Egyptian prototypes and then adapted to Israel's belief. "Wisdom" appears as the mediatrix of creation and salvation history, as

God's first creature in whom both the pure, primordial form of his creative will and the pure *answer*, which he discovers, find their expression; indeed, one can say that precisely this concept of the answer is formative for the Old Testament idea of wisdom. Creation answers, and the answer is as close to God as a playmate, as a lover.

We have previously noted that in order to interpret Mary, the New Testament refers back to the mothers of the Old Testament, to the theology of the daughter Zion, and probably also to Eve, and then ties these three lines of development together. We must now add that the Church's liturgy expands this Old Testament theology of woman insofar as it interprets the woman-saviors, Esther and Judith, in terms of Mary and refers the Wisdom texts to Mary. This has been sharply criticized by this century's liturgical movement in view of its Christocentric theology; it has been argued that these texts can and should allow only a Christological interpretation. After years of wholehearted agreement with this latter view, it is ever clearer to me that it actually misjudges what is most characteristic in those Wisdom texts. While it is correct to observe that Christology assimilated essential elements of the wisdom idea, so that one must speak of a Christological strand in the New Testament's continuation of the notion of wisdom, a remainder, nevertheless, resists total integration into Christology. In both Hebrew and Greek, "wisdom" is a feminine noun, and this is no empty grammatical phenomenon in antiquity's vivid awareness of language. "Sophia," a feminine noun, stands on that side of reality which is represented by the woman, by what is purely and simply feminine. It signifies the answer which emerges from the divine call of creation and election. It expresses precisely this: that there is a pure answer and that God's love finds its irrevocable dwelling place within it. In order to deal with the full complexity of the facts of the case, one must certainly consider that the word for "Spirit" in Hebrew (not, however, in Greek) is feminine. In that respect, because of the teaching about the Spirit, one can as it were practically have a presentiment of the primordial type of the feminine, in a mysterious, veiled manner, within God himself. Nevertheless, the doctrine of the Spirit and the doctrine of wisdom represent separate strands of tradition. From the viewpoint of the New Testament, wisdom refers, on one side, to the Son as the Word, in whom God creates, but on the other side to the creature, to the true Israel, who is personified in the humble maid whose whole existence is marked by the attitude of *Fiat mihi secundum verbum tuum.* Sophia refers to the Logos, the Word who establishes wisdom, and also to the womanly answer which receives wisdom and brings it to fruition. The eradication of the Marian interpretation of sophiology ultimately leaves out an entire dimension of the biblical and Christian mystery.

CHAPTER 29

The Mother of God

This short excerpt comes from Ratzinger's conversation with Peter Seewald published in *God and the World*. Included in this selection is a beautiful passage on Ratzinger's personal devotion to the Blessed Mother. Seewald's words are in italics.

The Mother of God

Basically, the story of our way of reckoning time began with a woman. "And the angel of the Lord brought the message to Mary," the Gospel tells us. She was a girl from the unknown little town of Nazareth, and she obviously had no idea what was happening to her.

The true stature of this event has only gradually been recognized in the course of history. First there is the meeting with the angel, when Mary is, as it were, suddenly overcome by this unusual message: She has found favor with God; she has been specially selected to be the Mother of his Son. That must have been a terrifying moment for Mary.

A human being as the Mother of God!

This is in fact the great paradox. God becomes small. He becomes man; he accepts thereby the limitations of human conception and childbirth. He has a mother and is thus truly woven into the tapestry of our human history, so that in fact a woman is able to say to him who is her child, a human child: The Lord of the world is within you.

For a long time, there was a great deal of controversy about the expression *Mother of God*. There were the Nestorians, who said she did not of course give birth to God; she gave birth to the man Jesus. Accordingly, she can be called Mother of Christ, but not Mother of God. It was basically a matter of the question of how profound a unity there is between God and man in this person Jesus Christ, whether it is so great that we can say, Yes, the one who is born is God, and so she is God's mother. Obviously she is not God's mother in the sense of his having come from her. But she was in the sense of having been the mother of that man who was entirely at one with God. In this way she entered into a quite unique union with God.

Mary is honored as Queen of heaven, as the prototype of the Church, and likewise as Mother of mercy. The power and outreach of this Madonna, who again and again provides the motivation for millions of people, cannot be measured by conventional standards.

What happened has been understood in history, to an increasing extent, as at the same time honoring woman. The original image of woman is expressed in Mary, the pure figure of humanity and of the Church. And while Eve, the original first woman, the "mother of all," as they call her nowadays, the mother of all the living, gives birth in the end only for death, now Mary, in giving birth to the Savior, who rises from death and who brings life, becomes truly the pure fulfillment of what was meant with Eve, with the promise of woman and of her fruitfulness. She becomes the Mother of the One who is life and who gives life, Mother of life and of the living.

Ave Maria

The angel's greeting to Mary has become a fundamental prayer of the Catholic Church. Some of the greatest geniuses of mankind, Mozart, Rossini, and others, have set the Ave Maria to music: "Hail Mary, full of grace! The Lord is with you. Blessed are you among women, and blessed is the fruit of your womb, Jesus." And the angel then says: "Do not be afraid." And what does Mary say then?

"Behold, I am a maidservant of the Lord." Yes, she does learn this fearlessness. For we see that throughout Holy Scripture, whether in the case of the shepherds or that of the disciples: when man becomes aware of the closeness of God, he is afraid. He realizes how small he is, and

217

he is terrified by the overwhelming glory and holiness of God, since he plainly recognizes his incommensurability. This appears as one of the first messages of the gospel: "Do not be afraid." This God has not come to frighten us; rather in his greatness he makes himself small, puts aside what makes us afraid, because he comes to save us.

John Paul II took up the saying "Do not be afraid, have no fear of Christ" in one of his first addresses as Pope. I would say that this is a thread that ought to run throughout Christianity. We do not need to be afraid of this God, as if he were going to take something away from us or to threaten us, for it is from him that we have the security that overcomes even death.

As concerns the *Ave Maria*, the Church's prayer, it is composed of two pieces. One part is the angel's greeting; the other is what Elizabeth says when Mary comes to visit her: "Blessed is the fruit of your womb," and Elizabeth then adds: "All generations will call you blessed," thus also predicting the devotion offered to Mary. That is spoken prophetically, in the Holy Spirit. In other words: Christians will also give praise to God by rejoicing over people in whom he has shown how great and how good he is.

What does Mary mean to you, personally?

An expression of the closeness of God. It is with her involvement that the Incarnation becomes really concrete and comprehensible. It is very moving that the Son of God has a human mother and that we are all entrusted to her care. The saying of Jesus on the Cross, when he gives Mary to John as his mother, far transcends that moment and reaches right down through history. With this handing over of Mary, the prayer to Mary opens up for everyone a particular aspect of trust and intimacy and our relation to God as such. Personally, my attitude was shaped from the beginning by the strongly Christocentric aspect of the liturgical movement, and this has been further strengthened in dialogue with our Protestant friends. But over and above the liturgical feasts of Mary, the May devotions, the October Rosary, the places of pilgrimage—the popular devotion to Mary, that is—have always meant a lot to me. And the older I am, the more the Mother of God is important to me and close to me.

There are really not many places in the Gospels where we are told about Mary. There are important parts of Jesus' life during which she doesn't appear at all, and if she does, then it's not always a positive appearance as the loving mother.

That's correct, in the Gospel tradition Mary is quite marginal. In Matthew the Mother plays almost no part; the story of Jesus' childhood is written more from the point of view of Joseph. Obviously, I would say here, people were discreet so long as she was alive. And obviously she herself was always discreet.

Jesus is building a new family, and whenever the woman who gave him birth and who suckled him is praised, he corrects the traditional view of family and upbringing. He says what is important to him: "Blessed are those who hear the Word of God and follow it." That is the new family membership, the new motherhood. He describes it in this way: Whoever does my will shall be brother, mother, sister to me. Understood thus, the departure from the normal human familial relationship, moving toward the great family of community with the will of God, which is now to be built up, is essential. Luke, who tells us about this reprimand, has in any case linked this saying on a literary level with the childhood story, with the meeting with Elizabeth. There, Mary appears as the Mother who embodies not only physical motherhood but also quite fully the hearing and believing, as the one who stands within the divine community. She is portrayed by the Gospel of Luke as the one who hears and keeps the Word in exemplary fashion.

CHAPTER 30

The Faith of Mary

In this text from a general audience given toward the end of his papacy, Benedict XVI reflects on the faith of Mary, a woman who "lived entirely from and in her relationship with the Lord."

The Virgin Mary has a special place in the journey of Advent as the One who, in a unique way, awaited the fulfilment of God's promises, welcoming Jesus the Son of God in faith and in the flesh and with full obedience to the divine will. Today, I wish to ponder briefly with you on Mary's faith, starting from the great mystery of the Annunciation.

"*Chaîre kecharitomene, ho Kyrios meta sou*," "Hail, [rejoice] full of grace, the Lord is with you" (Luke 1:28). These are the words—recorded by Luke the Evangelist—with which the Archangel Gabriel addresses Mary. At first sight the term *chaire* "rejoice," seems an ordinary greeting, typical in the Greek world, but if this word is interpreted against the background of the biblical tradition it acquires a far deeper meaning. The same term occurs four times in the Greek version of the Old Testament and always as a proclamation of joy in the coming of the Messiah (cf. Zeph. 3:14, Joel 2:21; Zech. 9:9; Lam. 4:21).

The Angel's greeting to Mary is therefore an invitation to joy, deep joy. It announces an end to the sadness that exists in the world because of life's limitations, suffering, death, wickedness, in all that seems to block out the light of the divine goodness. It is a greeting that marks the beginning of the Gospel, the Good News.

But why is Mary invited to rejoice in this way? The answer is to be found in the second part of the greeting: "The Lord is with you." Here too, if we are to understand correctly the meaning of these words we must turn to the Old Testament. In the Book of Zephaniah, we find these words: "Sing aloud, O daughter of Zion. . . . The King of Israel, the Lord, is in your midst. . . . The Lord, your God, in your midst, a warrior who gives victory" (3:14–17).

In these words a twofold promise is made to Israel, to the daughter of Zion: God will come as a savior and will pitch his tent in his people's midst, in the womb of the daughter of Zion. This promise is fulfilled to the letter in the dialogue between the Angel and Mary. Mary is identified with the people espoused by God, she is truly the daughter of Zion in person; in her the expectation of the definitive coming of God is fulfilled, in her the Living God makes his dwelling place.

In the greeting of the Angel Mary is called "full of grace." In Greek, the term "grace," *charis*, has the same linguistic root as the word "joy." In this term too the source of Mary's exultation is further clarified: her joy comes from grace, that is, from being in communion with God, from having such a vital connection with him, from being the dwelling place of the Holy Spirit, totally fashioned by God's action. Mary is the creature who opened the door to her Creator in a special way, placing herself in his hands without reserve. She lived entirely *from* and *in* her relationship with the Lord; she was disposed to listen, alert to recognizing the signs of God in the journey of his people; she was integrated into a history of faith and hope in God's promises with which the fabric of her life was woven. And she submitted freely to the word received, to the divine will in the obedience of faith.

The Evangelist Luke tells Mary's story by aligning it closely to the history of Abraham. Just as the great Patriarch is the father of believers who responded to God's call to leave the land in which he lived, to leave behind all that guaranteed his security in order to start out on the journey to an unknown land, assured only in the divine promise, so Mary trusts implicitly in the word that the messenger of God has announced to her, and becomes the model and Mother of all believers.

I would like to emphasize another important point: the opening of the soul to God and to his action in faith also includes an element of obscurity. The relationship of human beings with God does not delete the distance between Creator and creature, it does not eliminate what the Apostle Paul said before the depth of God's wisdom: "How unsearchable are his judgements and how inscrutable his ways!" (Rom. 11:33).

Yet those who—like Mary—open themselves totally to God, come to accept the divine will, even though it is mysterious, although it often does not correspond with their own wishes, and is a sword that pierces their soul, as the elderly Simeon would say prophetically to Mary when Jesus was presented in the Temple (cf. Luke 2:35). Abraham's journey of faith included the moment of joy in the gift of his son Isaac, but also the period of darkness, when he had to climb Mount Moriah to execute a paradoxical order: God was asking him to sacrifice the son he had just given him. On the mountain, the Angel told him: "Do not lay your hand on the lad or do anything to him; for now I know that you fear God, seeing you have not withheld your son, your only son, from me" (Gen. 22:12). Abraham's full trust in the God who is faithful to his promises did not fail, even when his word was mysterious and difficult, almost impossible to accept. So it is with Mary. Her faith experienced the joy of the Annunciation, but also passed through the gloom of the crucifixion of the Son to be able to reach the light of the Resurrection.

It is exactly the same on the journey of faith of each one of us: we encounter patches of light, but we also encounter stretches in which God seems absent, when his silence weighs on our hearts and his will does not correspond with ours, with our inclination to do as we like. However, the more we open ourselves to God, welcome the gift of faith and put our whole trust in him—like Abraham, like Mary—the more capable he will make us, with his presence, of living every situation of life in peace and assured of his faithfulness and his love. However, this means coming out of ourselves and our own projects so that the word of God may be the lamp that guides our thoughts and actions.

I would like once again to ponder on an aspect that surfaces in the infancy narratives of Jesus recounted by St. Luke. Mary and Joseph take their Son to Jerusalem, to the Temple, to present him to the Lord and to consecrate him as required by Mosaic Law: "Every firstborn male shall be designated as holy to the Lord" (cf. Luke 2:22–24). The Holy Family's action acquires an even more profound meaning if we interpret it in the light of the evangelical knowledge of the 12-year-old Jesus. After three days of searching he was found in the Temple in conversation with the teachers. The deeply anxious words of Mary and Joseph: "Son, why have you treated us so? Behold, your father and I have been looking for you anxiously," are in conformity with Jesus' mysterious answer: "How is it that you sought me? Did you not know that I must be in my Father's house?" (Luke 2:48–49). The significance lies in the Father's property, "in my Father's house," as a son is.

Mary is obliged to renew the profound faith with which she said "yes" at the Annunciation; she must accept that it is the true and proper Father of Jesus who has precedence; she must be able to leave the Son she has brought forth free to follow his mission. And Mary's "yes" to God's will, in the obedience of faith, is repeated throughout her life, until the most difficult moment, that of the Cross.

Confronting all this, we may ask ourselves: how was Mary able to journey on beside her Son with such a strong faith, even in darkness, without losing her full trust in the action of God? Mary assumes a fundamental approach in facing what happens in her life. At the Annunciation, on hearing the Angel's words she is distressed—it is the fear a person feels when moved by God's closeness—but it is not the attitude of someone who is afraid of what God might ask. Mary reflects, she ponders on the meaning of this greeting (cf. Luke 1:29). The Greek word used in the Gospel to define this "reflection," "*dielogizeto*," calls to mind the etymology of the word "dialogue."

This means that Mary enters into a deep conversation with the Word of God that has been announced to her, she does not consider it superficially but meditates on it, lets it sink into her mind and her heart so as to understand what the Lord wants of her, the meaning of the announcement.

We find another hint of Mary's inner attitude to God's action—again in the Gospel according to St. Luke—at the time of Jesus' birth, after the adoration of the shepherds. Luke affirms that Mary "kept all these things, pondering them in her heart" (Luke 2:19). In Greek the term is *symballon*, we could say that she "kept together," "pieced together" in her heart all the events that were happening to her; she placed every individual element, every word, every event, within the whole and confronted it, cherished it, recognizing that it all came from the will of God.

Mary does not stop at a first superficial understanding of what is happening in her life, but can look in depth, she lets herself be called into question by events, digests them, discerns them, and attains the understanding that only faith can provide. It is the profound humility of the obedient faith of Mary, who welcomes within her even what she does not understand in God's action, leaving it to God to open her mind and heart. "Blessed is she who believed that there would be a fulfilment of what was spoken to her from the Lord" (Luke 1:45), her kinswoman Elizabeth exclaims. It is exactly because of this faith that all generations will call her blessed.

Dear friends, the Solemnity of the Nativity of the Lord which we shall soon be celebrating invites us to practice this same humility and obedience of faith. The glory of God is not expressed in the triumph and power of a king, it does not shine out in a famous city or a sumptuous palace, but makes its abode in a virgin's womb and is revealed in the poverty of a child. In our lives too, the almightiness of God acts with the force—often in silence—of truth and love. Thus faith tells us that in the end the defenseless power of that Child triumphs over the clamor of worldly powers. Many thanks!

PART IX

THE CHURCH FATHERS

In 2007 and 2008, Benedict XVI devoted a number of his weekly Wednesday general audiences to the Church Fathers, influential theologians between the first and seventh centuries whose writings—together with Sacred Scripture—helped to shape the early Church's life and thought. Benedict XVI himself was deeply influenced by the Church Fathers in his own theology and spirituality. The following chapters are excerpted from these audiences.

CHAPTER 31

St. Clement of Rome

St. Clement, Bishop of Rome in the last years of the first century, was the third Successor of Peter, after Linus and Anacletus. The most important testimony concerning his life comes from St. Irenaeus, Bishop of Lyons until 202. He attests that Clement "had seen the blessed Apostles," "had been conversant with them," and "might be said to have the preaching of the apostles still echoing [in his ears], and their traditions before his eyes" (*Adversus Haer.* 3, 3, 3).

Later testimonies which date back to between the fourth and sixth centuries attribute to Clement the title of martyr.

The authority and prestige of this Bishop of Rome were such that various writings were attributed to him, but the only one that is certainly his is the *Letter to the Corinthians*. Eusebius of Caesarea, the great "archivist" of Christian beginnings, presents it in these terms: "There is extant an Epistle of this Clement which is acknowledged to be genuine and is of considerable length and of remarkable merit. He wrote it in the name of the Church of Rome to the Church of Corinth, when a sedition had arisen in the latter Church. We know that this Epistle also has been publicly used in a great many Churches both in former times and in our own" (*Hist. Eccl.* 3, 16).

An almost canonical character was attributed to this Letter. At the beginning of this text—written in Greek—Clement expressed his regret that "the sudden and successive calamitous events which have happened to ourselves" (1, 1) had prevented him from intervening sooner. These "calamitous events" can be identified with Domitian's persecution: therefore, the Letter must have been written just after the Emperor's death and at the end of the persecution, that is, immediately after the year 96.

227

Clement's intervention—we are still in the first century—was prompted by the serious problems besetting the Church in Corinth: the elders of the community, in fact, had been deposed by some young contestants. The sorrowful event was recalled once again by St. Irenaeus who wrote: "In the time of this Clement, no small dissension having occurred among the brethren in Corinth, the Church in Rome dispatched a most powerful Letter to the Corinthians exhorting them to peace, renewing their faith and declaring the tradition which it had lately received from the Apostles" (*Adv. Haer.* 3, 3, 3).

Thus, we could say that this Letter was a first exercise of the Roman primacy after St. Peter's death. Clement's Letter touches on topics that were dear to St. Paul, who had written two important Letters to the Corinthians, in particular the theological dialectic, perennially current, between the *indicative* of salvation and the *imperative* of moral commitment.

First of all came the joyful proclamation of saving grace. The Lord forewarns us and gives us his forgiveness, gives us his love and the grace to be Christians, his brothers and sisters. It is a proclamation that fills our life with joy and gives certainty to our action: the Lord always forewarns us with his goodness and the Lord's goodness is always greater than all our sins.

However, we must commit ourselves in a way that is consistent with the gift received and respond to the proclamation of salvation with a generous and courageous journey of conversion.

In comparison with the Pauline model, the innovation is that Clement adds to the doctrinal and practical sections, found in all the Pauline Letters, a "great prayer" that virtually concludes the Letter.

The Letter's immediate circumstances provided the Bishop of Rome with ample room for an intervention on the Church's identity and mission. If there were abuses in Corinth, Clement observed, the reason should be sought in the weakening of charity and of the other indispensable Christian virtues.

He therefore calls the faithful to humility and fraternal love, two truly constitutive virtues of being in the Church: "Seeing, therefore, that we are the portion of the Holy One," he warned, "let us do all those things which pertain to holiness" (30, 1).

In particular, the Bishop of Rome recalls that the Lord himself, "has established where and by whom he wishes liturgical functions to be carried out, so that all may be devoutly performed in accordance with his wishes and in a manner acceptable to him. . . . For his own peculiar services are assigned to the high priest, and their own proper place is prescribed to the priests, and their own special ministries devolve on the Levites. The layman is bound by the laws that pertain to laymen" (40, 1–5: it can be noted that here, in this early first-century Letter, the Greek word "laikós" appears for the first time in Christian literature, meaning "a member of the laos," that is, "of the People of God").

In this way, referring to the liturgy of ancient Israel, Clement revealed his ideal Church. She was assembled by "the one Spirit of grace poured out upon us" which breathes on the various members of the Body of Christ, where all, united without any divisions, are "members of one another" (46, 6–7).

The clear distinction between the "lay person" and the hierarchy in no way signifies opposition, but only this organic connection of a body, an organism with its different functions. The Church, in fact, is not a place of confusion and anarchy where one can do what one likes all the time: each one in this organism, with an articulated structure, exercises his ministry in accordance with the vocation he has received.

With regard to community leaders, Clement clearly explains the doctrine of Apostolic Succession. The norms that regulate it derive ultimately from God himself. The Father sent Jesus Christ, who in turn sent the Apostles. They then sent the first heads of communities and established that they would be succeeded by other worthy men.

Everything, therefore, was made "in an orderly way, according to the will of God" (42). With these words, these sentences, St. Clement underlined that the Church's structure was sacramental and not political.

The action of God who comes to meet us in the liturgy precedes our decisions and our ideas. The Church is above all a gift of God and not something we ourselves created; consequently, this sacramental structure does not only guarantee the common order but also this precedence of God's gift which we all need.

Finally, the "great prayer" confers a cosmic breath to the previous reasoning. Clement praises and thanks God for his marvelous providence of love that created the world and continues to save and sanctify it.

The prayer for rulers and governors acquires special importance. Subsequent to the New Testament texts, it is the oldest prayer extant for political institutions. Thus, in the period following their persecution, Christians, well aware that the persecutions would continue, never ceased to pray for the very authorities who had unjustly condemned them.

The reason is primarily Christological: it is necessary to pray for one's persecutors as Jesus did on the Cross.

But this prayer also contains a teaching that guides the attitude of Christians towards politics and the State down the centuries. In praying for the Authorities, Clement recognized the legitimacy of political institutions in the order established by God; at the same time, he expressed his concern that the Authorities would be docile to God, "devoutly in peace and meekness exercising the power given them by [God]" (61, 2).

Caesar is not everything. Another sovereignty emerges whose origins and essence are not of this world but of "the heavens above": it is that of Truth, which also claims a right to be heard by the State.

Thus, Clement's Letter addresses numerous themes of perennial timeliness. It is all the more meaningful since it represents, from the first century, the concern of the Church of Rome which presides in charity over all the other Churches.

In this same Spirit, let us make our own the invocations of the "great prayer" in which the Bishop of Rome makes himself the voice of the entire world: "Yes, O Lord, make your face to shine upon us for good in peace, that we may be shielded by your mighty hand . . . through the High Priest and Guardian of our souls, Jesus Christ, through whom be glory and majesty to you both now and from generation to generation, for evermore" (60–61).

CHAPTER 32

St. Ignatius of Antioch

St. Ignatius . . . was the third Bishop of Antioch from 70 to 107, the date of his martyrdom. At that time, Rome, Alexandria, and Antioch were the three great metropolises of the Roman Empire. The Council of Nicaea mentioned three "primacies": Rome, but also Alexandria and Antioch participated in a certain sense in a "primacy."

St. Ignatius was Bishop of Antioch, which today is located in Turkey. Here in Antioch, as we know from the Acts of the Apostles, a flourishing Christian community developed. Its first Bishop was the Apostle Peter—or so tradition claims—and it was there that the disciples were *"for the first time called Christians"* (Acts 11:26). Eusebius of Caesarea, a fourth-century historian, dedicated an entire chapter of his *Church History* to the life and literary works of Ignatius (cf. 3:36).

Eusebius writes: "The Report says that he [Ignatius] was sent from Syria to Rome, and became food for wild beasts on account of his testimony to Christ. And as he made the journey through Asia under the strictest military surveillance" (he called the guards "ten leopards" in his *Letter to the Romans*, 5:1), "he fortified the parishes in the various cities where he stopped by homilies and exhortations, and warned them above all to be especially on their guard against the heresies that were then beginning to prevail, and exhorted them to hold fast to the tradition of the Apostles."

The first place Ignatius stopped on the way to his martyrdom was the city of Smyrna, where St. Polycarp, a disciple of St. John, was Bishop. Here, Ignatius wrote four letters, respectively to the Churches of Ephesus, Magnesia, Tralli, and Rome. "Having left Smyrna," Eusebius continues, Ignatius reached Troas and "wrote again": two letters to the Churches of Philadelphia and Smyrna, and one to Bishop Polycarp.

Thus, Eusebius completes the list of his letters, which have come down to us from the Church of the first century as a precious treasure. In reading these texts one feels the freshness of the faith of the generation which had still known the Apostles. In these letters, the ardent love of a saint can also be felt.

Lastly, the martyr travelled from Troas to Rome, where he was thrown to fierce wild animals in the Flavian Amphitheatre.

No Church Father has expressed the longing for *union* with Christ and for *life* in him with the intensity of Ignatius. We therefore read the Gospel passage on the vine, which according to John's Gospel is Jesus. In fact, two spiritual "currents" converge in Ignatius, that of Paul, straining with all his might for *union* with Christ, and that of John, concentrated on *life* in him. In turn, these two currents translate into the *imitation* of Christ, whom Ignatius several times proclaimed as "my" or "our God."

Thus, Ignatius implores the Christians of Rome not to prevent his martyrdom since he is impatient "to attain to Jesus Christ." And he explains, "It is better for me to die on behalf of Jesus Christ than to reign over all the ends of the earth. . . . Him I seek, who died for us: him I desire, who rose again for our sake. . . . Permit me to be an imitator of the Passion of my God!" (*Romans*, 5–6).

One can perceive in these words on fire with love, the pronounced Christological "realism" typical of the Church of Antioch, more focused than ever on the Incarnation of the Son of God and on his true and concrete humanity: "Jesus Christ," St. Ignatius wrote to the Smyrnaeans, "was *truly* of the seed of David," "he was *truly* born of a virgin," "and was *truly* nailed [to the Cross] for us" (1:1). Ignatius' irresistible longing for union with Christ was the foundation of a real "mysticism of unity." He describes himself: "I therefore did what befitted me as a man devoted to unity" (*Philadelphians*, 8:1).

For Ignatius unity was first and foremost a prerogative of God, who, since he exists as Three Persons, is One in absolute unity. Ignatius often used to repeat that God is unity and that in God alone is unity found in its pure and original state. Unity to be brought about on this earth by Christians is no more than an imitation as close as possible to the divine archetype.

Thus, Ignatius reached the point of being able to work out a vision of the Church strongly reminiscent of certain expressions in Clement of Rome's *Letter to the Corinthians.*

For example, he wrote to the Christians of Ephesus: "It is fitting that you should concur with the will of your Bishop, which you also do. For your justly renowned presbytery, worthy of God, is fitted as exactly to the Bishop as the strings are to the harp. Therefore, in your concord and harmonious love, Jesus Christ is sung. And man by man, you become a choir, that being harmonious in love and taking up the song of God in unison you may with one voice sing to the Father . . ." (4:1–2).

And after recommending to the Smyrnaeans: "Let no man do anything connected with Church without the Bishop," he confides to Polycarp: "I offer my life for those who are submissive to the Bishop, to the presbyters, and to the deacons, and may I along with them obtain my portion in God! Labor together with one another; strive in company together; run together; suffer together; sleep together; and awake together as the stewards and associates and servants of God. Please him under whom you fight, and from whom you receive your wages. Let none of you be found a deserter. Let your Baptism endure as your arms; your faith as your helmet; your love as your spear; your patience as a complete panoply" (*Polycarp*, 6:1–2).

Overall, it is possible to grasp in the *Letters* of Ignatius a sort of constant and fruitful dialectic between two characteristic aspects of Christian life: on the one hand, the hierarchical structure of the Ecclesial Community, and on the other, the fundamental unity that binds all the faithful in Christ.

Consequently, their roles cannot be opposed to one another. On the contrary, the insistence on communion among believers and of believers with their Pastors was constantly reformulated in eloquent images and analogies: the harp, strings, intonation, the concert, the symphony. The special responsibility of Bishops, priests, and deacons in building the community is clear.

This applies first of all to their invitation to love and unity. "Be one," Ignatius wrote to the Magnesians, echoing the prayer of Jesus at the Last Supper: "one supplication, one mind, one hope in love. . . . Therefore, all run together as into one temple of God, as to one altar, as to one Jesus Christ who came forth from one Father, and is with and has gone to one" (7:1–2).

Ignatius was the first person in Christian literature to attribute to the Church the adjective "catholic" or "universal": "Wherever Jesus Christ is," he said, "there is the Catholic Church" (*Smyrnaeans*, 8:2). And precisely in the service of unity to the Catholic Church, the Christian community of Rome exercised a sort of primacy of love: "The Church which presides in the place of the region of the Romans, and which is worthy of God, worthy of honor, worthy of the highest happiness . . . and which presides over love, is named from Christ, and from the Father . . ." (*Romans*, Prologue).

As can be seen, Ignatius is truly the "Doctor of Unity": unity of God and unity of Christ (despite the various heresies gaining ground which separated the human and the divine in Christ), unity of the Church, unity of the faithful in "faith and love, to which nothing is to be preferred" (*Smyrnaeans*, 6:1).

Ultimately, Ignatius' realism invites the faithful of yesterday and today, invites us all, to make a gradual synthesis between *configuration to Christ* (union with him, life in him) and *dedication to his Church* (unity with the Bishop, generous service to the community and to the world).

To summarize, it is necessary to achieve a synthesis between *communion* of the Church within herself and *mission*, the proclamation of the Gospel to others, until the other speaks through one dimension and believers increasingly "have obtained the inseparable Spirit, who is Jesus Christ" (*Magnesians*, 15).

Imploring from the Lord this "grace of unity" and in the conviction that the whole Church presides in charity (cf. *Romans*, Prologue), I address to you yourselves the same hope with which Ignatius ended his *Letter to the Trallians*: "Love one another with an undivided heart. Let my spirit be sanctified by yours, not only now, but also when I shall attain to God. . . . In [Jesus Christ] may you be found unblemished" (13).

And let us pray that the Lord will help us to attain this unity and to be found at last unstained, because it is love that purifies souls.

CHAPTER 33

St. Justin Martyr

St. Justin, Philosopher and Martyr, [was] the most important of the second-century apologist Fathers.

The word "apologist" designates those ancient Christian writers who set out to defend the new religion from the weighty accusations of both pagans and Jews, and to spread the Christian doctrine in terms suited to the culture of their time.

Thus, the apologists had a twofold concern: that most properly called "apologetic," to defend the newborn Christianity (*apologhía* in Greek means, precisely, "defense"), and the pro-positive, "missionary" concern, to explain the content of the faith in a language and on a wavelength comprehensible to their contemporaries.

Justin was born in about the year 100 near ancient Shechem, Samaria, in the Holy Land; he spent a long time seeking the truth, moving through the various schools of the Greek philosophical tradition.

Finally, as he himself recounts in the first chapters of his *Dialogue with Tryphon*, a mysterious figure, an old man he met on the seashore, initially leads him into a crisis by showing him that it is impossible for the human being to satisfy his aspiration to the divine solely with his own forces. He then pointed out to him the ancient prophets as the people to turn to in order to find the way to God and "true philosophy."

In taking his leave, the old man urged him to pray that the gates of light would be opened to him. The story foretells the crucial episode in Justin's life: at the end of a long philosophical journey, a quest for the truth, he arrived at the Christian faith. He founded a school in Rome where, free of charge, he initiated students into the new religion, considered as the true philosophy. Indeed, in it he had found the truth, hence, the art of living virtuously.

For this reason he was reported and beheaded in about 165 during the reign of Marcus Aurelius, the philosopher-emperor to whom Justin had actually addressed one of his *Apologia*.

These—the two *Apologies* and the *Dialogue with the Hebrew, Tryphon*—are his only surviving works. In them, Justin intends above all to illustrate the divine project of creation and salvation, which is fulfilled in Jesus Christ, the *Logos*, that is, the eternal Word, eternal Reason, creative Reason.

Every person as a rational being shares in the *Logos*, carrying within himself a "seed," and can perceive glimmers of the truth. Thus, the same *Logos* who revealed himself as a prophetic figure to the Hebrews of the ancient Law also manifested himself partially, in "seeds of truth," in Greek philosophy.

Now, Justin concludes, since Christianity is the historical and personal manifestation of the *Logos* in his totality, it follows that "whatever things were rightly said among all men are the property of us Christians" (*Second Apology of St. Justin Martyr*, 13:4).

In this way, although Justin disputed Greek philosophy and its contradictions, he decisively oriented any philosophical truth to the *Logos*, giving reasons for the unusual "claim" to truth and universality of the Christian religion. If the Old Testament leaned towards Christ, just as the symbol is a guide to the reality represented, then Greek philosophy also aspired to Christ and the Gospel, just as the part strives to be united with the whole.

And he said that these two realities, the Old Testament and Greek philosophy, are like two paths that lead to Christ, to the *Logos*. This is why Greek philosophy cannot be opposed to Gospel truth, and Christians can draw from it confidently as from a good of their own.

Therefore, my venerable Predecessor, Pope John Paul II, described St. Justin as a "pioneer of positive engagement with philosophical thinking—albeit with cautious discernment. . . . Although he continued to hold Greek philosophy in high esteem after his conversion, Justin claimed with power and clarity that he had found in Christianity 'the only sure and profitable philosophy' (*Dial.* 8:1)" (*Fides et Ratio*, no. 38).

Overall, the figure and work of Justin mark the ancient Church's forceful option for philosophy, for reason, rather than for the religion of the pagans. With the pagan religion, in fact, the early Christians strenuously rejected every compromise. They held it to be idolatry, at the cost of being accused for this reason of "impiety" and "atheism."

Justin in particular, especially in his first *Apology*, mercilessly criticized the pagan religion and its myths, which he considered to be diabolically misleading on the path of truth.

Philosophy, on the other hand, represented the privileged area of the encounter between paganism, Judaism, and Christianity, precisely at the level of the criticism of pagan religion and its false myths. "Our philosophy . . .": this is how another apologist, Bishop Melito of Sardis, a contemporary of Justin, came to define the new religion in a more explicit way (*Ap. Hist. Eccl.* 4, 26, 7).

In fact, the pagan religion did not follow the ways of the *Logos*, but clung to myth, even if Greek philosophy recognized that mythology was devoid of consistency with the truth.

Therefore, the decline of the pagan religion was inevitable: it was a logical consequence of the detachment of religion—reduced to an artificial collection of ceremonies, conventions, and customs—from the truth of being.

Justin, and with him other apologists, adopted the clear stance taken by the Christian faith for the God of the philosophers against the false gods of the pagan religion.

It was the choice of the *truth* of being against the myth of *custom*. Several decades after Justin, Tertullian defined the same option of Christians with a lapidary sentence that still applies: "*Dominus noster Christus veritatem se, non consuetudinem, cognominavit*—Christ has said that he is truth, not fashion" (*De Virgin. Vel.* 1, 1).

238

It should be noted in this regard that the term *consuetudo*, used here by Tertullian in reference to the pagan religion, can be translated into modern languages with the expressions: "cultural fashion," "current fads."

In a time like ours, marked by relativism in the discussion on values and on religion—as well as in interreligious dialogue—this is a lesson that should not be forgotten.

To this end, I suggest to you once again—and thus I conclude—the last words of the mysterious old man whom Justin the Philosopher met on the seashore: "Pray that, above all things, the gates of light may be opened to you; for these things cannot be perceived or understood by all, but only by the man to whom God and his Christ have imparted wisdom" (*Dial.* 7:3).

CHAPTER 34

St. Irenaeus of Lyons

The biographical information on [St. Irenaeus of Lyons] comes from his own testimony, handed down to us by Eusebius in his fifth book on Church History.

Irenaeus was in all probability born in Smyrna (today, Izmir in Turkey) in about 135–140, where in his youth, he attended the school of Bishop Polycarp, a disciple in his turn of the Apostle John. We do not know when he moved from Asia Minor to Gaul, but his move must have coincided with the first development of the Christian community in Lyons: here, in 177, we find Irenaeus listed in the college of presbyters. In that very year, he was sent to Rome bearing a letter from the community in Lyons to Pope Eleutherius. His mission to Rome saved Irenaeus from the persecution of Marcus Aurelius which took a toll of at least 48 martyrs, including the 90-year-old Bishop Pontinus of Lyons, who died from ill-treatment in prison. Thus, on his return Irenaeus was appointed Bishop of the city. The new Pastor devoted himself without reserve to his episcopal ministry which ended in about 202–203, perhaps with martyrdom.

Irenaeus was first and foremost a man of faith and a Pastor. Like a good Pastor, he had a good sense of proportion, a wealth of doctrine, and missionary enthusiasm. As a writer, he pursued a twofold aim: to defend true doctrine from the attacks of heretics, and to explain the truth of the faith clearly. His two extant works—the five books of *The Detection and Overthrow of the False Gnosis* and *Demonstration of the Apostolic Teaching* (which can also be called the oldest "catechism of Christian doctrine")—exactly corresponded with these aims. In short, Irenaeus can be defined as the champion in the fight against heresies.

The second-century Church was threatened by the so-called *Gnosis*, a doctrine which affirmed that the faith taught in the Church was merely a symbolism for the simple who were unable to grasp difficult concepts; instead, the initiates, the intellectuals—Gnostics, they were called—claimed to understand what was behind these symbols and thus formed an elitist and intellectualist Christianity. Obviously, this intellectual Christianity became increasingly fragmented, splitting into different currents with ideas that were often bizarre and extravagant, yet attractive to many. One element these different currents had in common was "dualism": they denied faith in the one God and Father of all, Creator and Savior of man and of the world. To explain evil in the world, they affirmed the existence, besides the Good God, of a negative principle. This negative principle was supposed to have produced material things, matter.

Firmly rooted in the biblical doctrine of creation, Irenaeus refuted the Gnostic dualism and pessimism which debased corporeal realities. He decisively claimed the original holiness of matter, of the body, of the flesh no less than of the spirit. But his work went far beyond the confutation of heresy: in fact, one can say that he emerges as the first great Church theologian who created systematic theology; he himself speaks of the system of theology, that is, of the internal coherence of all faith. At the heart of his doctrine is the question of the "rule of faith" and its transmission. For Irenaeus, the "rule of faith" coincided in practice with the *Apostles' Creed*, which gives us the key for interpreting the Gospel, for interpreting the Creed in light of the Gospel. The Creed, which is a sort of Gospel synthesis, helps us understand what it means and how we should read the Gospel itself.

In fact, the Gospel preached by Irenaeus is the one he was taught by Polycarp, Bishop of Smyrna, and Polycarp's Gospel dates back to the Apostle John, whose disciple Polycarp was. The true teaching, therefore, is not that invented by intellectuals which goes beyond the Church's simple faith. The true Gospel is the one imparted by the Bishops who received it in an uninterrupted line from the Apostles. They taught nothing except this simple faith, which is also the true depth of God's revelation. Thus, Irenaeus tells us, there is no secret doctrine concealed in the Church's common Creed. There is no superior Christianity for intellectuals. The faith publicly confessed by the Church is the common faith of all. This faith alone is apostolic, it is handed down from the Apostles, that is, from Jesus and from God. In adhering to this faith, publicly transmitted by the Apostles to their successors, Christians must observe what their Bishops say and must give special consideration to the teaching of the Church of Rome, pre-eminent and very ancient. It is because of her antiquity that this Church has the greatest apostolicity; in fact, she originated in Peter and Paul, pillars of the Apostolic College. All Churches must agree with the Church of Rome, recognizing in her the measure of the true Apostolic Tradition, the Church's one common faith. With these arguments, summed up very briefly here, Irenaeus refuted the claims of these Gnostics, these intellectuals, from the start. First of all, they possessed no truth superior to that of the ordinary faith, because what they said was not of apostolic origin, it was invented by them. Secondly, truth and salvation are not the privilege or monopoly of the few, but are available to all through the preaching of the Successors of the Apostles, especially of the Bishop of Rome. In particular—once again disputing the "secret" character of the Gnostic tradition and noting its multiple and contradictory results—Irenaeus was concerned to describe the genuine concept of the Apostolic Tradition which we can sum up here in three points.

a) Apostolic Tradition is "public," not private or secret. Irenaeus did not doubt that the content of the faith transmitted by the Church is that received from the Apostles and from Jesus, the Son of God. There is no other teaching than this. Therefore, for anyone who wishes to know true doctrine, it suffices to know "the Tradition passed down by the Apostles and the faith proclaimed to men": a tradition and faith that "have come down to us through the succession of Bishops" (*Adversus Haereses*, 3, 3, 3–4). Hence, the succession of Bishops, the personal principle, and Apostolic Tradition, the doctrinal principle, coincide.

b) Apostolic Tradition is "one." Indeed, whereas Gnosticism was divided into multiple sects, Church Tradition is one in its fundamental content, which—as we have seen—Irenaeus calls precisely *regula fidei* or *veritatis:* and thus, because it is one, it creates unity through the peoples, through the different cultures, through the different peoples; it is a common content like the truth, despite the diversity of languages and cultures. A very precious saying of St. Irenaeus is found in his book *Adversus Haereses:* "The Church, though dispersed throughout the world . . . having received [this faith from the Apostles] . . . as if occupying but one house, carefully preserves it. She also believes these points [of doctrine] just as if she had but one soul and one and the same heart, and she proclaims them, and teaches them and hands them down with perfect harmony as if she possessed only one mouth. For, although the languages of the world are dissimilar, yet the import of the tradition is one and the same. For the Churches which have been planted in Germany do not believe or hand down anything different, nor do those in Spain, nor those in Gaul, nor those in the East, nor those in Egypt, nor those in Libya, nor those which have been established in the central regions of the world" (1, 10, 1–2). Already at that time—we are in the year 200—it was possible to perceive the Church's universality, her catholicity and the unifying power of the truth that unites these very different realities, from Germany, to Spain, to Italy, to Egypt, to Libya, in the common truth revealed to us by Christ.

c) Lastly, the Apostolic Tradition, as he says in the Greek language in which he wrote his book, is "pneumatic," in other words, spiritual, guided by the Holy Spirit: in Greek, the word for "spirit" is "*pneuma.*" Indeed, it is not a question of a transmission entrusted to the ability of more or less learned people, but to God's Spirit who guarantees fidelity to the transmission of the faith. This is the "life" of the Church, what makes the Church ever young and fresh, fruitful with multiple charisms.

For Irenaeus, Church and Spirit were inseparable: "This faith," we read again in the third book of *Adversus Haereses,* "which, having been received from the Church, we do preserve, and which always, by the

Spirit of God, renewing its youth as if it were some precious deposit in an excellent vessel, causes the vessel itself containing it to renew its youth also. . . . For where the Church is, there is the Spirit of God; and where the Spirit of God is, there is the Church and every kind of grace" (3, 24, 1). As can be seen, Irenaeus did not stop at defining the concept of Tradition. His tradition, uninterrupted Tradition, is not traditionalism, because this Tradition is always enlivened from within by the Holy Spirit, who makes it live anew, causes it to be interpreted and understood in the vitality of the Church. Adhering to her teaching, the Church should transmit the faith in such a way that it must be what it appears, that is, "public," "one," "pneumatic," "spiritual." Starting with each one of these characteristics, a fruitful discernment can be made of the authentic transmission of the faith in the *today* of the Church. More generally, in Irenaeus' teaching, the dignity of man, body and soul, is firmly anchored in divine creation, in the image of Christ and in the Spirit's permanent work of sanctification. This doctrine is like a "high road" in order to discern together with all people of good will the object and boundaries of the dialogue of values, and to give an ever new impetus to the Church's missionary action, to the force of the truth which is the source of all true values in the world.

CHAPTER 35

Origen of Alexandria

Origen of Alexandria truly was a figure crucial to the whole development of Christian thought. He gathered up the legacy of Clement of Alexandria . . . and launched it for the future in a way so innovative that he impressed an irreversible turning point on the development of Christian thought.

He was a true "maestro," and so it was that his pupils remembered him with nostalgia and emotion: he was not only a brilliant theologian but also an exemplary witness of the doctrine he passed on. Eusebius of Caesarea, his enthusiastic biographer, said "his manner of life was as his doctrine, and his doctrine as his life. Therefore, by the divine power working with him he aroused a great many to his own zeal" (cf. *Church History*, 6, 3, 7).

His whole life was pervaded by a ceaseless longing for martyrdom. He was 17 years old when, in the 10th year of the reign of Emperor Septimius Severus, the persecution against Christians was unleashed in Alexandria. Clement, his teacher, fled the city, and Origen's father, Leonides, was thrown into prison. His son longed ardently for martyrdom but was unable to realize his desire. So he wrote to his father, urging him not to shrink from the supreme witness of faith. And when Leonides was beheaded, the young Origen felt bound to welcome the example of his father's life.

Forty years later, while preaching in Caesarea, he confessed: "It is of no use to me to have a martyr father if I do not behave well and honor the nobility of my ancestors, that is, the martyrdom of my father and the witness that made him illustrious in Christ" (*Hom. Ez.* 4, 8). In a later homily—when, thanks to the extreme tolerance of the Emperor,

Philip the Arab, the possibility of bearing witness by shedding one's blood seemed no longer to exist—Origen exclaims: "If God were to grant me to be washed in my blood so as to receive the second Baptism after accepting death for Christ, I would depart this world with assurance. . . . But those who deserve such things are blessed" (*Hom. Iud.* 7, 12). These words reveal the full force of Origen's longing for Baptism with blood.

And finally, this irresistible yearning was granted to him, at least in part. In the year 250, during Decius' persecution, Origen was arrested and cruelly tortured. Weakened by the suffering to which he had been subjected, he died a few years later. He was not yet 70.

We have mentioned the "irreversible turning point" that Origen impressed upon the history of theology and Christian thought. But of what did this turning point, this innovation so pregnant with consequences, consist? It corresponds in substance to theology's foundation in the explanation of the Scriptures.

Theology to him was essentially explaining, understanding Scripture; or we might also say that his theology was a perfect symbiosis between theology and exegesis. In fact, the proper hallmark of Origen's doctrine seems to lie precisely in the constant invitation to move from the letter to the spirit of the Scriptures, to progress in knowledge of God. Furthermore, this so-called "allegorism," as von Balthasar wrote, coincides exactly "with the development of Christian dogma, effected by the teaching of the Church Doctors," who in one way or another accepted Origen's "lessons."

Thus, Tradition and the Magisterium, the foundation and guarantee of theological research, come to take the form of "scripture in action" (cf. *Origene: Il mondo, Cristo e la Chiesa*, Milan, 1972, p. 43). We can therefore say that the central nucleus of Origen's immense literary opus consists in his "threefold interpretation" of the Bible.

But before describing this "interpretation" it would be right to take an overall look at the Alexandrian's literary production.

St. Jerome, in his *Epistle* 33, lists the titles of 320 books and 310 homilies by Origen. Unfortunately, most of these works have been lost, but even the few that remain make him the most prolific author of Christianity's first three centuries. His field of interest extended from exegesis to dogma, to philosophy, apologetics, ascetical theology and mystical theology. It was a fundamental and global vision of Christian life.

The inspiring nucleus of this work, as we have said, was the "threefold interpretation" of the Scriptures that Origen developed in his lifetime. By this phrase, we wish to allude to the three most important ways in which Origen devoted himself to studying the Scriptures: they are not in sequence; on the contrary, more often than not they overlap.

First of all, he read the Bible, determined to do his utmost to ascertain the biblical text and offer the most reliable version of it. This, for example, was the first step: to know truly what is written and what a specific scriptural passage intentionally and principally meant.

He studied extensively for this purpose and drafted an edition of the Bible with six parallel columns, from left to right, with the Hebrew text in Hebrew characters—he was even in touch with rabbis to make sure he properly understood the Bible's original Hebrew text—then the Hebrew text transliterated into Greek characters, and then four different translations in Greek that enabled him to compare the different possibilities for its translation. Hence comes the title of "*Hexapla*" ("six columns"), attributed to this enormous synopsis.

This is the first point: to know exactly what was written, the text as such.

Secondly, Origen read the Bible systematically with his famous *Commentaries.* They reproduced faithfully the explanations that the teacher offered during his lessons at Alexandria and Caesarea.

Origen proceeded verse by verse with a detailed, broad, and analytical approach, with philological and doctrinal notes. He worked with great precision in order to know completely what the sacred authors meant.

Lastly, even before his ordination to the priesthood, Origen was deeply dedicated to preaching the Bible and adapted himself to a varied public. In any case, the teacher can also be perceived in his *Homilies*, wholly dedicated as he was to the systematic interpretation of the passage under examination, which he analyzed step by step in the sequence of the verses.

Also in his *Homilies*, Origen took every opportunity to recall the different dimensions of the sense of Sacred Scripture that encourage or express a process of growth in the faith: there is the "literal" sense, but this conceals depths that are not immediately apparent.

The second dimension is the "moral" sense: what we must do in living the word; and finally, the "spiritual" sense, the unity of Scripture which throughout its development speaks of Christ.

It is the Holy Spirit who enables us to understand the Christological content, hence, the unity in diversity of Scripture. It would be interesting to demonstrate this. I have made a humble attempt in my book, *Jesus of Nazareth*, to show in today's context these multiple dimensions of the Word, of Sacred Scripture, whose historical meaning must in the first place be respected.

But this sense transcends us, moving us towards God in the light of the Holy Spirit, and shows us the way, shows us how to live. Mention of it is found, for example, in the ninth *Homily on Numbers*, where Origen likens Scripture to [fresh] walnuts: "The doctrine of the Law and the Prophets at the school of Christ is like this," the homilist says; "the letter is bitter, like the [green-covered] skin; secondly, you will come to the shell, which is the moral doctrine; thirdly, you will discover the meaning of the mysteries, with which the souls of the saints are nourished in the present life and the future" (*Hom. Num.* 9, 7).

It was especially on this route that Origen succeeded in effectively promoting the "Christian interpretation" of the Old Testament, brilliantly countering the challenge of the heretics, especially the Gnostics and Marcionites, who made the two Testaments disagree to the extent that they rejected the Old Testament.

In this regard, in the same *Homily on Numbers,* the Alexandrian says, "I do not call the Law an 'Old Testament' if I understand it in the Spirit. The Law becomes an 'Old Testament' only for those who wish to understand it carnally," that is, for those who stop at the literal meaning of the text.

But "for us, who understand it and apply it in the Spirit and in the Gospel sense, the Law is ever new and the two Testaments are a new Testament for us, not because of their date in time but because of the newness of the meaning. . . . Instead, for the sinner and those who do not respect the covenant of love, even the Gospels age" (cf. ibid., 9, 4).

I invite you—and so I conclude—to welcome into your hearts the teaching of this great master of faith. He reminds us with deep delight that in the prayerful reading of Scripture and in consistent commitment to life, the Church is ever renewed and rejuvenated. The Word of God, which never ages and is never exhausted, is a privileged means to this end. Indeed, it is the Word of God, through the action of the Holy Spirit, which always guides us to the whole truth (cf. Benedict XVI, *Address at the International Congress for the 50th Anniversary of* Dei Verbum, *L'Osservatore Romano* English edition, September 21, 2005, p. 7).

And let us pray to the Lord that he will give us thinkers, theologians and exegetes who discover this multifaceted dimension, this ongoing timeliness of Sacred Scripture, its newness for today. Let us pray that the Lord will help us to read Sacred Scripture in a prayerful way, to be truly nourished with the true Bread of Life, with his Word.

CHAPTER 36

St. Athanasius

Let us focus our attention today on St. Athanasius of Alexandria.

Only a few years after his death, this authentic protagonist of the Christian tradition was already hailed as "the pillar of the Church" by Gregory of Nazianzus, the great theologian and Bishop of Constantinople (*Orationes*, 21, 26), and he has always been considered a model of orthodoxy in both East and West.

As a result, it was not by chance that Gian Lorenzo Bernini placed his statue among those of the four holy Doctors of the Eastern and Western Churches—together with the images of Ambrose, John Chrysostom, and Augustine—which surround the Chair of St. Peter in the marvelous apse of the Vatican Basilica.

Athanasius was undoubtedly one of the most important and revered early Church Fathers. But this great Saint was above all the impassioned theologian of the Incarnation of the *Logos*, the Word of God who—as the Prologue of the fourth Gospel says—"became flesh and dwelt among us" (John 1:14).

For this very reason Athanasius was also the most important and tenacious adversary of the Arian heresy, which at that time threatened faith in Christ, reduced to a creature "halfway" between God and man, according to a recurring tendency in history which we also see manifested today in various forms.

In all likelihood Athanasius was born in Alexandria, Egypt, in about the year 300 A.D. He received a good education before becoming a deacon and secretary to the Bishop of Alexandria, the great Egyptian metropolis. As a close collaborator of his Bishop, the young cleric took part with him in the Council of Nicaea, the first Ecumenical Council, convoked by the Emperor Constantine in May 325 A.D. to ensure Church unity. The Nicene Fathers were thus able to address various issues and primarily the serious problem that had arisen a few years earlier from the preaching of the Alexandrian priest, Arius.

With his theory, Arius threatened authentic faith in Christ, declaring that the *Logos* was not a true God but a created God, a creature "halfway" between God and man who hence remained forever inaccessible to us. The Bishops gathered in Nicaea responded by developing and establishing the "Symbol of faith" ["Creed"] which, completed later at the First Council of Constantinople, has endured in the traditions of various Christian denominations and in the liturgy as the *Niceno-Constantinopolitan Creed.*

In this fundamental text—which expresses the faith of the undivided Church and which we also recite today, every Sunday, in the Eucharistic celebration—the Greek term *homooúsios* is featured, in Latin *consubstantialis*: it means that the Son, the *Logos,* is "of the same substance" as the Father, he is God of God, he is his substance. Thus, the full divinity of the Son, which was denied by the Arians, was brought into the limelight.

In 328 A.D., when Bishop Alexander died, Athanasius succeeded him as Bishop of Alexandria. He showed straightaway that he was determined to reject any compromise with regard to the Arian theories condemned by the Council of Nicaea.

His intransigence—tenacious and, if necessary, at times harsh—against those who opposed his episcopal appointment and especially against adversaries of the Nicene Creed, provoked the implacable hostility of the Arians and philo-Arians.

Despite the unequivocal outcome of the Council, which clearly affirmed that the Son is of the same substance as the Father, these erroneous ideas shortly thereafter once again began to prevail—in this situation even Arius was rehabilitated—and they were upheld for political reasons by the Emperor Constantine himself and then by his son Constantius II.

Moreover, Constantine was not so much concerned with theological truth but rather with the unity of the Empire and its political problems; he wished to politicize the faith, making it more accessible—in his opinion—to all his subjects throughout the Empire.

Thus, the Arian crisis, believed to have been resolved at Nicaea, persisted for decades with complicated events and painful divisions in the Church. At least five times—during the 30 years between 336 and 366 A.D.—Athanasius was obliged to abandon his city, spending 17 years in exile and suffering for the faith. But during his forced absences from Alexandria, the Bishop was able to sustain and to spread in the West, first at Trier and then in Rome, the Nicene faith as well as the ideals of monasticism, embraced in Egypt by the great hermit, Anthony, with a choice of life to which Athanasius was always close.

St. Anthony, with his spiritual strength, was the most important champion of St. Athanasius' faith. Reinstated in his See once and for all, the Bishop of Alexandria was able to devote himself to religious pacification and the reorganization of the Christian communities. He died on May 2, 373, the day when we celebrate his liturgical Memorial.

The most famous doctrinal work of the holy Alexandrian Bishop is his treatise: *De Incarnatione* (*On the Incarnation of the Word*), the divine *Logos* who was made flesh, becoming like one of us for our salvation.

In this work Athanasius says with an affirmation that has rightly become famous that the Word of God "was made man so that we might be made God; and he manifested himself through a body so that we might receive the idea of the unseen Father; and he endured the insolence of men that we might inherit immortality" (54, 3). With his Resurrection, in fact, the Lord banished death from us like "straw from the fire" (8, 4).

The fundamental idea of Athanasius' entire theological battle was precisely that God is accessible. He is not a secondary God, he is the true God and it is through our communion with Christ that we can truly be united to God. He has really become "God-with-us."

Among the other works of this great Father of the Church—which remain largely associated with the events of the Arian crisis—let us remember the four epistles he addressed to his friend Serapion, Bishop of Thmuis, on the divinity of the Holy Spirit which he clearly affirmed, and approximately 30 "Festal" Letters addressed at the beginning of each year to the Churches and monasteries of Egypt to inform them of the date of the Easter celebration, but above all to guarantee the links between the faithful, reinforcing their faith and preparing them for this great Solemnity.

Lastly, Athanasius also wrote meditational texts on the Psalms, subsequently circulated widely, and in particular, a work that constitutes the *bestseller* of early Christian literature: *The Life of Anthony*, that is, the biography of St. Anthony, Abbot. It was written shortly after this Saint's death precisely while the exiled Bishop of Alexandria was staying with monks in the Egyptian desert.

Athanasius was such a close friend of the great hermit that he received one of the two sheepskins which Anthony left as his legacy, together with the mantle that the Bishop of Alexandria himself had given to him.

The exemplary biography of this figure dear to Christian tradition soon became very popular, almost immediately translated into Latin, in two editions, and then into various Oriental languages; it made an important contribution to the spread of monasticism in the East and in the West.

It was not by chance that the interpretation of this text, in Trier, was at the center of a moving tale of the conversion of two imperial officials which Augustine incorporated into his *Confessions* (cf. VIII, 6, 15) as the preamble to his own conversion.

Moreover, Athanasius himself showed he was clearly aware of the influence that Anthony's fine example could have on Christian people. Indeed, he wrote at the end of this work: "The fact that his fame has been blazoned everywhere, that all regard him with wonder, and that those who have never seen him long for him, is clear proof of his virtue

253

and God's love of his soul. For not from writings, nor from worldly wisdom, nor through any art, was Anthony renowned, but solely from his piety towards God. That this was the gift of God no one will deny.

"For from whence into Spain and into Gaul, how into Rome and Africa, was the man heard of who dwelt hidden in a mountain, unless it was God who makes his own known everywhere, who also promised this to Anthony at the beginning? For even if they work secretly, even if they wish to remain in obscurity, yet the Lord shows them as lamps to lighten all, that those who hear may thus know that the precepts of God are able to make men prosper and thus be zealous in the path of virtue" (*Life of Anthony*, 93, 5–6).

Yes, brothers and sisters! We have many causes for which to be grateful to St. Athanasius. His life, like that of Anthony and of countless other saints, shows us that "those who draw near to God do not withdraw from men, but rather become truly close to them" (*Deus Caritas Est*, no. 42).

CHAPTER 37

St. Basil

St. Basil [is] described by Byzantine liturgical texts as "a luminary of the Church."

He was an important Bishop in the fourth century to whom the entire Church of the East, and likewise the Church of the West, looks with admiration because of the holiness of his life, the excellence of his teaching and the harmonious synthesis of his speculative and practical gifts.

He was born in about 330 A.D. into a family of saints, "a true domestic Church," immersed in an atmosphere of deep faith. He studied with the best teachers in Athens and Constantinople.

Unsatisfied with his worldly success and realizing that he had frivolously wasted much time on vanities, he himself confessed: "One day, like a man roused from deep sleep, I turned my eyes to the marvelous light of the truth of the Gospel . . . and I wept many tears over my miserable life" (cf. *Letter* 223: PG 32, 824a).

Attracted by Christ, Basil began to look and listen to him alone (cf. *Moralia*, 80, 1: PG 31, 860bc). He devoted himself with determination to the monastic life through prayer, meditation on the Sacred Scriptures and the writings of the Fathers of the Church, and the practice of charity (cf. *Letters* 2, 22), also following the example of his sister, St. Macrina, who was already living the ascetic life of a nun. He was then ordained a priest and finally, in the year 370, Bishop of Caesarea in Cappadocia in present-day Turkey.

Through his preaching and writings, he carried out immensely busy pastoral, theological, and literary activities.

With a wise balance, he was able to combine service to souls with dedication to prayer and meditation in solitude. Availing himself of his personal experience, he encouraged the foundation of numerous "fraternities," in other words, communities of Christians consecrated to God, which he visited frequently (cf. Gregory of Nazianzus, *Oratio* 43, 29, *in laudem Basilii: PG* 36, 536b).

He urged them with his words and his writings, many of which have come down to us (cf. *Regulae brevius tractatae,* Proemio: *PG* 31, 1080ab), to live and to advance in perfection.

Various legislators of ancient monasticism drew on his works, including St. Benedict, who considered Basil his teacher (cf. *Rule* 73, 5).

Indeed, Basil created a very special monasticism: it was not closed to the community of the local Church but instead was open to it. His monks belonged to the particular Church; they were her life-giving nucleus and, going before the other faithful in the following of Christ and not only in faith, showed a strong attachment to him—love for him—especially through charitable acts. These monks, who ran schools and hospitals, were at the service of the poor and thus demonstrated the integrity of Christian life.

In speaking of monasticism, the Servant of God John Paul II wrote: "For this reason many people think that the essential structure of the life of the Church, monasticism, was established, for all time, mainly by St. Basil; or that, at least, it was not defined in its more specific nature without his decisive contribution" (Apostolic Letter *Patres Ecclesiae,* no. 2, January 1980; *L'Osservatore Romano* English edition, February 25, p. 6).

As the Bishop and Pastor of his vast Diocese, Basil was constantly concerned with the difficult material conditions in which his faithful lived; he firmly denounced the evils; he did all he could on behalf of the poorest and most marginalized people; he also intervened with rulers to alleviate the sufferings of the population, especially in times of disaster; he watched over the Church's freedom, opposing even the powerful in order to defend the right to profess the true faith (cf. Gregory of Nazianzus, *Oratio* 43, 48–51 *in laude Basilii: PG* 36, 557c–561c).

Basil bore an effective witness to God, who is love and charity, by building for the needy various institutions (cf. Basil, *Letter* 94: *PG* 32, 488bc), virtually a "city" of mercy, called *"Basiliade"* after him (cf. Sozomeno, *Historia Eccl.* 6, 34: *PG* 67, 1397a). This was the origin of the modern hospital structures where the sick are admitted for treatment.

Aware that "the liturgy is the summit toward which the activity of the Church is directed," and "also the fount from which all her power flows" (*Sacrosanctum Concilium*, no. 10), and in spite of his constant concern to do charitable acts which is the hallmark of faith, Basil was also a wise "liturgical reformer" (cf. Gregory Nazianzus, *Oratio* 43, 34 *in laude Basilii: PG* 36, 541c).

Indeed, he has bequeathed to us a great Eucharistic Prayer [or *anaphora*] which takes its name from him and has given a fundamental order to prayer and psalmody: at his prompting, the people learned to know and love the Psalms and even went to pray them during the night (cf. Basil, *In Psalmum* 1, 1–2: *PG* 29, 212a–213c). And we thus see how liturgy, worship, prayer with the Church, and charity go hand in hand and condition one another.

With zeal and courage Basil opposed the heretics who denied that Jesus Christ was God as Father (cf. Basil, *Letter* 9, 3: *PG* 32, 272a; *Letter* 52, 1–3: *PG* 32, 392b–396a; *Adv. Eunomium* 1, 20: *PG* 29, 556c). Likewise, against those who would not accept the divinity of the Holy Spirit, he maintained that the Spirit is also God and "must be equated and glorified with the Father and with the Son (cf. *De Spiritu Sancto: SC* 17ff., 348). For this reason Basil was one of the great Fathers who formulated the doctrine on the Trinity: the one God, precisely because he is love, is a God in three Persons who form the most profound unity that exists: divine unity.

In his love for Christ and for his Gospel, the great Cappadocian also strove to mend divisions within the Church (cf. *Letters*, 70, 243), doing his utmost to bring all to convert to Christ and to his word (cf. *De Iudicio* 4: PG 31, 660b–661a), a unifying force which all believers were bound to obey (cf. ibid. 1–3: PG 31, 653a–656c).

To conclude, Basil spent himself without reserve in faithful service to the Church and in the multiform exercise of the episcopal ministry. In accordance with the program that he himself drafted, he became an "apostle and minister of Christ, steward of God's mysteries, herald of the Kingdom, a model and rule of piety, an eye of the Body of the Church, a Pastor of Christ's sheep, a loving doctor, father and nurse, a coopera-tor of God, a farmer of God, a builder of God's temple" (cf. *Moralia* 80, 11–20: PG 31, 864b–868b).

This is the program which the holy Bishop consigns to preachers of the Word—in the past as in the present—a program which he him-self was generously committed to putting into practice. In 379 A.D. Basil, who was not yet 50, returned to God "in the hope of eternal life, through Jesus Christ Our Lord" (*De Baptismo*, 1, 2, 9).

He was a man who truly lived with his gaze fixed on Christ. He was a man of love for his neighbor. Full of the hope and joy of faith, Basil shows us how to be true Christians.

CHAPTER 38

St. Gregory Nazianzus

I would like to speak of [St. Basil's] friend, Gregory Nazianzus; like Basil, he too was a native of Cappadocia. As a distinguished theologian, orator, and champion of the Christian faith in the fourth century, he was famous for his eloquence, and as a poet, he also had a refined and sensitive soul.

Gregory was born into a noble family in about 330 A.D. and his mother consecrated him to God at birth. After his education at home, he attended the most famous schools of his time: he first went to Caesarea in Cappadocia, where he made friends with Basil, the future Bishop of that city, and went on to stay in other capitals of the ancient world, such as Alexandria, Egypt, and in particular Athens, where once again he met Basil (cf. *Orationes* 43: 14–24; SC 384: 146–180).

Remembering this friendship, Gregory was later to write: "Then not only did I feel full of veneration for my great Basil because of the seriousness of his morals and the maturity and wisdom of his speeches, but he induced others who did not yet know him to be like him. . . . The same eagerness for knowledge motivated us. . . . This was our competition: not who was first but who allowed the other to be first. It seemed as if we had one soul in two bodies" (*Orationes* 43: 16, 20; SC 384: 154–156, 164).

These words more or less paint the self-portrait of this noble soul. Yet, one can also imagine how this man, who was powerfully cast beyond earthly values, must have suffered deeply for the things of this world.

On his return home, Gregory received Baptism and developed an inclination for monastic life: solitude as well as philosophical and spiritual meditation fascinated him.

He himself wrote: "Nothing seems to me greater than this: to silence one's senses, to emerge from the flesh of the world, to withdraw into oneself, no longer to be concerned with human things other than what is strictly necessary; to converse with oneself and with God, to lead a life that transcends the visible; to bear in one's soul divine images, ever pure, not mingled with earthly or erroneous forms; truly to be a perfect mirror of God and of divine things, and to become so more and more, taking light from light . . . ; to enjoy, in the present hope, the future good, and to converse with angels; to have already left the earth even while continuing to dwell on it, borne aloft by the spirit" (*Orationes* 2: 7; SC 247: 96).

As he confides in his autobiography (cf. *Carmina [historica]* 2: 1, 11, *De Vita Sua* 340–349; PG 37: 1053), he received priestly ordination with a certain reluctance for he knew that he would later have to be a Bishop, to look after others and their affairs, hence, could no longer be absorbed in pure meditation.

However, he subsequently accepted this vocation and took on the pastoral ministry in full obedience, accepting, as often happened to him in his life, to be carried by Providence where he did not wish to go (cf. John 21:18).

In 371, his friend Basil, Bishop of Caesarea, against Gregory's own wishes, desired to ordain him Bishop of Sasima, a strategically important locality in Cappadocia. Because of various problems, however, he never took possession of it and instead stayed on in the city of Nazianzus.

In about 379, Gregory was called to Constantinople, the capital, to head the small Catholic community faithful to the Council of Nicaea and to belief in the Trinity. The majority adhered instead to Arianism, which was "politically correct" and viewed by emperors as politically useful.

Thus, he found himself in a condition of minority, surrounded by hostility. He delivered five *Theological Orations* (*Orationes* 27–31; SC 2 50: 70–343) in the little Church of the Anastasis precisely in order to defend the Trinitarian faith and to make it intelligible.

These discourses became famous because of the soundness of his doctrine and his ability to reason, which truly made clear that this was the divine logic. And the splendor of their form also makes them fascinating today.

It was because of these orations that Gregory acquired the nickname: "The Theologian."

This is what he is called in the Orthodox Church: the "Theologian." And this is because to his way of thinking theology was not merely human reflection or even less, only a fruit of complicated speculation, but rather sprang from a life of prayer and holiness, from a persevering dialogue with God. And in this very way he causes the reality of God, the mystery of the Trinity, to appear to our reason.

In the silence of contemplation, interspersed with wonder at the marvels of the mystery revealed, his soul was engrossed in beauty and divine glory.

While Gregory was taking part in the Second Ecumenical Council in 381, he was elected Bishop of Constantinople and presided over the Council; but he was challenged straightaway by strong opposition, to the point that the situation became untenable. These hostilities must have been unbearable to such a sensitive soul.

What Gregory had previously lamented with heartfelt words was repeated: "We have divided Christ, we who so loved God and Christ! We have lied to one another because of the Truth, we have harbored sentiments of hatred because of Love, we are separated from one another" (*Orationes* 6: 3; SC 405: 128).

Thus, in a tense atmosphere, the time came for him to resign.

In the packed cathedral, Gregory delivered a farewell discourse of great effectiveness and dignity (cf. *Orationes* 42; SC 384: 48–114). He ended his heartrending speech with these words: "Farewell, great city, beloved by Christt. . . . My children, I beg you, jealously guard the deposit [of faith] that has been entrusted to you (cf. 1 Tim. 6:20), remember my suffering (cf. Col. 4:18). May the grace of Our Lord Jesus Christ be with you all" (cf. *Orationes* 42: 27; SC 384: 112–114).

Gregory returned to Nazianzus and for about two years devoted himself to the pastoral care of this Christian community. He then withdrew definitively to solitude in nearby Arianzo, his birthplace, and dedicated himself to studies and the ascetic life.

It was in this period that he wrote the majority of his poetic works and especially his autobiography: the *De Vita Sua*, a reinterpretation in verse of his own human and spiritual journey, an exemplary journey of a suffering Christian, of a man of profound interiority in a world full of conflicts.

He is a man who makes us aware of God's primacy, hence, also speaks to us, to this world of ours: without God, man loses his grandeur; without God, there is no true humanism.

Consequently, let us too listen to this voice and seek to know God's Face.

In one of his poems he wrote, addressing himself to God: "May you be benevolent, You, the hereafter of all things" (*Carmina [dogmatica]* 1: 1, 29; PG 37: 508).

And in 390, God welcomed into his arms this faithful servant who had defended him in his writings with keen intelligence and had praised him in his poetry with such great love.

CHAPTER 39

St. John Chrysostom

This year is the 16th centenary of St. John Chrysostom's death (407–2007). It can be said that John of Antioch, nicknamed "Chrysostom," that is, "golden-mouthed," because of his eloquence, is also still alive today because of his works. An anonymous copyist left in writing that "they cross the whole globe like flashes of lightening."

Chrysostom's writings also enable us, as they did the faithful of his time whom his frequent exiles deprived of his presence, to live with his books, despite his absence. This is what he himself suggested in a letter when he was in exile (*To Olympias,* Letter 8, 45).

He was born in about the year 349 A.D. in Antioch, Syria (today Antakya in Southern Turkey). He carried out his priestly ministry there for about 11 years, until 397, when, appointed Bishop of Constantinople, he exercised his episcopal ministry in the capital of the Empire prior to his two exiles, which succeeded one close upon the other—in 403 and 407. Let us limit ourselves today to examining the years Chrysostom spent in Antioch.

He lost his father at a tender age and lived with Anthusa, his mother, who instilled in him exquisite human sensitivity and a deep Christian faith.

After completing his elementary and advanced studies crowned by courses in philosophy and rhetoric, he had as his teacher, Libanius, a pagan and the most famous rhetorician of that time. At his school John became the greatest orator of late Greek antiquity.

He was baptized in 368 and trained for the ecclesiastical life by Bishop Meletius, who instituted him as lector in 371. This event marked Chrysostom's official entry into the ecclesiastical *cursus.* From 367 to 372, he attended the *Asceterius*, a sort of seminary in Antioch, together with a group of young men, some of whom later became Bishops, under the guidance of the exegete Diodore of Tarsus, who initiated John into the literal and grammatical exegesis characteristic of Antiochean tradition.

He then withdrew for four years to the hermits on the neighboring Mount Silpius. He extended his retreat for a further two years, living alone in a cave under the guidance of an "old hermit." In that period, he dedicated himself unreservedly to meditating on "the laws of Christ," the Gospels and especially the Letters of Paul. Having fallen ill, he found it impossible to care for himself unaided, and therefore had to return to the Christian community in Antioch (cf. Palladius, *Dialogue on the Life of St. John Chrysostom*, 5).

The Lord, his biographer explains, intervened with the illness at the right moment to enable John to follow his true vocation. In fact, he himself was later to write that were he to choose between the troubles of Church government and the tranquility of monastic life, he would have preferred pastoral service a thousand times (cf. *On the Priesthood*, 6, 7): it was precisely to this that Chrysostom felt called.

It was here that he reached the crucial turning point in the story of his vocation: a full-time pastor of souls! Intimacy with the Word of God, cultivated in his years at the hermitage, had developed in him an irresistible urge to preach the Gospel, to give to others what he himself had received in his years of meditation. The missionary ideal thus launched him into pastoral care, his heart on fire.

Between 378 and 379, he returned to the city. He was ordained a deacon in 381 and a priest in 386, and became a famous preacher in his city's churches. He preached homilies against the Arians, followed by homilies commemorating the Antiochean martyrs and other important liturgical celebrations: this was an important teaching of faith in Christ and also in the light of his Saints.

The year 387 was John's "heroic year," that of the so-called "revolt of the statues." As a sign of protest against levied taxes, the people destroyed the Emperor's statues. It was in those days of Lent and the fear of the Emperor's impending reprisal that Chrysostom gave his 22 vibrant *Homilies on the Statues,* whose aim was to induce repentance and conversion. This was followed by a period of serene pastoral care (387–397).

Chrysostom is among the most prolific of the Fathers: 17 treatises, more than 700 authentic homilies, commentaries on Matthew and on Paul (Letters to the Romans, Corinthians, Ephesians, and Hebrews), and 241 letters are extant. He was not a speculative theologian.

Nevertheless, he passed on the Church's tradition and reliable doctrine in an age of theological controversies, sparked above all by Arianism or, in other words, the denial of Christ's divinity. He is therefore a trustworthy witness of the dogmatic development achieved by the Church from the fourth to the fifth centuries.

His is a perfectly pastoral theology in which there is constant concern for consistency between thought expressed via words and existential experience. It is this in particular that forms the main theme of the splendid catecheses with which he prepared catechumens to receive Baptism.

On approaching death, he wrote that the value of the human being lies in "exact knowledge of true doctrine and in rectitude of life" (*Letter from Exile).* Both these things, knowledge of truth and rectitude of life, go hand in hand: knowledge has to be expressed in life. All his discourses aimed to develop in the faithful the use of intelligence, of true reason, in order to understand and to put into practice the moral and spiritual requirements of faith.

John Chrysostom was anxious to accompany his writings with the person's integral development in his physical, intellectual, and religious dimensions. The various phases of his growth are compared to as many seas in an immense ocean: "The first of these seas is childhood" (*Homily,* 81, 5 *on Matthew's Gospel).*

Indeed, "it is precisely at this early age that inclinations to vice or virtue are manifest." Thus, God's law must be impressed upon the soul from the outset "as on a wax tablet" (*Homily* 3, 1 *on John's Gospel).* This is indeed the most important age. We must bear in mind how fundamentally important it is that the great orientations which give man a proper outlook on life truly enter him in this first phase of life.

Chrysostom therefore recommended: "From the tenderest age, arm children with spiritual weapons and teach them to make the Sign of the Cross on their forehead with their hand" (*Homily*, 12, 7 *on First Corinthians*).

Then come adolescence and youth: "Following childhood is the sea of adolescence, where violent winds blow . . . , for concupiscence . . . grows within us" (*Homily 81, 5 on Matthew's Gospel*).

Lastly comes engagement and marriage: "Youth is succeeded by the age of the mature person who assumes family commitments: this is the time to seek a wife" (ibid.).

He recalls the aims of marriage, enriching them—referring to virtue and temperance—with a rich fabric of personal relationships. Properly prepared spouses therefore bar the way to divorce: everything takes place with joy and children can be educated in virtue. Then when the first child is born, he is "like a bridge; the three become one flesh, because the child joins the two parts" (*Homily* 12, 5 on the Letter to the Colossians), and the three constitute "a family, a Church in miniature" (*Homily 20, 6 on the Letter to the Ephesians*).

Chrysostom's preaching usually took place during the liturgy, the "place" where the community is built with the Word and the Eucharist. The assembly gathered here expresses the one Church (*Homily 8, 7 on the Letter to the Romans*), the same word is addressed everywhere to all (*Homily 24, 2 on First Corinthians*), and Eucharistic Communion becomes an effective sign of unity (*Homily 32, 7 on Matthew's Gospel*).

His pastoral project was incorporated into the Church's life, in which the lay faithful assume the priestly, royal, and prophetic office with Baptism. To the lay faithful he said: "Baptism will also make you king, priest, and prophet" (*Homily 3, 5 on Second Corinthians*).

From this stems the fundamental duty of the mission, because each one is to some extent responsible for the salvation of others: "This is the principle of our social life . . . not to be solely concerned with ourselves!" (*Homily 9, 2 on Genesis*). This all takes place between two poles: the great Church and the "Church in miniature," the family, in a reciprocal relationship.

As you can see, dear brothers and sisters, Chrysostom's lesson on the authentically Christian presence of the lay faithful in the family and in society is still more timely than ever today. Let us pray to the Lord to make us docile to the teachings of this great Master of the faith.

CHAPTER 40

St. Hilary of Poitiers

I would like to talk about a great Father of the Church of the West, St. Hilary of Poitiers, one of the important Episcopal figures of the fourth century. In the controversy with the Arians, who considered Jesus the Son of God to be an excellent human creature but only human, Hilary devoted his whole life to defending faith in the divinity of Jesus Christ, Son of God and God as the Father who generated him from eternity.

We have no reliable information on most of Hilary's life. Ancient sources say that he was born in Poitiers, probably in about the year 310 A.D. From a wealthy family, he received a solid literary education, which is clearly recognizable in his writings. It does not seem that he grew up in a Christian environment. He himself tells us of a quest for the truth which led him little by little to recognize God the Creator and the incarnate God who died to give us eternal life. Baptized in about 345, he was elected Bishop of his native city around 353–354. In the years that followed, Hilary wrote his first work, *Commentary on St. Matthew's Gospel*. It is the oldest extant commentary in Latin on this Gospel. In 356, Hilary took part as a Bishop in the Synod of Béziers in the South of France, the "synod of false apostles," as he himself called it since the assembly was in the control of Philo-Arian Bishops who denied the divinity of Jesus Christ. "These false apostles" asked the Emperor Constantius to have the Bishop of Poitiers sentenced to exile. Thus, in the summer of 356, Hilary was forced to leave Gaul.

Banished to Phrygia in present-day Turkey, Hilary found himself in contact with a religious context totally dominated by Arianism. Here too, his concern as a Pastor impelled him to work strenuously to re-establish the unity of the Church on the basis of right faith as formulated by the Council of Nicaea. To this end he began to draft his own best-known and most important dogmatic work: *De Trinitate (On the Trinity)*. Hilary explained in it his personal journey towards knowledge of God and took pains to show that not only in the New Testament but also in many Old Testament passages, in which Christ's mystery already appears, Scripture clearly testifies to the divinity of the Son and his equality with the Father. To the Arians he insisted on the truth of the names of Father and Son, and developed his entire Trinitarian theology based on the formula of Baptism given to us by the Lord himself: "In the name of the Father and of the Son and of the Holy Spirit."

The Father and the Son are of the same nature. And although several passages in the New Testament might make one think that the Son was inferior to the Father, Hilary offers precise rules to avoid misleading interpretations: some Scriptural texts speak of Jesus as God, others highlight instead his humanity. Some refer to him in his pre-existence with the Father; others take into consideration his state of emptying of self *(kenosis)*, his descent to death; others, finally, contemplate him in the glory of the Resurrection. In the years of his exile, Hilary also wrote the *Book of Synods* in which, for his brother Bishops of Gaul, he reproduced confessions of faith and commented on them and on other documents of synods which met in the East in about the middle of the fourth century. Ever adamant in opposing the radical Arians, St. Hilary showed a conciliatory spirit to those who agreed to confess that the Son was essentially *similar* to the Father, seeking of course to lead them to the true faith, according to which there is not only a likeness but a true equality of the Father and of the Son in divinity. This too seems to me to be characteristic: the spirit of reconciliation that seeks to understand those who have not yet arrived and helps them with great theological intelligence to reach full faith in the true divinity of the Lord Jesus Christ.

In 360 or 361, Hilary was finally able to return home from exile and immediately resumed pastoral activity in his Church, but the influence of his magisterium extended in fact far beyond its boundaries. A synod celebrated in Paris in 360 or 361 borrows the language of the Council of Nicaea. Several ancient authors believe that this anti-Arian turning point of the Gaul episcopate was largely due to the fortitude and docility of the Bishop of Poitiers. This was precisely his gift: to combine strength in the faith and docility in interpersonal relations. In the last years of his life he also composed the *Treatises on the Psalms*, a commentary on 58 Psalms interpreted according to the principle highlighted in the introduction to the work: "There is no doubt that all the things that are said in the Psalms should be understood in accordance with Gospel proclamation, so that, whatever the voice with which the prophetic spirit has spoken, all may be referred nevertheless to the knowledge of the coming of Our Lord Jesus Christ, the Incarnation, Passion, and Kingdom, and to the power and glory of our resurrection" (*Instructio Psalmorum*, 5). He saw in all the Psalms this transparency of the mystery of Christ and of his Body which is the Church. Hilary met St. Martin on various occasions: the future Bishop of Tours founded a monastery right by Poitiers, which still exists today. Hilary died in 367. His liturgical Memorial is celebrated on January 13. In 1851 Blessed Pius IX proclaimed him a Doctor of the universal Church.

To sum up the essentials of his doctrine, I would like to say that Hilary found the starting point for his theological reflection in baptismal faith. In *De Trinitate*, Hilary writes: Jesus "has commanded us to baptize *in the name of the Father and of the Son and of the Holy Spirit* (cf. Matt. 28:19), that is, in the confession of the Author, of the Only-Begotten One, and of the Gift. The Author of all things is one alone, for *one alone is God the Father, from whom all things proceed. And one alone is Our Lord Jesus Christ, through whom all things exist* (cf. 1 Cor. 8:6), *and one alone is the Spirit* (cf. Eph. 4:4), a gift in all. . . . In nothing can be found to be lacking so great a fullness, in which the immensity in the Eternal One, the revelation in the Image, joy in the Gift, converge in the Father, in the Son, and in the Holy Spirit" (*De Trinitate* 2, 1). God the Father, being wholly love, is able to communicate his divinity to his Son in its fullness. I find particularly beautiful the following formula of St. Hilary: "God knows not how to be anything other than love, he knows not how to be anyone other than the Father. Those who love are not envious and the one who is the Father is so in his totality. This name admits no compromise, as if God were father in some aspects and not in others" (ibid., 9, 61).

For this reason the Son is fully God without any gaps or diminishment. "The One who comes from the perfect is perfect because he has all, he has given all" (ibid., 2, 8). Humanity finds salvation in Christ alone, Son of God and Son of man. In assuming our human nature, he has united himself with every man, "he has become the flesh of us all" (*Tractatus super Psalmos* 54, 9); "he took on himself the nature of all flesh and through it became true life, he has in himself the root of every vine shoot" (ibid., 51, 16). For this very reason the way to Christ is open to all—because he has drawn all into his being as a man—even if personal conversion is always required: "Through the relationship with his flesh, access to Christ is open to all, on condition that they divest themselves of their former self (cf. Eph. 4:22), nailing it to the Cross (cf. Col. 2:14); provided we give up our former way of life and convert in order to be buried with him in his baptism, in view of life (cf. Col. 1:12; Rom. 6:4)" (ibid., 91, 9).

Fidelity to God is a gift of his grace. Therefore, St. Hilary asks, at the end of his Treatise on the Trinity, to be able to remain ever faithful to the baptismal faith. It is a feature of this book: reflection is transformed into prayer and prayer returns to reflection. The whole book is a dialogue with God.

I would like to end today's Catechesis with one of these prayers, which thus becomes our prayer: "Obtain, O Lord," St. Hilary recites with inspiration, "that I may keep ever faithful to what I have professed in the symbol of my regeneration, when I was baptized in the Father, in the Son, and in the Holy Spirit. That I may worship you, our Father, and with you, your Son; that I may deserve your Holy Spirit, who proceeds from you through your Only Begotten Son . . . Amen" (*De Trinitate* 12, 57).

CHAPTER 41

St. Ambrose

Holy Bishop Ambrose—about whom I shall speak to you today—died in Milan in the night between April 3 and 4 [in] 397. It was dawn on Holy Saturday. The day before, at about five o'clock in the afternoon, he had settled down to pray, lying on his bed with his arms wide open in the form of a cross. Thus, he took part in the solemn Easter Triduum, in the death and Resurrection of the Lord. "*We saw his lips moving*," said Paulinus, the faithful deacon who wrote his *Life* at St. Augustine's suggestion, "but we could not hear his voice." The situation suddenly became dramatic. Honoratus, Bishop of Vercelli, who was assisting Ambrose and was sleeping on the upper floor, was awoken by a voice saying again and again, "Get up quickly! Ambrose is dying . . ." "Honoratus hurried downstairs," Paulinus continues, "and offered the Saint the Body of the Lord. As soon as he had received and swallowed it, Ambrose gave up his spirit, taking the good Viaticum with him. His soul, thus refreshed by the virtue of that food, now enjoys the company of Angels" (*Life*, 47). On that Holy Friday 397, the wide open arms of the dying Ambrose expressed his mystical participation in the death and Resurrection of the Lord. This was his last catechesis: in the silence of the words, he continued to speak with the witness of his life.

Ambrose was not old when he died. He had not even reached the age of 60, since he was born in about 340 A.D. in Treves, where his father was Prefect of the Gauls. His family was Christian. Upon his father's death while he was still a boy, his mother took him to Rome and educated him for a civil career, assuring him a sound instruction in rhetoric and jurisprudence. In about 370 he was sent to govern the Provinces of Emilia and Liguria, with headquarters in Milan. It was precisely there that the struggle between orthodox and Arians was raging and became particularly heated after the death of the Arian Bishop Auxentius. Ambrose intervened to pacify the members of the two opposing factions; his authority was such that although he was merely a catechumen, the people acclaimed him Bishop of Milan.

Until that moment, Ambrose had been the most senior magistrate of the Empire in northern Italy. Culturally well-educated but at the same time ignorant of the Scriptures, the new Bishop briskly began to study them. From the works of Origen, the indisputable master of the "Alexandrian School," he learned to know and to comment on the Bible. Thus, Ambrose transferred to the Latin environment the meditation on the Scriptures which Origen had begun, introducing in the West the practice of *lectio divina*. The method of *lectio* served to guide all of Ambrose's preaching and writings, which stemmed precisely from *prayerful listening* to the Word of God. The famous introduction of an Ambrosian catechesis shows clearly how the holy Bishop applied the Old Testament to Christian life: "Every day, when we were reading about the lives of the Patriarchs and the maxims of the Proverbs, we addressed morality," the Bishop of Milan said to his catechumens and neophytes, "so that formed and instructed by them you may become accustomed to taking the path of the Fathers and to following the route of obedience to the divine precepts" (*On the Mysteries* 1, 1). In other words, the neophytes and catechumens, in accordance with the Bishop's decision, after having learned the art of a well-ordered life, could henceforth consider themselves prepared for Christ's great mysteries. Thus, Ambrose's preaching—which constitutes the structural nucleus of his immense literary opus—starts with the reading of the Sacred Books ("the Patriarchs" or the historical Books and "Proverbs," or in other words, the Wisdom Books) in order to live in conformity with divine Revelation.

It is obvious that the preacher's personal testimony and the level of exemplarity of the Christian community condition the effectiveness of the preaching. In this perspective, a passage from St. Augustine's *Confessions* is relevant. He had come to Milan as a teacher of rhetoric;

he was a skeptic and not Christian. He was seeking the Christian truth but was not capable of truly finding it.

What moved the heart of the young African rhetorician, skeptic and downhearted, and what impelled him to definitive conversion was not above all Ambrose's splendid homilies (although he deeply appreciated them). It was rather the testimony of the Bishop and his Milanese Church that prayed and sang as one intact body. It was a Church that could resist the tyrannical ploys of the Emperor and his mother, who in early 386 again demanded a church building for the Arians' celebrations. In the building that was to be requisitioned, Augustine relates, "the devout people watched, ready to die with their Bishop." This testimony of the *Confessions* is precious because it points out that something was moving in Augustine, who continues: "We too, although spiritually tepid, shared in the excitement of the whole people" (*Confessions* 9, 7).

Augustine learned from the life and example of Bishop Ambrose to believe and to preach. We can refer to a famous sermon of the African, which centuries later merited citation in the conciliar Constitution on Divine Revelation, *Dei Verbum:* "Therefore, all clerics, particularly priests of Christ and others who, as deacons or catechists, are officially engaged in the ministry of the Word," *Dei Verbum* recommends, "should immerse themselves in the Scriptures by constant sacred reading and diligent study. For it must not happen that anyone becomes"—and this is Augustine's citation—"'an empty preacher of the Word of God to others, not being a hearer of the Word in his own heart'" (no. 25). Augustine had learned precisely from Ambrose how to "hear in his own heart" this perseverance in reading Sacred Scripture with a prayerful approach, so as truly to absorb and assimilate the Word of God in one's heart.

Dear brothers and sisters, I would like further to propose to you a sort of "patristic icon," which, interpreted in the light of what we have said, effectively represents "the heart" of Ambrosian doctrine. In the sixth book of the *Confessions*, Augustine tells of his meeting with Ambrose, an encounter that was indisputably of great importance in the history of the Church. He writes in his text that whenever he went to see the Bishop of Milan, he would regularly find him taken up with *catervae* of people full of problems for whose needs he did his utmost. There was always a long queue waiting to talk to Ambrose, seeking in him consolation and hope. When Ambrose was not with them, with the people (and this happened for the space of the briefest of moments), he was either restoring his body with the necessary food or nourishing his spirit with reading. Here Augustine marvels because Ambrose read the Scriptures with his mouth shut, only with his eyes (cf. *Confessions*, 6, 3). Indeed, in the early Christian centuries reading was conceived of strictly for proclamation, and reading aloud also facilitated the reader's understanding. That Ambrose could scan the pages with his eyes alone suggested to the admiring Augustine a rare ability for reading and familiarity with the Scriptures. Well, in that "reading under one's breath," where the heart is committed to achieving knowledge of the Word of God—this is the "icon" to which we are referring—one can glimpse the method of Ambrosian catechesis; it is Scripture itself, intimately assimilated, which suggests the content to proclaim that will lead to the conversion of hearts.

Thus, with regard to the magisterium of Ambrose and of Augustine, catechesis is inseparable from witness of life. What I wrote on the theologian in the *Introduction to Christianity* might also be useful to the catechist. An educator in the faith cannot risk appearing like a sort of clown who recites a part "by profession." Rather—to use an image dear to Origen, a writer who was particularly appreciated by Ambrose—he must be like the beloved disciple who rested his head against his Master's heart and there learned the way to think, speak, and act. The true disciple is ultimately the one whose proclamation of the Gospel is the most credible and effective.

Like the Apostle John, Bishop Ambrose—who never tired of saying: "*Omnia Christus est nobis!* To us Christ is all!"—continues to be a genuine witness of the Lord. Let us thus conclude our Catechesis with his same words, full of love for Jesus: "*Omnia Christus est nobis!* If you have a wound to heal, he is the doctor; if you are parched by fever, he

275

is the spring; if you are oppressed by injustice, he is justice; if you are in need of help, he is strength; if you fear death, he is life; if you desire Heaven, he is the way; if you are in the darkness, he is light. . . . Taste and see how good is the Lord: blessed is the man who hopes in him!" (*De Virginitate*, 16, 99). Let us also hope in Christ. We shall thus be blessed and shall live in peace.

CHAPTER 42

St. Jerome

We turn our attention to St. Jerome, a Church Father who centered his life on the Bible: he translated it into Latin, commented on it in his works, and above all, strove to live it in practice throughout his long earthly life, despite the well-known difficult, hot-tempered character with which nature had endowed him.

Jerome was born into a Christian family in about 347 A.D. in Stridon. He was given a good education and was even sent to Rome to fine-tune his studies. As a young man he was attracted by the worldly life (cf. *Ep* 22, 7), but his desire for and interest in the Christian religion prevailed.

He received Baptism in about 366 and opted for the ascetic life. He went to Aquileia and joined a group of fervent Christians that had formed around Bishop Valerian and which he described as almost "a choir of blesseds" (*Chron. ad ann.* 374). He then left for the East and lived as a hermit in the Desert of Chalcis, south of Aleppo (*Ep* 14, 10), devoting himself assiduously to study. He perfected his knowledge of Greek, began learning Hebrew (cf. *Ep* 125, 12), and transcribed codices and Patristic writings (cf. *Ep* 5, 2). Meditation, solitude, and contact with the Word of God helped his Christian sensibility to mature. He bitterly regretted the indiscretions of his youth (cf. *Ep.* 22, 7) and was keenly aware of the contrast between the pagan mentality and the Christian life: a contrast made famous by the dramatic and lively "vision"—of which he has left us an account—in which it seemed to him that he was being scourged before God because he was "Ciceronian rather than Christian" (cf. *Ep.* 22, 30).

277

In 382 he moved to Rome: here, acquainted with his fame as an ascetic and his ability as a scholar, Pope Damasus engaged him as secretary and counsellor; the Pope encouraged him, for pastoral and cultural reasons, to embark on a new Latin translation of the Biblical texts. Several members of the Roman aristocracy, especially noblewomen such as Paula, Marcella, Asella, Lea, and others, desirous of committing themselves to the way of Christian perfection and of deepening their knowledge of the Word of God, chose him as their spiritual guide and teacher in the methodical approach to the sacred texts. These noblewomen also learned Greek and Hebrew.

After the death of Pope Damasus, Jerome left Rome in 385 and went on pilgrimage, first to the Holy Land, a silent witness of Christ's earthly life, and then to Egypt, the favorite country of numerous monks (cf. *Contra Rufinum*, 3, 22; *Ep.* 108, 6–14). In 386 he stopped in Bethlehem, where male and female monasteries were built through the generosity of the noblewoman, Paula, as well as a hospice for pilgrims bound for the Holy Land, "remembering Mary and Joseph who had found no room there" (*Ep.* 108, 14). He stayed in Bethlehem until he died, continuing to do a prodigious amount of work: he commented on the Word of God; he defended the faith, vigorously opposing various heresies; he urged the monks on to perfection; he taught classical and Christian culture to young students; he welcomed with a pastor's heart pilgrims who were visiting the Holy Land. He died in his cell close to the Grotto of the Nativity on September 30, 419 or 420.

Jerome's literary studies and vast erudition enabled him to revise and translate many biblical texts: an invaluable undertaking for the Latin Church and for Western culture. On the basis of the original Greek and Hebrew texts, and thanks to the comparison with previous versions, he revised the four Gospels in Latin, then the Psalter and a large part of the Old Testament. Taking into account the original Hebrew and Greek texts of the Septuagint, the classical Greek version of the Old Testament that dates back to pre-Christian times, as well as the earlier Latin versions, Jerome was able, with the assistance later of other collaborators, to produce a better translation: this constitutes the so-called "*Vulgate*," the "official" text of the Latin Church which was recognized as such by the Council of Trent and which, after the recent revision, continues to be the "official" Latin text of the Church. It is interesting to point out the criteria which the great biblicist abided by in his work as a translator. He himself reveals them when he says that he respects even the order of the words of the Sacred Scriptures, for in them, he says, "the order of the words is also a mystery" (*Ep.* 57, 5), that is, a revelation. Furthermore, he reaffirms the need to refer to the original texts: "Should an argument on the New Testament arise between Latins because of interpretations of the manuscripts that fail to agree, let us turn to the original, that is, to the Greek text in which the New Testament was written. Likewise, with regard to the Old Testament, if there are divergences between the Greek and Latin texts we should have recourse to the original Hebrew text; thus, we shall be able to find in the streams all that flows from the source" (*Ep.* 106, 2). Jerome also commented on many biblical texts. For him the commentaries had to offer multiple opinions "so that the shrewd reader, after reading the different explanations and hearing many opinions—to be accepted or rejected—may judge which is the most reliable, and, like an expert moneychanger, may reject the false coin" (*Contra Rufinum* 1, 16).

Jerome refuted with energy and liveliness the heretics who contested the tradition and faith of the Church. He also demonstrated the importance and validity of Christian literature, which had by then become a real culture that deserved to be compared with classical literature: he did so by composing his *De Viris Illustribus,* a work in which Jerome presents the biographies of more than a hundred Christian authors. Further, he wrote biographies of monks, comparing among other things their spiritual itineraries as well as monastic ideal. In addition, he translated various works by Greek authors. Lastly, in the important *Epistulae,* a masterpiece of Latin literature, Jerome emerges with the profile of a man of culture, an ascetic, and a guide of souls.

What can we learn from St. Jerome? It seems to me, this above all; to love the Word of God in Sacred Scripture. St. Jerome said: "Ignorance of the Scriptures is ignorance of Christ." It is therefore important that every Christian live in contact and in personal dialogue with the Word of God given to us in Sacred Scripture. This dialogue with Scripture must always have two dimensions: on the one hand, it must be a truly personal dialogue because God speaks with each one of us through Sacred Scripture and it has a message for each one. We must not read Sacred Scripture as a word of the past but as the Word of God that is also addressed to us, and we must try to understand what it is that the Lord wants to tell us. However, to avoid falling into individualism, we must bear in mind that the Word of God has been given to us precisely in order to build communion and to join forces in the truth on our journey towards God. Thus, although it is always a personal Word, it is also a Word that builds community, that builds the Church. We must therefore read it in communion with the living Church. The privileged place for reading and listening to the Word of God is the liturgy, in which, celebrating the Word and making Christ's Body present in the Sacrament, we actualize the Word in our lives and make it present among us. We must never forget that the Word of God transcends time. Human opinions come and go. What is very modern today will be very antiquated tomorrow. On the other hand, the Word of God is the Word of eternal life, it bears within it eternity and is valid for ever. By carrying the Word of God within us, we therefore carry within us eternity, eternal life.

I thus conclude with a word St. Jerome once addressed to St. Paulinus of Nola. In it the great exegete expressed this very reality, that is, in the Word of God we receive eternity, eternal life. St. Jerome said: "Seek to learn on earth those truths which will remain ever valid in Heaven" (*Ep.* 53, 10).

CHAPTER 43

St. Augustine

I would like to . . . speak today of the greatest Father of the Latin Church, St. Augustine. This man of passion and faith, of the highest intelligence and tireless in his pastoral care, a great Saint and Doctor of the Church is often known, at least by hearsay, even by those who ignore Christianity or who are not familiar with it, because he left a very deep mark on the cultural life of the West and on the whole world. Because of his special importance St. Augustine's influence was widespread. It could be said on the one hand that all the roads of Latin Christian literature led to Hippo (today Annaba, on the coast of Algeria), the place where he was Bishop from 395 to his death in 430, and, on the other, that from this city of Roman Africa, many other roads of later Christianity and of Western culture itself branched out.

A civilization has seldom encountered such a great spirit who was able to assimilate Christianity's values and exalt its intrinsic wealth, inventing ideas and forms that were to nourish the future generations, as Paul VI also stressed: "It may be said that all the thought-currents of the past meet in his works and form the source which provides the whole doctrinal tradition of succeeding ages" (Inaugural Address at the Patristic Institute of the "Augustinianum," May 4, 1970; L'Osservatore Romano English edition, May 21, 1970, p. 8). Augustine is also the Father of the Church who left the greatest number of works. Possidius, his biographer, said that it seemed impossible that one man could have written so many things in his lifetime. We shall speak of these different works at one of our meetings soon. Today, we shall focus on his life, which is easy to reconstruct from his writings, in particular the *Confessions*, his extraordinary spiritual autobiography written in praise of God. This is his most famous work; and rightly so, since it is precisely Augustine's *Confessions*, with their focus on interiority and psychology, that constitute a unique model in Western (and not only Western) literature—including non-religious literature—up to modern times. This attention to the spiritual life, to the mystery of the "I," to the mystery of God who is concealed in the "I," is something quite extraordinary, without precedent, and remains forever, as it were, a spiritual "peak."

But to come back to his life: Augustine was born in Tagaste in the Roman Province of Numidia, Africa, on November 13, 354, to Patricius, a pagan who later became a catechumen, and Monica, a fervent Christian. This passionate woman, venerated as a saint, exercised an enormous influence on her son and raised him in the Christian faith. Augustine had also received the salt, a sign of acceptance in the catechumenate, and was always fascinated by the figure of Jesus Christ; indeed, he said that he had always loved Jesus but had drifted further and further away from ecclesial faith and practice, as also happens to many young people today.

Augustine also had a brother, Navigius, and a sister whose name is unknown to us and who, after being widowed, subsequently became the head of a monastery for women. As a boy with a very keen intelligence, Augustine received a good education although he was not always an exemplary student. However, he learned grammar well, first in his native town and then in Madaura, and from 370, he studied rhetoric in Carthage, the capital of Roman Africa. He mastered Latin perfectly but was not quite as successful with Greek and did not learn Punic, spoken by his contemporaries. It was in Carthage itself that for the first time Augustine read the *Hortensius*, a writing by Cicero later lost, an event that can be placed at the beginning of his journey towards conversion. In fact, Cicero's text awoke within him love for wisdom, as, by then a Bishop, he was to write in his *Confessions*: "The book changed my feelings," to the extent that "every vain hope became empty to me, and

I longed for the immortality of wisdom with an incredible ardor in my heart" (III, 4, 7).

However, since he was convinced that without Jesus the truth cannot be said effectively to have been found and since Jesus' Name was not mentioned in this book, immediately after he read it he began to read Scripture, the Bible. But it disappointed him. This was not only because the Latin style of the translation of the Sacred Scriptures was inadequate but also because to him their content itself did not seem satisfying. In the scriptural narratives of wars and other human vicissitudes, he discovered neither the loftiness of philosophy nor the splendor of the search for the truth which is part of it. Yet he did not want to live without God and thus sought a religion which corresponded to his desire for the truth and also with his desire to draw close to Jesus. Thus, he fell into the net of the Manicheans, who presented themselves as Christians and promised a totally rational religion. They said that the world was divided into two principles: good and evil. And in this way the whole complexity of human history can be explained. Their dualistic morals also pleased St. Augustine, because it included a very high morality for the elect: and those like him who adhered to it could live a life better suited to the situation of the time, especially for a young man. He therefore became a Manichean, convinced at that time that he had found the synthesis between rationality and the search for the truth and love of Jesus Christ. Manicheanism also offered him a concrete advantage in life: joining the Manicheans facilitated the prospects of a career. By belonging to that religion, which included so many influential figures, he was able to continue his relationship with a woman and to advance in his career. By this woman he had a son, Adeodatus, who was very dear to him and very intelligent, who was later to be present during the preparation for Baptism near Lake Como, taking part in those "Dialogues" which St. Augustine has passed down to us. The boy unfortunately died prematurely. Having been a grammar teacher since his twenties in the city of his birth, he soon returned to Carthage, where he became a brilliant and famous teacher of rhetoric.

However, with time Augustine began to distance himself from the faith of the Manicheans. They disappointed him precisely from the intellectual viewpoint since they proved incapable of dispelling his doubts. He moved to Rome and then to Milan, where the imperial court resided at that time and where he obtained a prestigious post through the good offices and recommendations of the Prefect of Rome, Symmacus, a pagan hostile to St. Ambrose, Bishop of Milan.

In Milan, Augustine acquired the habit of listening—at first for the purpose of enriching his rhetorical baggage—to the eloquent preaching of Bishop Ambrose, who had been a representative of the Emperor for Northern Italy. The African rhetorician was fascinated by the words of the great Milanese Prelate; and not only by his rhetoric. It was above all the content that increasingly touched Augustine's heart. The great difficulty with the Old Testament, because of its lack of rhetorical beauty and lofty philosophy was resolved in St. Ambrose's preaching through his typological interpretation of the Old Testament: Augustine realized that the whole of the Old Testament was a journey toward Jesus Christ. Thus, he found the key to understanding the beauty and even the philosophical depth of the Old Testament and grasped the whole unity of the mystery of Christ in history, as well as the synthesis between philosophy, rationality, and faith in the *Logos*, in Christ, the Eternal Word who was made flesh.

Augustine soon realized that the allegorical interpretation of Scripture and the Neo-Platonic philosophy practiced by the Bishop of Milan enabled him to solve the intellectual difficulties which, when he was younger during his first approach to the biblical texts, had seemed insurmountable to him.

Thus, Augustine followed his reading of the philosophers' writings by reading Scripture anew, especially the Pauline Letters. His conversion to Christianity on 15 August 386 therefore came at the end of a long and tormented inner journey—of which we shall speak in another catechesis—and the African moved to the countryside, north of Milan by Lake Como—with his mother Monica, his son Adeodatus, and a small group of friends—to prepare himself for Baptism. So it was that at the age of 32 Augustine was baptized by Ambrose in the Cathedral of Milan on 24 April 387, during the Easter Vigil.

After his Baptism, Augustine decided to return to Africa with his friends, with the idea of living a community life of the monastic kind at the service of God. However, while awaiting their departure in Ostia, his mother fell ill unexpectedly and died shortly afterwards, breaking her son's heart. Having returned to his homeland at last, the convert settled in Hippo for the very purpose of founding a monastery. In this city on the African coast he was ordained a priest in 391, despite his reticence, and with a few companions began the monastic life which had long been in his mind, dividing his time between prayer, study, and preaching. All he wanted was to be at the service of the truth. He did not feel he had a vocation to pastoral life but realized later that God was calling him to be a pastor among others and thus to offer people the gift of the truth. He was ordained a Bishop in Hippo four years later, in 395. Augustine continued to deepen his study of Scripture and of the texts of the Christian tradition and was an exemplary Bishop in his tireless pastoral commitment: he preached several times a week to his faithful, supported the poor and orphans, supervised the formation of the clergy and the organization of mens' and womens' monasteries. In short, the former rhetorician asserted himself as one of the most important exponents of Christianity of that time. He was very active in the government of his Diocese—with remarkable, even civil, implications—in the more than 35 years of his Episcopate, and the Bishop of Hippo actually exercised a vast influence in his guidance of the Catholic Church in Roman Africa and, more generally, in the Christianity of his time, coping with religious tendencies and tenacious, disruptive heresies such as Manichaeism, Donatism, and Pelagianism, which endangered the Christian faith in the one God, rich in mercy.

And Augustine entrusted himself to God every day until the very end of his life: smitten by fever, while for almost three months his Hippo was being besieged by vandal invaders, the Bishop—his friend Possidius recounts in his *Vita Augustini*—asked that the penitential psalms be transcribed in large characters, "and that the sheets be attached to the wall, so that while he was bedridden during his illness he could see and read them and he shed constant hot tears" (31, 2). This is how Augustine spent the last days of his life. He died on August 28, 430, when he was not yet 76.

CHAPTER 44

St. Leo the Great

Today we encounter a Pope who in 1754 Benedict XIV proclaimed a Doctor of the Church: St. Leo the Great. As the nickname soon attributed to him by tradition suggests, he was truly one of the greatest Pontiffs to have honored the Roman See and made a very important contribution to strengthening its authority and prestige. He was the first Bishop of Rome to have been called Leo, a name used subsequently by another 12 Supreme Pontiffs, and was also the first Pope whose preaching to the people who gathered round him during celebrations has come down to us. We spontaneously think of him also in the context of today's Wednesday General Audiences, events that in past decades have become a customary meeting of the Bishop of Rome with the faithful and the many visitors from every part of the world.

Leo was a Tuscan native. In about the year 430 A.D., he became a deacon of the Church of Rome, in which he acquired over time a very important position. In the year 440 his prominent role induced Galla Placidia, who then ruled the Empire of the West, to send him to Gaul to heal a difficult situation. But in the summer of that year, Pope Sixtus III, whose name is associated with the magnificent mosaics in St. Mary Major's, died, and it was Leo who was elected to succeed him. Leo heard the news precisely while he was carrying out his peace mission in Gaul. Having returned to Rome, the new Pope was consecrated on September 29, 440. This is how his Pontificate began. It lasted more than 21 years and was undoubtedly one of the most important in the Church's history. Pope Leo died on November 10, 461, and was buried near the tomb of St. Peter. Today, his relics are preserved in one of the altars in the Vatican Basilica.

The times in which Pope Leo lived were very difficult: constant barbarian invasions, the gradual weakening of imperial authority in the West and the long, drawn-out social crisis forced the Bishop of Rome— as was to happen even more obviously a century and a half later during the Pontificate of Gregory the Great—to play an important role in civil and political events. This, naturally, could only add to the importance and prestige of the Roman See. The fame of one particular episode in Leo's life has endured. It dates back to 452 when the Pope, together with a Roman delegation, met Attila, chief of the Huns, in Mantua and dissuaded him from continuing the war of invasion by which he had already devastated the northeastern regions of Italy. Thus, he saved the rest of the Peninsula. This important event soon became memorable and lives on as an emblematic sign of the Pontiff's action for peace. Unfortunately, the outcome of another Papal initiative three years later was not as successful, yet it was a sign of courage that still amazes us: in the spring of 455 Leo did not manage to prevent Genseric's Vandals, who had reached the gates of Rome, from invading the undefended city that they plundered for two weeks. This gesture of the Pope—who, defenseless and surrounded by his clergy, went forth to meet the invader to implore him to desist—nevertheless prevented Rome from being burned and assured that the Basilicas of St. Peter, St. Paul, and St. John, in which part of the terrified population sought refuge, were spared.

We are familiar with Pope Leo's action thanks to his most beau-tiful sermons—almost 100 in a splendid and clear Latin have been preserved—and thanks to his approximately 150 letters. In these texts the Pontiff appears in all his greatness, devoted to the service of truth in charity through an assiduous exercise of the Word which shows him to us as both Theologian and Pastor. Leo the Great, constantly thought-ful of his faithful and of the people of Rome but also of communion between the different Churches and of their needs, was a tireless cham-pion and upholder of the Roman Primacy, presenting himself as the Apostle Peter's authentic heir: the many Bishops who gathered at the

Council of Chalcedon, the majority of whom came from the East, were well aware of this.

This Council, held in 451 and in which 350 Bishops took part, was the most important assembly ever to have been celebrated in the history of the Church. Chalcedon represents the sure goal of the Christology of the three previous Ecumenical Councils: Nicaea in 325, Constantinople in 381, and Ephesus in 431. By the sixth century these four Councils that sum up the faith of the ancient Church were already being compared to the four Gospels. This is what Gregory the Great affirms in a famous letter (I, 24): "I confess that I receive and revere, as the four books of the Gospel so also the four Councils," because on them, Gregory explains further, "as on a four-square stone, rises the structure of the holy faith." The Council of Chalcedon, which rejected the heresy of Eutyches who denied the true human nature of the Son of God, affirmed the union in his one Person, without confusion and without separation, of his two natures, human and divine.

The Pope asserted this faith in Jesus Christ, true God and true man, in an important doctrinal text addressed to the Bishop of Constantinople, the so-called *Tome to Flavian* which, read at Chalcedon, was received by the Bishops present with an eloquent acclamation. Information on it has been preserved in the proceedings of the Council: "Peter has spoken through the mouth of Leo," the Council Fathers announced in unison. From this intervention in particular, but also from others made during the Christological controversy in those years, it is clear that the Pope felt with special urgency his responsibilities as Successor of Peter, whose role in the Church is unique since "to one Apostle alone was entrusted what was communicated to all the Apostles," as Leo said in one of his sermons for the Feast of Sts. Peter and Paul (83, 2). And the Pontiff was able to exercise these responsibilities, in the West as in the East, intervening in various circumstances with caution, firmness, and lucidity through his writings and legates. In this manner he showed how exercising the Roman Primacy was as necessary then as it is today to effectively serve communion, a characteristic of Christ's one Church.

Aware of the historical period in which he lived and of the change that was taking place—from pagan Rome to Christian Rome—in a period of profound crisis, Leo the Great knew how to make himself close to the people and the faithful with his pastoral action and his preaching. He enlivened charity in a Rome tried by famines, an influx of refugees, injustice, and poverty. He opposed pagan superstitions and the actions of Manichaean groups. He associated the liturgy with the daily life of Christians: for example, by combining the practice of fasting with charity and almsgiving above all on the occasion of the *Quattro tempora,* which in the course of the year marked the change of seasons. In particular, Leo the Great taught his faithful—and his words still apply for us today—that the Christian liturgy is not the memory of past events, but the actualization of invisible realities which act in the lives of each one of us. This is what he stressed in a sermon (cf. 64, 1–2) on Easter, to be celebrated in every season of the year "not so much as something of the past as rather an event of the present." All this fits into a precise project, the Holy Pontiff insisted: just as, in fact, the Creator enlivened with the breath of rational life man formed from the dust of the ground, after the original sin he sent his Son into the world to restore to man his lost dignity and to destroy the dominion of the devil through the new life of grace.

This is the Christological mystery to which St. Leo the Great, with his Letter to the Council of Ephesus, made an effective and essential contribution, confirming for all time—through this Council—what St. Peter said at Caesarea Philippi. With Peter and as Peter, he professed: "You are the Christ, the Son of the living God." And so it is that God and man together "are not foreign to the human race but alien to sin" (cf. *Serm.* 64). Through the force of this Christological faith he was a great messenger of peace and love. He thus shows us the way: in faith we learn charity. Let us therefore learn with St. Leo the Great to believe in Christ, true God and true Man, and to implement this faith every day in action for peace and love of neighbor.

CHAPTER 45

St. Benedict

Today, I would like to speak about Benedict, the Founder of Western Monasticism and also the Patron of my Pontificate. I begin with words that St. Gregory the Great wrote about St. Benedict: "The man of God who shone on this earth among so many miracles was just as brilliant in the eloquent exposition of his teaching" (cf. *Dialogues II, 36*). The great Pope wrote these words in 592 A.D. The holy monk, who had died barely 50 years earlier, lived on in people's memories and especially in the flourishing religious Order he had founded. St. Benedict of Norcia, with his life and his work, had a fundamental influence on the development of European civilization and culture. The most important source on Benedict's life is the second book of St. Gregory the Great's *Dialogues*. It is not a biography in the classical sense. In accordance with the ideas of his time, by giving the example of a real man—St. Benedict, in this case—Gregory wished to illustrate the ascent to the peak of contemplation which can be achieved by those who abandon themselves to God. He therefore gives us a model for human life in the climb towards the summit of perfection. St. Gregory the Great also tells in this book of the *Dialogues* of many miracles worked by the Saint, and here too he does not merely wish to recount something curious but rather to show how God, by admonishing, helping, and even punishing, intervenes in the practical situations of man's life. Gregory's aim was to demonstrate that God is not a distant hypothesis placed at the origin of the world but is present in the life of man, of every man.

This perspective of the "biographer" is also explained in light of the general context of his time: straddling the fifth and sixth centuries, "the world was overturned by a tremendous crisis of values and institutions caused by the collapse of the Roman Empire, the invasion of new peoples and the decay of morals." But in this terrible situation, here, in this very city of Rome, Gregory presented St. Benedict as a "luminous star" in order to point the way out of the "black night of history" (cf. John Paul II, May 18, 1979). In fact, the Saint's work and particularly his *Rule* were to prove heralds of an authentic spiritual leaven which, in the course of the centuries, far beyond the boundaries of his country and time, changed the face of Europe following the fall of the political unity created by the Roman Empire, inspiring a new spiritual and cultural unity, that of the Christian faith shared by the peoples of the Continent. This is how the reality we call "Europe" came into being.

St. Benedict was born around the year 480. As St. Gregory said, he came *"ex provincia Nursiae"*—from the province of Norcia. His well-to-do parents sent him to study in Rome. However, he did not stay long in the Eternal City. As a fully plausible explanation, Gregory mentions that the young Benedict was put off by the dissolute lifestyle of many of his fellow students and did not wish to make the same mistakes. He wanted only to please God: *"soli Deo placere desiderans"* (II Dialogues, Prol. 1). Thus, even before he finished his studies, Benedict left Rome and withdrew to the solitude of the mountains east of Rome. After a short stay in the village of Enfide (today, Affile), where for a time he lived with a "religious community" of monks, he became a hermit in the neighboring locality of Subiaco. He lived there completely alone for three years in a cave which has been the heart of a Benedictine Monastery called the "Sacro Speco" (Holy Grotto) since the early Middle Ages. The period in Subiaco, a time of solitude with God, was a time of maturation for Benedict. It was here that he bore and overcame the three fundamental temptations of every human being: the temptation of self-affirmation and the desire to put oneself at the center, the temptation of sensuality and, lastly, the temptation of anger and revenge. In fact, Benedict was convinced that only after overcoming these temptations would he be able to say a useful word to others about their own situations of neediness. Thus, having tranquilized his soul, he could be in full control of the drive of his ego and thus create peace around him. Only then did he decide to found his first monasteries in the Valley of the Anio, near Subiaco.

In the year 529, Benedict left Subiaco and settled in Monte Cassino. Some have explained this move as an escape from the intrigues of an envious local cleric. However, this attempt at an explanation hardly proved convincing since the latter's sudden death did not induce Benedict to return (*II Dialogues*, 8). In fact, this decision was called for because he had entered a new phase of inner maturity and monastic experience. According to Gregory the Great, Benedict's exodus from the remote Valley of the Anio to Monte Cassio—a plateau dominating the vast surrounding plain which can be seen from afar—has a symbolic character: a hidden monastic life has its own *raison d'être* but a monastery also has its public purpose in the life of the Church and of society, and it must give visibility to the faith as a force of life. Indeed, when Benedict's earthly life ended on March 21, 547, he bequeathed with his *Rule* and the Benedictine family he founded a heritage that bore fruit in the passing centuries and is still bearing fruit throughout the world.

Throughout the second book of his *Dialogues*, Gregory shows us how St. Benedict's life was steeped in an atmosphere of prayer, the foundation of his existence. Without prayer there is no experience of God. Yet Benedict's spirituality was not an interiority removed from reality. In the anxiety and confusion of his day, he lived under God's gaze and in this very way never lost sight of the duties of daily life and of man with his practical needs. Seeing God, he understood the reality of man and his mission. In his *Rule* he describes monastic life as "a school for the service of the Lord" (Prol. 45) and advises his monks, "let nothing be preferred to the Work of God" [that is, the Divine Office or the Liturgy of the Hours] (43, 3). However, Benedict states that in the first place prayer is an act of listening (Prol. 9–11), which must then be expressed in action. "The Lord is waiting every day for us to respond to his holy admonitions by our deeds" (Prol. 35). Thus, the monk's life becomes a fruitful symbiosis between action and contemplation, "so that God may be glorified in all things" (57, 9). In contrast with a facile and egocentric self-fulfillment, today often exalted, the first and indispensable commitment of a disciple of St. Benedict is the sincere search for God (58, 7) on the path mapped out by the humble and obedient Christ (5, 13), whose love he must put before all else (4, 21; 72, 11), and in this way, in the service of the other, he becomes a man of service and peace. In the exercise of obedience practiced by faith inspired by love (5, 2), the monk achieves humility (5, 1), to which the *Rule* dedicates an entire chapter (7). In this way, man conforms ever more to Christ and attains true self-fulfillment as a creature in the image and likeness of God.

The obedience of the disciple must correspond with the wisdom of the Abbot who, in the monastery, "is believed to hold the place of Christ" (2, 2; 63, 13). The figure of the Abbot, which is described above all in Chapter II of the *Rule* with a profile of spiritual beauty and demanding commitment, can be considered a self-portrait of Benedict, since, as St. Gregory the Great wrote, "the holy man could not teach otherwise than as he himself lived" (cf. *II Dialogues*, 36). The Abbot must be at the same time a tender father and a strict teacher (cf. Rule, 2, 24), a true educator. Inflexible against vices, he is nevertheless called above all to imitate the tenderness of the Good Shepherd (27, 8), to "serve rather than to rule" (64, 8) in order "to show them all what is good and holy by his deeds more than by his words" and "illustrate the divine precepts by his example" (2, 12). To be able to decide responsibly, the Abbot must also be a person who listens to "the brethren's views" (3, 2), because "the Lord often reveals to the youngest what is best" (3, 3). This provision makes a *Rule* written almost 15 centuries ago surprisingly modern! A man with public responsibility even in small circles must always be a man who can listen and learn from what he hears.

Benedict describes the *Rule* he wrote as "minimal, just an initial outline" (cf. 73, 8); in fact, however, he offers useful guidelines not only for monks but for all who seek guidance on their journey toward

God. For its moderation, humanity, and sober discernment between the essential and the secondary in spiritual life, his *Rule* has retained its illuminating power even to today. By proclaiming St. Benedict Patron of Europe on October 24, 1964, Paul VI intended to recognize the marvelous work the Saint achieved with his *Rule* for the formation of the civilization and culture of Europe. Having recently emerged from a century that was deeply wounded by two World Wars and the collapse of the great ideologies, now revealed as tragic utopias, Europe today is in search of its own identity. Of course, in order to create new and lasting unity, political, economic, and juridical instruments are important, but it is also necessary to awaken an ethical and spiritual renewal which draws on the Christian roots of the Continent, otherwise a new Europe cannot be built. Without this vital sap, man is exposed to the danger of succumbing to the ancient temptation of seeking to redeem himself by himself—a utopia which in different ways, in 20th-century Europe, as Pope John Paul II pointed out, has caused "a regression without precedent in the tormented history of humanity" (*Address to the Pontifical Council for Culture*, January 12, 1990). Today, in seeking true progress, let us also listen to the *Rule* of St. Benedict as a guiding light on our journey. The great monk is still a true master at whose school we can learn to become proficient in true humanism.

CHAPTER 46

St. Gregory the Great

Today I would like to present the figure of one of the greatest Fathers in the history of the Church, one of four Doctors of the West, Pope St. Gregory, who was Bishop of Rome from 590 to 604, and who earned the traditional title of *Magnus* / the Great. Gregory was truly a great Pope and a great Doctor of the Church! He was born in Rome about 540 into a rich patrician family of the *gens Anicia*, who were distinguished not only for their noble blood but also for their adherence to the Christian faith and for their service to the Apostolic See. Two Popes came from this family: Felix III (483–492), the great-great grandfather of Gregory, and Agapetus (535–536). The house in which Gregory grew up stood on the Clivus Scauri, surrounded by majestic buildings that attested to the greatness of ancient Rome and the spiritual strength of Christianity. The example of his parents Gordian and Sylvia, both venerated as Saints, and those of his father's sisters, Aemiliana and Tharsilla, who lived in their own home as consecrated virgins following a path of prayer and self-denial, inspired lofty Christian sentiments in him.

In the footsteps of his father, Gregory entered early into an administrative career which reached its climax in 572 when he became Prefect of the city. This office, complicated by the sorry times, allowed him to apply himself on a vast range to every type of administrative problem, drawing light for future duties from them. In particular, he retained a deep sense of order and discipline: having become Pope, he advised Bishops to take as a model for the management of ecclesial affairs the diligence and respect for the law like civil functionaries. Yet this life could not have satisfied him since shortly after, he decided to leave every civil assignment in order to withdraw to his home to begin the monastic life, transforming his family home into the monastery of St. Andrew on the Coelian Hill. This period of monastic life, the life of permanent dialogue with the Lord in listening to his word, constituted a perennial nostalgia which he referred to ever anew and ever more in his homilies. In the midst of the pressure of pastoral worries, he often recalled it in his writings as a happy time of recollection in God, dedication to prayer and peaceful immersion in study. Thus, he could acquire that deep understanding of Sacred Scripture and of the Fathers of the Church that later served him in his work.

But the cloistered withdrawal of Gregory did not last long. The precious experience that he gained in civil administration during a period marked by serious problems, the relationships he had had in this post with the Byzantines, and the universal respect that he acquired induced Pope Pelagius to appoint him deacon and to send him to Constantinople as his "apocrisarius"—today one would say "Apostolic Nuncio"—in order to help overcome the last traces of the Monophysite controversy and above all to obtain the Emperor's support in the effort to check the Lombard invaders. The stay at Constantinople, where he resumed monastic life with a group of monks, was very important for Gregory, since it permitted him to acquire direct experience of the Byzantine world, as well as to approach the problem of the Lombards, who would later put his ability and energy to the test during the years of his Pontificate. After some years he was recalled to Rome by the Pope, who appointed him his secretary. They were difficult years: the continual rain, flooding due to overflowing rivers, the famine that afflicted many regions of Italy as well as Rome. Finally, even the plague broke out, which claimed numerous victims, among whom was also Pope Pelagius II. The clergy, people, and senate were unanimous in choosing Gregory as his successor to the See of Peter. He tried to resist, even attempting to flee, but to no avail: finally, he had to yield. The year was 590.

Recognizing the will of God in what had happened, the new Pontiff immediately and enthusiastically set to work. From the beginning he showed a singularly enlightened vision of [the] reality with which he had to deal, an extraordinary capacity for work confronting both ecclesial and civil affairs, a constant and even balance in making decisions, at times with courage, imposed on him by his office.

Abundant documentation has been preserved from his governance thanks to the Register of his Letters (approximately 800), reflecting the complex questions that arrived on his desk on a daily basis. They were questions that came from Bishops, Abbots, clergy, and even from civil authorities of every order and rank. Among the problems that afflicted Italy and Rome at that time was one of special importance both in the civil and ecclesial spheres: the Lombard question. The Pope dedicated every possible energy to it in view of a truly peaceful solution. Contrary to the Byzantine Emperor who assumed that the Lombards were only uncouth individuals and predators to be defeated or exterminated, St. Gregory saw this people with the eyes of a good pastor, and was concerned with proclaiming the word of salvation to them, establishing fraternal relationships with them in view of a future peace founded on mutual respect and peaceful coexistence between Italians, Imperials, and Lombards. He was concerned with the conversion of the young people and the new civil structure of Europe: the Visigoths of Spain, the Franks, the Saxons, the immigrants in Britain, and the Lombards, were the privileged recipients of his evangelizing mission. Yesterday we celebrated the liturgical memorial of St. Augustine of Canterbury, the leader of a group of monks Gregory assigned to go to Britain to evangelize England.

The Pope—who was a true peacemaker—deeply committed himself to establish an effective peace in Rome and in Italy by undertaking intense negotiations with Agilulf, the Lombard King. This negotiation led to a period of truce that lasted for about three years (598–601), after which, in 603, it was possible to stipulate a more stable armistice. This positive result was obtained also thanks to the parallel contacts that, meanwhile, the Pope undertook with Queen Theodolinda, a Bavarian princess who, unlike the leaders of other Germanic peoples, was Catholic, deeply Catholic. A series of Letters of Pope Gregory to this Queen has been preserved in which he reveals his respect and friendship for her. Theodolinda, little by little, was able to guide the King to Catholicism, thus preparing the way to peace. The Pope also was careful to send her relics for the Basilica of St. John the Baptist which she had had built in Monza, and did not fail to send his congratulations and precious gifts for the same Cathedral of Monza on the occasion of the birth and baptism of her son, Adaloald. The series of events concerning this Queen constitutes a beautiful testimony to the importance of women in the history of the Church. Gregory constantly focused on three basic objectives: to limit the Lombard expansion in Italy; to preserve Queen Theodolinda from the influence of schismatics and to strengthen the Catholic faith; and to mediate between the Lombards and the Byzantines in view of an accord that guaranteed peace in the peninsula and at the same time permitted the evangelization of the Lombards themselves. Therefore, in the complex situation his scope was constantly twofold: to promote understanding on the diplomatic-political level and to spread the proclamation of the true faith among the peoples.

Along with his purely spiritual and pastoral action, Pope Gregory also became an active protagonist in multifaceted social activities. With the revenues from the Roman See's substantial patrimony in Italy, especially in Sicily, he bought and distributed grain; assisted those in need, helped priests, monks, and nuns who lived in poverty; paid the ransom for citizens held captive by the Lombards; and purchased armistices and truces. Moreover, whether in Rome or other parts of Italy, he carefully carried out the administrative reorganization, giving precise instructions so that the goods of the Church, useful for her sustenance and evangelizing work in the world, were managed with absolute rectitude and according to the rules of justice and mercy. He demanded that the tenants on Church territory be protected from dishonest agents and, in cases of fraud, were to be quickly compensated, so that the face of the Bride of Christ was not soiled with dishonest profits.

Gregory carried out this intense activity notwithstanding his poor health, which often forced him to remain in bed for days on end. The

299

fasts practiced during the years of monastic life had caused him serious digestive problems. Furthermore, his voice was so feeble that he was often obliged to entrust the reading of his homilies to the deacon, so that the faithful present in the Roman Basilicas could hear him. On feast days he did his best to celebrate the *Missarum sollemnia,* that is the solemn Mass, and then he met personally with the people of God, who were very fond of him, because they saw in him the authoritative reference from whom to draw security: not by chance was the title *consul Dei* quickly attributed to him. Notwithstanding the very difficult conditions in which he had to work, he gained the faithful's trust, thanks to his holiness of life and rich humanity, achieving truly magnificent results for his time and for the future. He was a man immersed in God: his desire for God was always alive in the depths of his soul and precisely because of this he was always close to his neighbor, to the needy people of his time. Indeed, during a desperate period of havoc, he was able to create peace and give hope. This man of God shows us the true sources of peace, from which true hope comes. Thus, he becomes a guide also for us today.

PART X

PRAYER

CHAPTER 47

Prayer and the Natural Desire for God

In this address, taken from one of his weekly audiences in 2011, Benedict XVI discusses the "essential search for God" found in all the great civilizations of the world, and notes that prayer "is written on the heart of every person and of every civilization." But, he concludes, this longing finds its fulfillment only in the God who reveals himself in Jesus Christ.

We live in an age in which the signs of secularism are glaringly obvious. God seems to have disappeared from the horizon of some people or to have become a reality that meets with indifference. Yet at the same time we see many signs of a reawakening of the religious sense, a rediscovery of the importance of God to the human being's life, a need for spirituality, for going beyond a purely horizontal and materialistic vision of human life.

A look at recent history reveals the failure of the predictions of those who, in the age of the Enlightenment, foretold the disappearance of religions and who exalted absolute reason, detached from faith, a reason that was to dispel the shadows of religious dogmatism and was to dissolve the "world of the sacred," restoring to the human being freedom, dignity, and autonomy from God. The experience of the past century, with the tragedy of the two World Wars, disrupted the progress that autonomous reason, man without God, seemed to have been able to guarantee.

The *Catechism of the Catholic Church* says: "In the act of creation, God calls every being from nothingness into existence. . . . Even after losing through his sin his likeness to God, man remains an image of his Creator, and retains the desire for the one who calls him into existence.

All religions bear witness to man's essential search for God" (no. 2566). We could say—as I explained in my last Catecheses—that there has been no great civilization, from the most distant epoch to our day, which has not been religious.

Man is religious by nature, he is *homo religiosus* just as he is *homo sapiens* and *homo faber*: "The desire for God," the *Catechism* says further, "is written in the human heart, because man is created by God and for God" (no. 27). The image of the Creator is impressed on his being and he feels the need to find light to give a response to the questions that concern the deep sense of reality; a response that he cannot find in himself, in progress, in empirical science.

The *homo religiosus* does not only appear in the sphere of antiquity, he passes through the whole of human history. In this regard, the rich terrain of human experience has seen the religious sense develop in various forms, in the attempt to respond to the desire for fullness and happiness. The "digital" man, like the cave man, seeks in the religious experience ways to overcome his finiteness and to guarantee his precarious adventure on earth. Moreover, life without a transcendent horizon would not have its full meaning and happiness, for which we all seek, is spontaneously projected towards the future in a tomorrow that has yet to come.

In the Declaration *Nostra Aetate*, the Second Vatican Council stressed in summary form: "Men look to their different religions for an answer to the unsolved riddles of human existence. The problems that weigh heavily on the hearts of men are the same today as in the ages past. What is man?—[who am I?]—What is the meaning and purpose of life? What is upright behavior, and what is sinful? Where does suffering originate, and what end does it serve? How can genuine happiness be found? What happens at death? What is judgement? What reward follows death? And finally, what is the ultimate mystery, beyond human explanation, which embraces our entire existence, from which we take our origin and towards which we tend?" (no. 1).

Man knows that, by himself, he cannot respond to his own fundamental need to understand. However much he is deluded and still deludes himself that he is self-sufficient, he experiences his own insufficiency. He needs to open himself to something more, to something or to someone that can give him what he lacks, he must come out of himself towards the One who is able to fill the breadth and depth of his desire.

Man bears within him a thirst for the infinite, a longing for eternity, a quest for beauty, a desire for love, a need for light and for truth which impel him towards the Absolute; man bears within him the desire for God. And man knows, in a certain way, that he can turn to God, he knows he can pray to him.

St. Thomas Aquinas, one of the greatest theologians of history, defines prayer as "an expression of man's desire for God." This attraction to God, which God himself has placed in man, is the soul of prayer, that then takes on a great many forms, in accordance with the history, the time, the moment, the grace and even the sin of every person praying. Man's history has in fact known various forms of prayer, because he has developed different kinds of openness to the "Other" and to the Beyond, so that we may recognize prayer as an experience present in every religion and culture.

Indeed, dear brothers and sisters, as we saw last Wednesday, prayer is not linked to a specific context, but is written on the heart of every person and of every civilization. Of course, when we speak of prayer as an experience of the human being as such, of the *homo orans*, it is necessary to bear in mind that it is an inner attitude before being a series of practices and formulas, a manner of being in God's presence before performing acts of worship or speaking words.

Prayer is centered and rooted in the inmost depths of the person; it is therefore not easily decipherable and, for the same reason, can be subject to misunderstanding and mystification. In this sense too we can understand the expression: prayer is difficult. In fact, prayer is the place *par excellence* of free giving, of striving for the Invisible, the Unexpected, and the Ineffable. Therefore, the experience of prayer is a challenge to everyone, a "grace" to invoke, a gift of the One to whom we turn.

In prayer, in every period of history, man considers himself and his situation before God, from God, and in relation to God, and experiences being a creature in need of help, incapable of obtaining on his own the fulfilment of his life and his hope. The philosopher Ludwig Wittgenstein mentioned that "prayer means feeling that the world's meaning is outside the world."

In the dynamic of this relationship with the one who gives meaning to existence, with God, prayer has one of its typical expressions in the gesture of kneeling. It is a gesture that has in itself a radical ambivalence. In fact, I can be forced to kneel—a condition of indigence and slavery—but I can also kneel spontaneously, declaring my limitations and therefore my being in need of Another. To him I declare I am weak, needy, "a sinner."

In the experience of prayer, the human creature expresses all his self-awareness, all that he succeeds in grasping of his own existence and, at the same time, he turns with his whole being to the One before whom he stands, directs his soul to that Mystery from which he expects the fulfilment of his deepest desires and help to overcome the neediness of his own life. In this turning to "Another," in directing himself "beyond" lies the essence of prayer, as an experience of a reality that overcomes the tangible and the contingent.

Yet only in God who reveals himself does man's seeking find complete fulfilment. The prayer that is openness and elevation of the heart to God thus becomes a personal relationship with him. And even if man forgets his Creator, the living, true God does not cease to call man first to the mysterious encounter of prayer.

As the *Catechism* says: "in prayer, the faithful God's initiative of love always comes first; our own first step is always a response. As God gradually reveals himself and reveals man to himself, prayer appears as a reciprocal call, a covenant drama. Through words and actions, this drama engages the heart. It unfolds throughout the whole history of salvation" (no. 2567).

Dear brothers and sisters, let us learn to pause longer before God, who revealed himself in Jesus Christ, let us learn to recognize in silence, in our own hearts, his voice that calls us and leads us back to the depths of our existence, to the source of life, to the source of salvation, to enable us to go beyond the limitations of our life and to open ourselves to God's dimension, to the relationship with him, which is Infinite Love.

CHAPTER 48

Prayer and the Holy Spirit

In this passage drawn from a weekly audience in 2012, Benedict XVI urges us to see in prayer the work of the Holy Spirit, whose power unites us to Christ and helps us in our weakness, and explores three consequences for the Christian life that spring from this approach to dialogue with God.

I would like to . . . speak about prayer in the Letters of St. Paul, the Apostle to the Gentiles. First of all, I would like to note that it is by no accident that his Letters open and close with expressions of prayer: at the beginning thanksgiving and praise, and at the end the hope that the grace of God may guide the path of the community to whom the Letter is addressed. Between the opening formula: "I thank my God through Jesus Christ" (Rom. 1:8), and his final wish: "The grace of the Lord Jesus be with you all" (1 Cor. 16:23), the Apostle's letters unfold. St. Paul's prayer is one which manifests itself in a great many ways that move from thanksgiving to blessing, from praise to petitions and intercessions, from hymns to supplication. He uses a variety of expressions which demonstrate how prayer concerns and penetrates every one of life's situations, whether they be personal or of the communities, whom he is addressing.

One element that the Apostle would have us understand is that prayer should not be seen simply as a good deed done by us to God, our own action. It is, above all, a gift, the fruit of the living presence, the life-giving presence of the Father and of Jesus Christ in us. In the Letter to the Romans, he writes: "Likewise the Spirit helps us in our weakness; for we do not know how to pray as we ought, but the Spirit himself intercedes for us with sighs too deep for words" (8:26). And we know how true it is when the Apostle says: "we do not know how to pray as we ought." We want to pray, but God is far, we do not have the words, the language, to speak with God, not even the thought. We can only open ourselves, set our time at the disposal of God, waiting for him to help us enter into true dialogue. The Apostle says: this very lack of words, this absence of words, even the desire to enter into contact with God is a prayer that the Holy Spirit not only understands, but carries, interprets, to God. It is precisely our weakness which becomes, through the Holy Spirit, true prayer, true contact with God. The Holy Spirit is almost the interpreter who makes God and us ourselves understand what we want to say.

In prayer we experience, more so than in other dimensions of life, our weakness, our poverty, our being created, because we stand before the omnipotence and the transcendence of God. And the more we progress in listening to and dialoguing with God, for prayer becomes the daily breath of our soul, the more we perceive the meaning of our limits, not just before the concrete situations of every day but in our relationship with the Lord too. Growing within us is the need to trust, to trust ever more in him; we understand that "we do not know how to pray as we ought" (Rom 8:26). And it is the Holy Spirit who helps us in our incapacity, who illuminates our minds and warms our hearts, guiding us to turn to God. For St. Paul prayer is above all the work of the Spirit in our humanity, taking charge of our weakness and transforming us from men attached to the material world into spiritual men. In the First Letter to the Corinthians he writes: "Now we have received not the spirit of the world, but the Spirit which is from God, that we might understand the gifts bestowed on us by God. And we impart this in words not taught by human wisdom but taught by the Spirit, interpreting spiritual truths to those who possess the Spirit" (2:12–13). With his dwelling in our human frailty, the Holy Spirit changes us, intercedes for us, leads us toward the heights of God (cf. Rom 8:26).

With this presence of the Holy Spirit, our union with Christ is realized, for it is the Spirit of the Son of God in whom we are made children. St. Paul speaks of the Spirit of Christ (cf. Rom 8:9), and not only the Spirit of God. Clearly: if Christ is the Son of God, his Spirit is also the Spirit of God, and thus if the Spirit of God, the Spirit of Christ, had already become very close to us in the Son of God and the Son of man, the Spirit of God too becomes human spirit and touches us; we can enter into the communion of the Spirit.

It was as if he had said that not only God the Father was made visible in the Incarnation of the Son, but also the Spirit of God is manifest in the life and action of Jesus, of Jesus Christ who lived, was crucified, died and rose again. The Apostle reminds us that "No one can say 'Jesus is Lord' except by the Holy Spirit" (1 Cor. 12:3). Therefore, the Spirit directs our heart towards Jesus Christ, in such a way that "it is no longer we who live, but Christ who lives in us" (cf. Gal. 2:20). In his *De sacramentis*, reflecting on the Eucharist, St. Ambrose says: "Whoever is drunk of the Spirit is rooted in Christ" (5, 3, 12: *PL* 16, 450).

And now I would like to underline three consequences in Christian life when we let work within us not the spirit of the world but the Spirit of Christ as the interior principle of our entire action.

First, with prayer animated by the Spirit we are enabled to abandon and overcome every form of fear and slavery, living the authentic freedom of the children of God. Without prayer which every day nourishes our being in Christ, in an intimacy which progressively grows, we find ourselves in the state described by St. Paul in his Letter to the Romans: we do not do the good we want, but the evil we do not want (cf. Rom. 7:19). And this is the expression of the alienation of human beings, of the destruction of our freedom, the circumstances of our being because of original sin: we want the good that we do not do and we do what we do not want to do: evil. The Apostle wants to make us understand that it is not primarily our will that frees us from these conditions, nor even the law, but the Holy Spirit. And since "where the Spirit of the Lord is, there is freedom" (2 Cor. 3:17), in prayer we experience the freedom given by the Spirit: an authentic freedom, which is freedom from evil and sin for the good and for life, for God. The freedom of the Spirit, St. Paul continues, is never identified with licentiousness,

310

nor with the possibility to choose evil, but rather with "the fruit of the Spirit is love, joy, peace, patience, kindness, goodness, faithfulness, gentleness, self-control" (Gal. 5:22). This is true freedom: actually to be able to follow our desire for good, for true joy, for communion with God, and to be free from the oppression of circumstances that pull us in other directions.

A second consequence occurs in our life when we let work within us the Spirit of Christ and when the very relationship with God, becomes so profound that no other reality or situation affects it. We understand that with prayer we are not liberated from trials and suffering, but we can live through them in union with Christ, with his suffering, in the hope of also participating in his glory (cf. Rom. 8:17). Many times, in our prayer, we ask God to be freed from physical and spiritual evil, and we do it with great trust. However, often we have the impression of not being heard and we may well feel discouraged and fail to persevere. In reality, there is no human cry that is not heard by God and it is precisely in constant and faithful prayer that we comprehend with St. Paul that "the sufferings of this present time are not worth comparing with the glory that is to be revealed to us" (Rom. 8:18). Prayer does not exempt us from trial and suffering, indeed—St. Paul says—we "groan inwardly as we wait for adoption as sons, the redemption of our bodies" (Rom. 8:23). He says that prayer does not exempt us from suffering but prayer does permit us to live through it and face it with a new strength, with the confidence of Jesus, who—according to the Letter to the Hebrews—"In the days of his flesh, Jesus offered up prayers and supplications, with loud cries and tears, to him [God] who was able to save him from death, and he was heard for his godly fear" (5:7). The answer of God the Father to the Son, to his loud cries and tears, was not freedom from suffering, from the cross, from death, but a much greater fulfillment, an answer much more profound; through the cross and death God responded with the Resurrection of the Son, with new life. Prayer animated by the Holy Spirit leads us too to live every day a journey of life with its trials and sufferings, with the fullness of hope, with trust in God who answers us as he answered the Son.

And, the third, the prayer of the believer opens also to the dimensions of humanity and of all creation, in the expectation that "creation waits with eager longing for the revealing of the sons of God" (Rom. 8:19). This means that prayer, sustained by the Spirit of Christ speaking in the depths of each one of us, does not stay closed in on itself. It is never just prayer for me, but opens itself to sharing the suffering of our time, of others. It becomes intercession for others, and like this deliverance from me, a channel of hope for all creation, the expression of that love of God that is poured into our hearts through the Spirit whom he has given to us (cf. Rom. 5:5). And precisely this is a sign of true prayer, which does not end in us, but opens itself to others and like this delivers me, and thus helps in the redemption of the world.

Dear brothers and sisters, St. Paul teaches us that in our prayer we must open ourselves to the presence of the Holy Spirit, who prays in us with sighs too deep for words, to lead us to adhere to God with all our heart and with all our being. The Spirit of Christ becomes the strength of our "weak" prayers, the light of our "darkened" prayer, the fire of our "barren" prayer, giving us true inner freedom, teaching us to live facing the trials of existence, in the certainty of not being alone, opening us to the horizons of humanity and of creation which "has been groaning in travail" (Rom. 8:22).

CHAPTER 49

The Nature of Christian Prayer

In this selection, taken from a weekly audience in 2012, Benedict XVI encourages us to remember that, through Christ, we have been made children of God, and that Christian prayer is rooted in this intimacy with God our Father.

St. Paul says . . . [that] the Holy Spirit . . . teaches us to address God with the affectionate words that children use, calling him: "Abba, Father." This is what Jesus did; even in the most dramatic moment of his earthly life he never lost his trust in the Father and always called on him with the intimacy of the beloved Son. In Gethsemane, when he feels the anguish of his approaching death, his prayer is: "Abba, Father, all things are possible to you; remove this cup from me; yet not what I will, but what you will" (Mark 14:36).

Since the very first steps on her journey the Church has taken up this invocation and made it her own, especially in the prayer of the "Our Father," in which we say every day: "Our Father . . . Thy will be done, on earth as it is in heaven! (Matt. 6:9–10).

We find it twice in the Letters of St. Paul. The Apostle, as we have just heard, addresses these words to the Galatians: "And because you are sons, God has sent the Spirit of his Son into our hearts, crying, 'Abba! Father!'" (Gal. 4:6). And, at the center of that hymn to the Holy Spirit which is the eighth chapter of the Letter to the Romans, St. Paul declares: "For you did not receive the spirit of slavery to fall back into fear, but you have received the spirit of sonship. When we cry: 'Abba! Father!' it is the Spirit himself . . ." (Rom. 8:15).

Christianity is not a religion of fear but of trust and of love for the Father who loves us. Both these crucial affirmations speak to us of the sending forth and reception of the Holy Spirit, the gift of the

Risen One which makes us sons in Christ, the Only-Begotten Son, and places us in a filial relationship with God, a relationship of deep trust, like that of children; a filial relationship like that of Jesus, even though its origin and quality are different. Jesus is the eternal Son of God who took flesh; we instead become sons in him, in time, through faith and through the sacraments of Baptism and Confirmation. Thanks to these two sacraments we are immersed in the Paschal Mystery of Christ. The Holy Spirit is the precious and necessary gift that makes us children of God, that brings about that adoption as sons to which all human beings are called because, as the divine blessing in the Letter to the Ephesians explains, God, in Christ, "chose us in him before the foundation of the world, that we should be holy and blameless before him. He destined us in love to be his [adopted] sons through Jesus Christ" (Eph. 1:4).

Perhaps people today fail to perceive the beauty, greatness, and profound consolation contained in the word "father" with which we can turn to God in prayer because today the father figure is often not sufficiently present and all too often is not sufficiently positive in daily life. The father's absence, the problem of a father who is not present in a child's life, is a serious problem of our time. It therefore becomes difficult to understand what it means to say that God is really our Father. From Jesus himself, from his filial relationship with God, we can learn what "father" really means and what is the true nature of the Father who is in heaven.

Critics of religion have said that speaking of the "Father," of God, is a projection of our ancestors in heaven. But the opposite is true: in the Gospel Christ shows us who is the father and as he is a true father we can understand true fatherhood and even learn true fatherhood. Let us think of Jesus' words in the Sermon on the Mount where he says: "But I say to you, love your enemies and pray for those who persecute you, so that you may be sons of your Father who is in heaven" (Matt. 5:44–45). It is the very love of Jesus, the Only-Begotten Son—who goes even to the point of giving himself on the Cross—that reveals to us the true nature of the Father: he is Love and in our prayers as children we too enter this circuit of love, the love of God that purifies our desires, our attitudes marked by closure, self-sufficiency, and the typical selfishness of the former man.

We could therefore say that God in being Father has two dimensions. First of all God is our Father because he is our Creator. Each one of us, each man and each woman, is a miracle of God, is wanted by him and is personally known by him. When it says in the Book of Genesis that the human being is created in the image of God (cf. 1:27), it tries to express this precise reality: God is our Father, for him we are not anonymous, impersonal beings but have a name. And a phrase in the Psalms always moves me when I pray. "Your hands have made and fashioned me," says the Psalmist (Ps. 119[118]:73). In this beautiful image each one of us can express his personal relationship with God. "Your hands have fashioned me. You thought of me and created and wanted me."

Nonetheless this is still not enough. The Spirit of Christ opens us to a second dimension of God's fatherhood, beyond creation, since Jesus is the "Son" in the full sense of "one in being with the Father," as we profess in the Creed. Becoming a human being like us, with his Incarnation, death, and Resurrection, Jesus in his turn accepts us in his humanity and even in his being Son, so that we too may enter into his specific belonging to God. Of course, our being children of God does not have the fullness of Jesus. We must increasingly become so throughout the journey of our Christian existence, developing in the following of Christ and in communion with him so as to enter ever more intimately into the relationship of love with God the Father which sustains our life.

It is this fundamental reality that is disclosed to us when we open ourselves to the Holy Spirit and he makes us turn to God saying "Abba!," Father. We have truly preceded creation, entering into adoption with Jesus; united, we are really in God and are his children in a new way, in a new dimension.

Now I would like to return to St. Paul's two passages on this action of the Holy Spirit in our prayers on which we are reflecting. Here too

315

are two passages that correspond with each other but contain a different nuance. In the Letter to the Galatians, in fact, the Apostle says that the Spirit cries: "Abba! Father!" in us. In the Letter to the Romans he says that it is we who cry: "Abba! Father!" And St. Paul wants to make us understand that Christian prayer is never one way, never happens in one direction from us to God, it is never merely "an action of ours" but, rather, is the expression of a reciprocal relationship in which God is the first to act; it is the Holy Spirit who cries in us and we are able to cry because the impetus comes from the Holy Spirit.

We would not be able to pray were the desire for God, for being children of God, not engraved in the depths of our heart. Since he came into existence *homo sapiens* has always been in search of God and endeavors to speak with God because God has engraved himself in our hearts. The first initiative therefore comes from God and with Baptism, once again God acts in us, the Holy Spirit acts in us; he is the prime initiator of prayer so that we may really converse with God and say "Abba" to God. Hence his presence opens our prayers and our lives, it opens on to the horizons of the Trinity and of the Church.

We realize in addition—this is the second point—that the prayer of the Spirit of Christ in us and ours in him is not solely an individual act but an act of the entire Church. In praying our heart is opened, not only do we enter into communion with God but actually with all the children of God, because we are one body. When we address the Father in our inner room in silence and in recollection we are never alone. Those who speak to God are not alone. We are within the great prayer of the Church, we are part of a great symphony that the Christian community in all the parts of the earth and in all epochs, raises to God. Naturally, the musicians and instruments differ—and this is an element of enrichment—but the melody of praise is one and in harmony. Every time, then, that we shout or say: "Abba! Father!" it is the Church, the whole communion of people in prayer that supports our invocation and our invocation is an invocation of the Church.

This is also reflected in the wealth of charisms and of the ministries and tasks that we carry out in the community. St. Paul writes to the Christians of Corinth: "There are varieties of gifts, but the same Spirit; and there are varieties of service, but the same Lord; and there are varieties of working, but it is the same God who inspires them all in everyone" (1 Cor. 12:4–6).

Prayer guided by the Holy Spirit, who makes us say: "Abba! Father!" with Christ and in Christ, inserts us into the great mosaic of the family of God in which each one has a place and an important role, in profound unity with the whole.

One last remark: we also learn to cry "Abba! Father!" with Mary, Mother of the Son of God. The consummation of the fullness of time, of which St. Paul speaks in his Letter to the Galatians (cf. 4:4) is brought about at the moment when Mary said "yes," the moment of her full adherence to God's will: "Behold, I am the handmaid of the Lord" (Luke 1:38).

Dear brothers and sisters, let us learn to savor in our prayers the beauty of being friends, indeed children of God, of being able to call on him with the trust that a child has for the parents who love him. Let us open our prayers to the action of the Holy Spirit so that he may cry to God in us: "Abba! Father!," and so that our prayers may transform and constantly convert our way of thinking and our action to bring us ever more closely into line with Jesus Christ, the Only-Begotten Son of God.

PART XI

FAITH IN THE MODERN WORLD

CHAPTER 50

The Dictatorship of Relativism

In a homily just before the opening of the conclave that elected him pope, Cardinal Ratzinger warned of the growing "dictatorship of relativism," which "does not recognize anything as definitive and whose ultimate goal consists solely of one's own ego and desires." This became a key theme of his pontificate.

At this moment of great responsibility, let us listen with special attention to what the Lord says to us in his own words. I would like to examine just a few passages from the three readings that concern us directly at this time.

The first one offers us a prophetic portrait of the person of the Messiah—a portrait that receives its full meaning from the moment when Jesus reads the text in the synagogue at Nazareth and says, "Today this Scripture passage is fulfilled in your hearing" (Luke 4:21).

At the core of the prophetic text we find a word which seems contradictory, at least at first sight. The Messiah, speaking of himself, says that he was sent "to announce a year of favor from the Lord and a day of vindication by our God" (Isa. 61:2). We hear with joy the news of a year of favor: divine mercy puts a limit on evil, as the Holy Father told us. Jesus Christ is divine mercy in person: encountering Christ means encountering God's mercy.

Christ's mandate has become our mandate through the priestly anointing. We are called to proclaim, not only with our words but also with our lives and with the valuable signs of the sacraments, "the year of favor from the Lord."

But what does the prophet Isaiah mean when he announces "the day of vindication by our God"? At Nazareth, Jesus omitted these words in his reading of the prophet's text; he concluded by announcing the year of favor. Might this have been the reason for the outburst of scan-dal after his preaching? We do not know.

In any case, the Lord offered a genuine commentary on these words by being put to death on the cross. St. Peter says: "In his own body he brought your sins to the cross" (1 Pet. 2:24). And St. Paul writes in his Letter to the Galatians: "Christ has delivered us from the power of the law's curse by himself becoming a curse for us, as it is written, 'Accursed is anyone who is hanged on a tree.' This happened so that through Christ Jesus the blessing bestowed on Abraham might descend on the Gentiles in Christ Jesus, thereby making it possible for us to receive the promised Spirit through faith" (Gal. 3:13f.).

Christ's mercy is not a grace that comes cheap, nor does it imply the trivialization of evil. Christ carries the full weight of evil and all its destructive force in his body and in his soul. He burns and transforms evil in suffering, in the fire of his suffering love. The day of vindica-tion and the year of favor converge in the Paschal Mystery, in the dead and Risen Christ. This is the vengeance of God: he himself suffers for us, in the person of his Son. The more deeply stirred we are by the Lord's mercy, the greater the solidarity we feel with his suffering—and we become willing to complete in our own flesh "what is lacking in the afflictions of Christ" (Col. 1:24).

Let us move on to the second reading, the letter to the Ephesians. Here we see essentially three aspects: first of all, the ministries and charisms in the Church as gifts of the Lord who rose and ascended into heaven; then, the maturing of faith and the knowledge of the Son of God as the condition and content of unity in the Body of Christ; and lastly, our common participation in the growth of the Body of Christ, that is, the transformation of the world into communion with the Lord.

Let us dwell on only two points. The first is the journey towards "the maturity of Christ," as the Italian text says, simplifying it slightly. More precisely, in accordance with the Greek text, we should speak of the "measure of the fullness of Christ" that we are called to attain if we are to be true adults in the faith. We must not remain children in faith, in the condition of minors. And what does it mean to be children in faith? St. Paul answers: it means being "tossed here and there, carried about by every wind of doctrine" (Eph. 4:14). This description is very timely!

How many winds of doctrine have we known in recent decades, how many ideological currents, how many ways of thinking. The small boat of the thought of many Christians has often been tossed about by these waves—flung from one extreme to another: from Marxism to liberalism, even to libertinism; from collectivism to radical individualism; from atheism to a vague religious mysticism; from agnosticism to syncretism and so forth. Every day new sects spring up, and what St. Paul says about human deception and the trickery that strives to entice people into error (cf. Eph. 4:14) comes true.

Today, having a clear faith based on the Creed of the Church is often labeled as fundamentalism. Whereas relativism, that is, letting oneself be "tossed here and there, carried about by every wind of doctrine," seems the only attitude that can cope with modern times. We are building a dictatorship of relativism that does not recognize anything as definitive and whose ultimate goal consists solely of one's own ego and desires.

We, however, have a different goal: the Son of God, the true man. He is the measure of true humanism. An "adult" faith is not a faith that follows the trends of fashion and the latest novelty; a mature adult faith is deeply rooted in friendship with Christ. It is this friendship that opens us up to all that is good and gives us a criterion by which to distinguish the true from the false, and deceit from truth.

We must develop this adult faith; we must guide the flock of Christ to this faith. And it is this faith—only faith—that creates unity and is fulfilled in love.

On this theme, St. Paul offers us as a fundamental formula for Christian existence some beautiful words, in contrast to the continual vicissitudes of those who, like children, are tossed about by the waves: make truth in love. Truth and love coincide in Christ. To the extent that we draw close to Christ, in our own lives too, truth and love are blended. Love without truth would be blind; truth without love would be like "a clanging cymbal" (1 Cor. 13:1).

Let us now look at the Gospel, from whose riches I would like to draw only two small observations. The Lord addresses these wonderful words to us: "I no longer speak of you as slaves. . . . Instead, I call you friends" (John 15:15). We so often feel, and it is true, that we are only useless servants (cf. Luke 17:10).

Yet, in spite of this, the Lord calls us friends, he makes us his friends, he gives us his friendship. The Lord gives friendship a dual definition. There are no secrets between friends: Christ tells us all that he hears from the Father; he gives us his full trust and with trust, also knowledge. He reveals his face and his heart to us. He shows us the tenderness he feels for us, his passionate love that goes even as far as the folly of the Cross. He entrusts himself to us, he gives us the power to speak in his name: "this is my body . . ."; "I forgive you . . ." He entrusts his Body, the Church, to us.

To our weak minds, to our weak hands, he entrusts his truth—the mystery of God the Father, the Son, and the Holy Spirit; the mystery of God who "so loved the world that he gave his only Son" (John 3:16). He made us his friends—and how do we respond?

The second element Jesus uses to define friendship is the communion of wills. For the Romans *"Idem velle—idem nolle"* [same desires, same dislikes] was also the definition of friendship. "You are my friends if you do what I command you" (John 15:14). Friendship with Christ coincides with the third request of the *Our Father*: "Thy will be done on earth as it is in heaven." At his hour in the Garden of Gethsemane, Jesus transformed our rebellious human will into a will conformed and united with the divine will. He suffered the whole drama of our autonomy—and precisely by placing our will in God's hands, he gives us true freedom: "Not as I will, but as you will" (Matt. 26:39).

Our redemption is brought about in this communion of wills: being friends of Jesus, to become friends of God. The more we love Jesus, the more we know him, the more our true freedom develops and our joy in being redeemed flourishes. Thank you, Jesus, for your friendship!

The other element of the Gospel to which I wanted to refer is Jesus' teaching on bearing fruit: "It was I who chose you to go forth and bear fruit. Your fruit must endure" (John 15:16).

It is here that appears the dynamism of the life of a Christian, an apostle: *I chose you to go forth.* We must be enlivened by a holy restlessness: a restlessness to bring to everyone the gift of faith, of friendship with Christ. Truly, the love and friendship of God was given to us so that it might also be shared with others. We have received the faith to give it to others—we are priests in order to serve others. And we must bear fruit that will endure.

All people desire to leave a lasting mark. But what endures? Money does not. Even buildings do not, nor books. After a certain time, longer or shorter, all these things disappear. The only thing that lasts forever is the human soul, the human person created by God for eternity.

The fruit that endures is therefore all that we have sown in human souls: love, knowledge, a gesture capable of touching hearts, words that open the soul to joy in the Lord. So let us go and pray to the Lord to help us bear fruit that endures. Only in this way will the earth be changed from a valley of tears to a garden of God.

To conclude, let us return once again to the Letter to the Ephesians. The Letter says, with words from Psalm 68, that Christ, ascending into heaven, "gave gifts to men" (Eph. 4:8). The victor offers gifts. And these gifts are apostles, prophets, evangelists, pastors, and teachers. Our ministry is a gift of Christ to humankind, to build up his body—the new world. We live out our ministry in this way, as a gift of Christ to humanity!

CHAPTER 51

The Two Levels of Conscience

In this excerpt from his book *On Conscience*, Ratzinger offers insights into the true meaning of conscience, a concept that is often misunderstood in the modern world.

Anamnesis

After all these ramblings through intellectual history, it is finally time to arrive at some conclusions, that is, to formulate a concept of conscience. The medieval tradition was right, I believe, in according two levels to the concept of conscience. These levels, though they can be well distinguished, must be continually referred to each other. It seems to me that many unacceptable theses regarding conscience are the result of neglecting either the difference or the connection between the two. Mainstream scholasticism expressed these two levels in the concepts "synderesis" and "conscientia."

The word *synderesis* (*synteresis*) came into the medieval tradition of conscience from the Stoic doctrine of the microcosm. It remained unclear in its exact meaning, and for this reason became a hindrance to a careful development of this essential aspect of the whole question of conscience. I would like, therefore, without entering into philosophical disputes, to replace this problematic word with the much more clearly defined Platonic concept of anamnesis. It is not only linguistically clearer and philosophically deeper and purer, but anamnesis above all also harmonizes with key motifs of biblical thought and the anthropology derived from it.

The word *anamnesis* should be taken to mean exactly that which Paul expressed in the second chapter of his Letter to the Romans:

When Gentiles who have not the law do by nature what the law requires, they are a law to themselves, even though they do

326

not have the law. They show that what the law requires is written on their hearts, while their conscience also bears witness . . . (2:14–15)

The same thought is strikingly amplified in the great monastic rule of Saint Basil. Here we read:

The love of God is not founded on a discipline imposed on us from outside, but is constitutively established in us as the capacity and necessity of our rational nature.

Basil speaks in terms of "the spark of divine love which has been hidden in us," an expression that was to become important in medieval mysticism. In the spirit of Johannine theology Basil knows that love consists in keeping the commandments. For this reason, the spark of love, which has been put into us by the Creator, means this: "We have received interiorly beforehand the capacity and disposition for observing all divine commandments . . . These are not something imposed from without." Referring everything back to its simple core, Augustine adds, "We could never judge that one thing is better than another, if a basic understanding of the good had not already been instilled in us."

This means that the first so-called ontological level of the phenomenon conscience consists in the fact that something like an original memory of the good and true (they are identical) has been implanted in us, that there is an inner ontological tendency within man, who is created in the likeness of God, toward the divine. From its origin, man's being resonates with some things and clashes with others. This anamnesis of the origin, which results from the god-like constitution of our being, is not a conceptually articulated knowing, a store of retrievable contents. It is, so to speak, an inner sense, a capacity to recall, so that the one whom it addresses, if he is not turned in on himself, hears its echo from within. He sees: That's it! That is what my nature points to and seeks.

The possibility for and right to mission rest on this anamnesis of the Creator, which is identical to the ground of our existence. The gospel may, indeed must, be proclaimed to the pagans, because they themselves are yearning for it in the hidden recesses of their souls (see Isa. 42:4). Mission is vindicated, then, when those addressed recognize in the encounter with the word of the gospel that this indeed is what they have been waiting for.

In this sense Paul can say that the gentiles are a law to themselves—not in the sense of the modern liberal notions of autonomy, which preclude transcendence of the subject, but in the much deeper sense that nothing belongs less to me than I myself. My own "I" is the site of the profoundest surpassing of self and contact with him from whom I came and toward whom I am going.

In these sentences, Paul expresses the experience which he had had as missionary to the gentiles and which Israel may have experienced before him in dealings with the "god-fearing." Israel could have experienced among the gentiles what the ambassadors of Jesus Christ found reconfirmed. Their proclamation answered an expectation. Their proclamation encountered an antecedent basic knowledge of the essential constants of the will of God, which came to be written down in the commandments, which can be found in all cultures, and which can be all the more clearly elucidated the less an overbearing cultural bias distorts this primordial knowledge. The more man lives in "fear of the Lord" (consider the story of Cornelius, especially Acts 10:34–35), the more concretely and clearly effective this anamnesis becomes.

Again, let us take a formulation of St. Basil. The love of God, which is concrete in the commandments, is not imposed on us from without, the church father emphasizes, but has been implanted in us beforehand. The sense for the good has been stamped upon us, as Augustine puts it. We can now appreciate Newman's toast first to conscience and then to the pope. The pope cannot impose commandments on faithful Catholics because he wants to or finds it expedient. Such a modern, voluntaristic concept of authority can only distort the true theological meaning of the papacy. The true nature of the Petrine office has become so incomprehensible in the modern age no doubt because we think of authority only in terms that do not allow for bridges between subject and object. Accordingly, everything that does not come from the subject is thought to be externally imposed.

But the situation is really quite different according to the anthropology of conscience, of which we have tried to come to an appreciation in these reflections. The anamnesis instilled in our being needs, one might say, assistance from without so that it can become aware of itself. But this "from without" is not something set in opposition to anamnesis but is ordered to it. It has maieutic function, imposes nothing foreign, but brings to fruition what is proper to anamnesis, namely, its interior openness to the truth.

When we are dealing with the question of faith and church, whose radius extends from the redeeming Logos over the gift of creation, we must, however, take into account yet another dimension, which is especially developed in the Johannine writings. John is familiar with the anamnesis of the new "we," which is granted to us in the incorporation into Christ (one body, that is, one "I" with him). In remembering, they knew him, as the Gospel has it in a number of places.

The original encounter with Jesus gave the disciples what all generations thereafter receive in their foundational encounter with the Lord in baptism and the Eucharist, namely, the new anamnesis of faith, which unfolds, like the anamnesis of creation, in constant dialogue between *within* and *without*. In contrast to the presumption of gnostic teachers, who wanted to convince the faithful that their naive faith must be understood and applied much differently, John could say, You do not need such instruction; as anointed ones (baptized ones) you know everything (see 1 John 2:20).

This does not mean a factual omniscience on the part of the faithful. It does signify, however, the sureness of the Christian memory. This Christian memory, to be sure, is always learning, but proceeding from its sacramental identity, it also distinguishes *from within* between what is a genuine unfolding of its recollection and what is its destruction or falsification. In the crisis of the Church today, the power of this recollection and the truth of the apostolic word are experienced in an entirely new way, where (much more so than hierarchical direction) it is the power of memory of the simple faith that leads to the discernment of spirits.

One can comprehend the primacy of the pope and its correlation to Christian conscience only in this connection. The true sense of the teaching authority of the pope consists in his being the advocate of the Christian memory. The pope does not impose from without. Rather, he elucidates the Christian memory and defends it. For this reason the toast to conscience indeed must precede the toast to the pope, because without conscience there would not be a papacy. All power that the papacy has is power of conscience. It is service to the double memory on which the faith is based—and which again and again must be purified, expanded, and defended against the destruction of memory that is threatened by a subjectivity forgetful of its own foundation, as well as by the pressures of social and cultural conformity.

Conscientia

Having considered this first, essentially ontological level of the concept of conscience, we must now turn to its second level—that of judgment and decision, which the medieval tradition designates with the single word *conscientia*, conscience. Presumably this terminological tradition has not insignificantly contributed to the diminution of the concept of conscience. Saint Thomas, for example, designates only this second level as *conscientia*. For him it stands to reason that conscience is not a *habitus*, that is, a lasting ontic quality of man, but *actus*, an event in execution. Thomas, of course, assumes as given the ontological foundation of anamnesis (*synderesis*). He describes anamnesis as an inner repugnance to evil and attraction to the good.

The act of conscience applies this basic knowledge to the particular situation. It is divided, according to Thomas, into three elements: recognizing (*recognoscere*), bearing witness (*testificari*), and finally judging (*iudicare*). One might speak of an interaction between a function of control and a function of decision. Thomas sees this sequence according

330

to the Aristotelian tradition's model of deductive reasoning. But he is careful to emphasize what is peculiar to this knowledge of moral actions whose conclusions do not come from mere knowing or thinking.

Whether something is recognized or not depends too on the will, which can block the way to recognition or lead to it. It is dependent, that is to say, on an already formed moral character, which can either continue to deform or be further purified. On this level, the level of judgment (*conscientia* in the narrower sense), it can be said that even the erroneous conscience binds. This statement is completely intelligible from the rational tradition of scholasticism. No one may act against his convictions, as St. Paul had already said (Rom. 14:23). But this fact— that the conviction a person has come to certainly binds in the moment of acting—does not signify a canonization of subjectivity. It is never wrong to follow the convictions one has arrived at—in fact, one must do so. But it can very well be wrong to have come to such askew convictions in the first place, by having stifled the protest of the anamnesis of being.

The guilt lies then in a different place, much deeper—not in the present act, not in the present judgment of conscience, but in the neglect of my being that made me deaf to the internal promptings of truth. For this reason, criminals of conviction like Hitler and Stalin are guilty. These crass examples should not serve to put us at ease but should rouse us to take seriously the earnestness of the plea, "Free me from my unknown guilt" (Ps. 19:13).

CHAPTER 52

The Problem of Practical Atheism

In this passage, drawn from a weekly audience in 2012, Benedict XVI cautions against some of the modern challenges to faith, including a "practical" atheism in which a person affirms belief in God but lives "as though God did not exist."

Earlier, we reflected on the desire for God that human beings carry deep within them. . . . I would like to continue to examine this aspect, meditating briefly with you on some of the ways to attain knowledge of God. I wish to recall, however, that God's initiative always precedes every human initiative and on our journey towards him too it is he who first illuminates us, who directs and guides us, ever respecting our inner freedom. It is always he who admits us to intimacy with him, revealing himself and giving us the grace to be able to accept this revelation in faith. Let us never forget St. Augustine's experience: it is not we who possess the Truth after having sought it, but the Truth that seeks us out and possesses us.

Nonetheless there are ways that can open the human heart to knowledge of God, there are signs that lead to God. Of course, we often risk being dazzled by the glare of worldliness that makes us less able to follow these paths and to read these signs. Yet God never tires of seeking us, he is faithful to the human being whom he created and redeemed, he stays close to us in our life because he loves us. This is a certainty that must accompany us every day, even if a certain widespread mentality makes it harder for the Church and for Christians to communicate to every creature the joy of the Gospel and to lead everyone to the encounter with Jesus, the one Savior of the world.

However, this is our mission. It is the mission of the Church and every believer must carry it out joyously, feeling it his own, through an existence truly enlivened by faith, marked by charity, by service to God and to others, and that can radiate hope. This mission shines out above all in the holiness to which we are all called.

Today—as we know—faith, which is all too often not properly understood and contested or rejected, encounters no lack of difficulties and trials. St. Peter said to his Christians: "Always be prepared to make a defense to anyone who calls you to account for the hope that is in you, yet do it with gentleness and reverence" (1 Pet. 3:15). In the past, in the West, in a society deemed Christian, faith was the context in which people acted; the reference and adherence to God were part of daily life for the majority. Rather, it was the person who did not believe who had to justify his or her own incredulity. In our world the situation has changed and, increasingly, it is believers who must be able to account for their faith. In his Encyclical *Fides et Ratio* Blessed John Paul II stressed that faith is also put to the test in our day, riddled with subtle and captious forms of atheism, both theoretical and practical (cf. nos. 46–47). Ever since the Enlightenment the criticism of religion has been gathering momentum; history has also come to be marked by the presence of atheistic systems in which God was seen as a mere projection of the human mind, an illusion and the product of a society already misled by so many alienating factors. Moreover the past century experienced a strong process of secularization under the banner of the absolute autonomy of the human being, considered as the measure and architect of reality, but impoverished by being created "in the image and likeness of God." A particularly dangerous phenomenon for faith has arisen in our times: indeed a form of atheism exists which we define, precisely, as "practical," in which the truths of faith or religious rites are not denied but are merely deemed irrelevant to daily life, detached from life, pointless. So it is that people often believe in God in a superficial manner, and live "as though God did not exist" (*etsi Deus non daretur*). In the end, however, this way of life proves even more destructive because it leads to indifference to faith and to the question of God.

In fact human beings, separated from God, are reduced to a single dimension—the horizontal—and this reductionism itself is one of the fundamental causes of the various forms of totalitarianism that have had tragic consequences in the past century, as well as of the crisis of values that we see in the current situation. By obscuring the reference to God the ethical horizon has also been obscured, to leave room for relativism and for an ambiguous conception of freedom which, instead of being liberating, ends by binding human beings to idols. The temptations that Jesus faced in the wilderness before his public ministry vividly symbolize which "idols" entice human beings when they do not go beyond themselves. Were God to lose his centrality man would lose his rightful place, he would no longer fit into creation, into relations with others. What ancient wisdom evokes with the myth of Prometheus has not faded: man thinks he himself can become a "god," master of life and death.

With this picture before her, the Church, faithful to Christ's mandate, never ceases to affirm the truth about man and about his destiny. The Second Vatican Council affirms it concisely: "The dignity of man rests above all on the fact that he is called to communion with God. The invitation to converse with God is addressed to man as soon as he comes into being. For if man exists it is because God has created him through love, and through love continues to hold him in existence. He cannot live fully according to truth unless he freely acknowledges that love and unless he entrusts himself to his Creator" (Pastoral Constitution on the Church in the Modern World, *Gaudium et Spes*, no. 19).

What answers, therefore, is faith required to give, "with gentleness and reverence" to atheism, to skepticism, to indifference to the vertical dimension, in order that the people of our time may continue to ponder on the existence of God and take paths that lead to him? I want to point out several paths that derive both from natural reflection and from the power of faith itself. I would like to sum them up very briefly in three words: the world, man, faith.

The first word: the world. St. Augustine, who spent much of his life seeking the Truth and was grasped by the Truth, wrote a very beautiful and famous passage in which he said: "Question the beauty of the earth, question the beauty of the sea, question the beauty of the air distending and diffusing itself, question the beauty of the sky . . . question all these realities. All respond: 'See, we are beautiful.' Their beauty is a profession [*confessio*]. These beauties are subject to change. Who made them if not the Beautiful One [*Pulcher*] who is not subject to change?" (*Sermo* 241, 2: PL 38, 1134).

I think we should recover—and enable people today to recover—our capacity for contemplating creation, its beauty and its structure. The world is not a shapeless mass of magma, but the better we know it and the better we discover its marvelous mechanisms the more clearly we can see a plan, we see that there is a creative intelligence. Albert Einstein said that in natural law is revealed "an intelligence of such superiority that, compared with it, all the systematic thinking and acting of human beings is an utterly insignificant reflection" (*The World As I See It*, 1949). Consequently a first path that leads to the discovery of God is an attentive contemplation of creation.

The second word: man. Again, St. Augustine was to write a famous sentence in which he says that God is more intimate to me than I am to myself (cf. *Confessions* III, 6, 11).

Hence he formulates the invitation, "do not go outside yourself, return to yourself: the truth is higher than my highest and more inward than my innermost self" (*De Vera Religione*, 39, 72). This is another aspect that we risk losing in the noisy and dispersive world in which we live: the ability to pause and look deeply into ourselves and to reinterpret the thirst for the infinite that we bear within us, that impels us to go further and to refer to the One who can quench it. The *Catechism of the Catholic Church* says: "with his openness to truth and beauty, his sense of moral goodness, his freedom and the voice of his conscience, with his longings for the infinite and for happiness, man questions himself about God's existence" (no. 33).

The third word: faith. We must not forget, especially in the situation of our time, that the life of faith is a path which leads to the knowledge of and encounter with God. Those who believe are united to God and open to his grace, to the power of his love. Thus their existence becomes a witness, not of themselves but of the Risen One, and their faith does not hesitate to shine out in daily life, open to dialogue that expresses deep friendship for the journey of every human being and can bring hope to people in need of redemption, happiness, a future. Faith, in fact, is an encounter with God who speaks and works in history and converts our daily life, transforming within us mentalities, value judgements, decisions, and practical actions. Faith is not an illusion, a flight of fancy, a refuge, or sentimentalism; rather it is total involvement in the whole of life and is the proclamation of the Gospel, the Good News that can set the whole of the person free. A Christian and a community that are active and faithful to the plan of God who loved us first, are privileged paths for those immersed in indifference or in doubt about their life and action. However, this asks each and every one to make their testimony of faith ever more transparent, purifying their life so that it may be in conformity with Christ. Many people today have a limited idea of the Christian faith, because they identify it with a mere system of beliefs and values rather than with the truth of a God who revealed himself in history, anxious to communicate with human beings in a tête-à-tête, in a relationship of love with them. In fact, at the root of every doctrine or value is the event of the encounter between man and God in Jesus Christ. Christianity, before being a moral or an ethic, is the event of love, it is the acceptance of the Person of Jesus. For this reason the Christian and Christian communities must first look and make others look to Christ, the true Way that leads to God.

CHAPTER 53

Defending the Rationality
of Faith

In this selection, taken from his 2006 Regensburg Address, Benedict XVI argues for the critical role of reason in religion, affirming that God acts with "both reason and word—a reason which is creative and capable of self-communication, precisely as reason."

It is a moving experience for me to be back again in the university and to be able once again to give a lecture at this podium. I think back to those years when, after a pleasant period at the Freisinger Hochschule, I began teaching at the University of Bonn. That was in 1959, in the days of the old university made up of ordinary professors. The various chairs had neither assistants nor secretaries, but in recompense there was much direct contact with students and in particular among the professors themselves. We would meet before and after lessons in the rooms of the teaching staff. There was a lively exchange with historians, philosophers, philologists and, naturally, between the two theological faculties. Once a semester there was a *dies academicus*, when professors from every faculty appeared before the students of the entire university, making possible a genuine experience of *universitas*—something that you too, Magnificent Rector, just mentioned—the experience, in other words, of the fact that despite our specializations which at times make it difficult to communicate with each other, we made up a whole, working in everything on the basis of a single rationality with its various aspects and sharing responsibility for the right use of reason—this reality became a lived experience. The university was also very proud of its two theological faculties. It was clear that, by inquiring about the reasonableness of faith, they too carried out a work which is necessarily part of the "whole" of the *universitas scientiarum*, even if not everyone could share the faith which theologians seek to correlate with reason as a whole. This profound sense of coherence within the universe of reason was not troubled, even when it was once reported that a colleague had said there was something odd about our university: it had two faculties devoted to something that did not exist: God. That even in the face of such radical skepticism it is still necessary and reasonable to raise the question of God through the use of reason, and to do so in the context of the tradition of the Christian faith: this, within the university as a whole, was accepted without question.

I was reminded of all this recently, when I read the edition by Professor Theodore Khoury (Münster) of part of the dialogue carried on—perhaps in 1391 in the winter barracks near Ankara—by the erudite Byzantine emperor Manuel II Paleologus and an educated Persian on the subject of Christianity and Islam, and the truth of both. It was presumably the emperor himself who set down this dialogue, during the siege of Constantinople between 1394 and 1402; and this would explain why his arguments are given in greater detail than those of his Persian interlocutor. The dialogue ranges widely over the structures of faith contained in the Bible and in the Qur'an, and deals especially with the image of God and of man, while necessarily returning repeatedly to the relationship between—as they were called—three "Laws" or "rules of life": the Old Testament, the New Testament, and the Qur'an. It is not my intention to discuss this question in the present lecture; here I would like to discuss only one point—itself rather marginal to the dialogue as a whole—which, in the context of the issue of "faith and reason," I found interesting and which can serve as the starting-point for my reflections on this issue.

In the seventh conversation (διάλεξις—controversy) edited by Professor Khoury, the emperor touches on the theme of the holy war. The emperor must have known that surah 2, 256 reads: "There is no compulsion in religion." According to some of the experts, this is probably one of the suras of the early period, when Mohammed was still

338

powerless and under threat. But naturally the emperor also knew the instructions, developed later and recorded in the Qur'an, concerning holy war. Without descending to details, such as the difference in treatment accorded to those who have the "Book" and the "infidels," he addresses his interlocutor with a startling brusqueness, a brusqueness that we find unacceptable, on the central question about the relationship between religion and violence in general, saying: "Show me just what Mohammed brought that was new, and there you will find things only evil and inhuman, such as his command to spread by the sword the faith he preached."[1] The emperor, after having expressed himself so forcefully, goes on to explain in detail the reasons why spreading the faith through violence is something unreasonable. Violence is incompatible with the nature of God and the nature of the soul. "God," he says, "is not pleased by blood—and not acting reasonably (σὺν λόγω) is contrary to God's nature. Faith is born of the soul, not the body. Whoever would lead someone to faith needs the ability to speak well and to reason properly, without violence and threats. . . . To convince a reasonable soul, one does not need a strong arm, or weapons of any kind, or any other means of threatening a person with death . . ."

The decisive statement in this argument against violent conversion is this: not to act in accordance with reason is contrary to God's nature.[2] The editor, Theodore Khoury, observes: For the emperor, as a Byzantine shaped by Greek philosophy, this statement is self-evident. But for Muslim teaching, God is absolutely transcendent. His will is not bound up with any of our categories, even that of rationality. Here Khoury quotes a work of the noted French Islamist R. Arnaldez, who points out that Ibn Hazm went so far as to state that God is not bound

---

1. In the Muslim world, this quotation has unfortunately been taken as an expression of my personal position, thus arousing understandable indignation. I hope that the reader of my text can see immediately that this sentence does not express my personal view of the Qur'an, for which I have the respect due to the holy book of a great religion. In quoting the text of the Emperor Manuel II, I intended solely to draw out the essential relationship between faith and reason. On this point I am in agreement with Manuel II, but without endorsing his polemic.

2. It was purely for the sake of this statement that I quoted the dialogue between Manuel and his Persian interlocutor. In this statement the theme of my subsequent reflections emerges.

even by his own word, and that nothing would oblige him to reveal the truth to us. Were it God's will, we would even have to practice idolatry.

At this point, as far as understanding of God and thus the concrete practice of religion is concerned, we are faced with an unavoidable dilemma. Is the conviction that acting unreasonably contradicts God's nature merely a Greek idea, or is it always and intrinsically true? I believe that here we can see the profound harmony between what is Greek in the best sense of the word and the biblical understanding of faith in God. Modifying the first verse of the Book of Genesis, the first verse of the whole Bible, John began the prologue of his Gospel with the words: "In the beginning was the λόγος." This is the very word used by the emperor: God acts, σὺν λόγω, with *logos*. *Logos* means both reason and word—a reason which is creative and capable of self-communication, precisely as reason. John thus spoke the final word on the biblical concept of God, and in this word all the often toilsome and tortuous threads of biblical faith find their culmination and synthesis. In the beginning was the *logos*, and the *logos* is God, says the Evangelist. The encounter between the Biblical message and Greek thought did not happen by chance. The vision of Saint Paul, who saw the roads to Asia barred and in a dream saw a Macedonian man plead with him: "Come over to Macedonia and help us!" (cf. Acts 16:6–10)—this vision can be interpreted as a "distillation" of the intrinsic necessity of a rapprochement between Biblical faith and Greek inquiry.

In point of fact, this rapprochement had been going on for some time. The mysterious name of God, revealed from the burning bush, a name which separates this God from all other divinities with their many names and simply asserts being, "I am," already presents a challenge to the notion of myth, to which Socrates' attempt to vanquish and transcend myth stands in close analogy. Within the Old Testament, the process which started at the burning bush came to new maturity at the time of the Exile, when the God of Israel, an Israel now deprived of its land and worship, was proclaimed as the God of heaven and earth and described in a simple formula which echoes the words uttered at the burning bush: "I am." This new understanding of God is accompanied by a kind of enlightenment, which finds stark expression in the mockery of gods who are merely the work of human hands (cf. Ps. 115). Thus, despite the bitter conflict with those Hellenistic rulers who sought to accommodate it forcibly to the customs and idolatrous cult of the Greeks, biblical faith, in the Hellenistic period, encountered the best of Greek thought at a deep level, resulting in a mutual enrichment evident especially in the later wisdom literature. Today we know that the Greek translation of the Old Testament produced at Alexandria—the Septuagint—is more than a simple (and in that sense really less than satisfactory) translation of the Hebrew text: it is an independent textual witness and a distinct and important step in the history of revelation, one which brought about this encounter in a way that was decisive for the birth and spread of Christianity. A profound encounter of faith and reason is taking place here, an encounter between genuine enlightenment and religion. From the very heart of Christian faith and, at the same time, the heart of Greek thought now joined to faith, Manuel II was able to say: Not to act "with *logos*" is contrary to God's nature.

In all honesty, one must observe that in the late Middle Ages we find trends in theology which would sunder this synthesis between the Greek spirit and the Christian spirit. In contrast with the so-called intellectualism of Augustine and Thomas, there arose with Duns Scotus a voluntarism which, in its later developments, led to the claim that we can only know God's *voluntas ordinata*. Beyond this is the realm of God's freedom, in virtue of which he could have done the opposite of everything he has actually done. This gives rise to positions which clearly approach those of Ibn Hazm and might even lead to the image of a capricious God, who is not even bound to truth and goodness. God's transcendence and otherness are so exalted that our reason, our sense of the true and good, are no longer an authentic mirror of God, whose deepest possibilities remain eternally unattainable and hidden behind his actual decisions. As opposed to this, the faith of the Church has always insisted that between God and us, between his eternal Creator

Spirit and our created reason there exists a real analogy, in which—
as the Fourth Lateran Council in 1215 stated—unlikeness remains
infinitely greater than likeness, yet not to the point of abolishing analogy and its language. God does not become more divine when we push
him away from us in a sheer, impenetrable voluntarism; rather, the truly
divine God is the God who has revealed himself as *logos* and, as *logos*,
has acted and continues to act lovingly on our behalf. Certainly, love,
as Saint Paul says, "transcends" knowledge and is thereby capable of
perceiving more than thought alone (cf. Eph. 3:19); nonetheless it continues to be love of the God who is *Logos*. Consequently, Christian
worship is, again to quote Paul, "λογικη λατρεία," worship in harmony
with the eternal Word and with our reason (cf. Rom. 12:1).

This inner rapprochement between Biblical faith and Greek philosophical inquiry was an event of decisive importance not only from
the standpoint of the history of religions, but also from that of world
history—it is an event which concerns us even today. Given this convergence, it is not surprising that Christianity, despite its origins and
some significant developments in the East, finally took on its historically decisive character in Europe. We can also express this the other
way around: this convergence, with the subsequent addition of the
Roman heritage, created Europe and remains the foundation of what
can rightly be called Europe.

The thesis that the critically purified Greek heritage forms an
integral part of Christian faith has been countered by the call for a
dehellenization of Christianity—a call which has more and more dominated theological discussions since the beginning of the modern age.
Viewed more closely, three stages can be observed in the program of
dehellenization: although interconnected, they are clearly distinct from
one another in their motivations and objectives.

Dehellenization first emerges in connection with the postulates
of the Reformation in the sixteenth century. Looking at the tradition
of scholastic theology, the Reformers thought they were confronted
with a faith system totally conditioned by philosophy, that is to say an

articulation of the faith based on an alien system of thought. As a result, faith no longer appeared as a living historical Word but as one element of an overarching philosophical system. The principle of *sola scriptura*, on the other hand, sought faith in its pure, primordial form, as originally found in the biblical Word. Metaphysics appeared as a premise derived from another source, from which faith had to be liberated in order to become once more fully itself. When Kant stated that he needed to set thinking aside in order to make room for faith, he carried this program forward with a radicalism that the Reformers could never have foreseen. He thus anchored faith exclusively in practical reason, denying it access to reality as a whole.

The liberal theology of the nineteenth and twentieth centuries ushered in a second stage in the process of dehellenization, with Adolf von Harnack as its outstanding representative. When I was a student, and in the early years of my teaching, this program was highly influential in Catholic theology too. It took as its point of departure Pascal's distinction between the God of the philosophers and the God of Abraham, Isaac, and Jacob. In my inaugural lecture at Bonn in 1959, I tried to address the issue, and I do not intend to repeat here what I said on that occasion, but I would like to describe at least briefly what was new about this second stage of dehellenization. Harnack's central idea was to return simply to the man Jesus and to his simple message, underneath the accretions of theology and indeed of Hellenization: this simple message was seen as the culmination of the religious development of humanity. Jesus was said to have put an end to worship in favor of morality. In the end he was presented as the father of a humanitarian moral message. Fundamentally, Harnack's goal was to bring Christianity back into harmony with modern reason, liberating it, that is to say, from seemingly philosophical and theological elements, such as faith in Christ's divinity and the triune God. In this sense, historical-critical exegesis of the New Testament, as he saw it, restored to theology its place within the university: theology, for Harnack, is something essentially historical and therefore strictly scientific. What it is able to say critically about Jesus is, so to speak, an expression of practical reason and consequently it can take its rightful place within the university. Behind this thinking lies the modern self-limitation of reason, classically expressed in Kant's "Critiques," but in the meantime further radicalized by the impact of the natural sciences. This modern concept of reason is based, to put it briefly, on a synthesis between Platonism (Cartesianism) and empiricism, a synthesis confirmed by the success of technology. On the one hand it presupposes the mathematical structure of matter, its intrinsic rationality, which makes it possible to understand how matter works and use it efficiently: this basic premise is, so to speak, the Platonic element in the modern understanding of nature. On the other hand, there is nature's capacity to be exploited for our purposes, and here only the possibility of verification or falsification through experimentation can yield decisive certainty. The weight between the two poles can, depending on the circumstances, shift from one side to the other. As strongly positivistic a thinker as J. Monod has declared himself a convinced Platonist/Cartesian.

This gives rise to two principles which are crucial for the issue we have raised. First, only the kind of certainty resulting from the interplay of mathematical and empirical elements can be considered scientific. Anything that would claim to be science must be measured against this criterion. Hence the human sciences, such as history, psychology, sociology, and philosophy, attempt to conform themselves to this canon of scientificity. A second point, which is important for our reflections, is that by its very nature this method excludes the question of God, making it appear an unscientific or pre-scientific question. Consequently, we are faced with a reduction of the radius of science and reason, one which needs to be questioned.

I will return to this problem later. In the meantime, it must be observed that from this standpoint any attempt to maintain theology's claim to be "scientific" would end up reducing Christianity to a mere fragment of its former self. But we must say more: if science as a whole is this and this alone, then it is man himself who ends up being reduced, for the specifically human questions about our origin and destiny, the questions raised by religion and ethics, then have no place within the purview of collective reason as defined by "science," so understood, and must thus be relegated to the realm of the subjective. The subject then decides, on the basis of his experiences, what he considers tenable in matters of religion, and the subjective "conscience" becomes the sole arbiter of what is ethical. In this way, though, ethics and religion lose their power to create a community and become a completely personal matter. This is a dangerous state of affairs for humanity, as we see from the disturbing pathologies of religion and reason which necessarily erupt when reason is so reduced that questions of religion and ethics no longer concern it. Attempts to construct an ethic from the rules of evolution or from psychology and sociology end up being simply inadequate.

Before I draw the conclusions to which all this has been leading, I must briefly refer to the third stage of dehellenization, which is now in progress. In the light of our experience with cultural pluralism, it is often said nowadays that the synthesis with Hellenism achieved in the early Church was an initial inculturation which ought not to be binding on other cultures. The latter are said to have the right to return to the simple message of the New Testament prior to that inculturation, in order to inculturate it anew in their own particular milieux. This thesis is not simply false, but it is coarse and lacking in precision. The New Testament was written in Greek and bears the imprint of the Greek spirit, which had already come to maturity as the Old Testament developed. True, there are elements in the evolution of the early Church which do not have to be integrated into all cultures. Nonetheless, the fundamental decisions made about the relationship between faith and the use of human reason are part of the faith itself; they are developments consonant with the nature of faith itself.

And so I come to my conclusion. This attempt, painted with broad strokes, at a critique of modern reason from within has nothing to do with putting the clock back to the time before the Enlightenment and rejecting the insights of the modern age. The positive aspects of modernity are to be acknowledged unreservedly: we are all grateful for the marvelous possibilities that it has opened up for mankind and for the progress in humanity that has been granted to us. The scientific ethos, moreover, is—as you yourself mentioned, Magnificent Rector—the will to be obedient to the truth, and, as such, it embodies an attitude which belongs to the essential decisions of the Christian spirit. The intention here is not one of retrenchment or negative criticism, but of broadening our concept of reason and its application. While we rejoice in the new possibilities open to humanity, we also see the dangers arising from these possibilities and we must ask ourselves how we can overcome them. We will succeed in doing so only if reason and faith come together in a new way, if we overcome the self-imposed limitation of reason to the empirically falsifiable, and if we once more disclose its vast horizons. In this sense theology rightly belongs in the university and within the wide-ranging dialogue of sciences, not merely as a historical discipline and one of the human sciences, but precisely as theology, as inquiry into the rationality of faith.

Only thus do we become capable of that genuine dialogue of cultures and religions so urgently needed today. In the Western world it is widely held that only positivistic reason and the forms of philosophy based on it are universally valid. Yet the world's profoundly religious cultures see this exclusion of the divine from the universality of reason as an attack on their most profound convictions. A reason which is deaf to the divine and which relegates religion into the realm of subcultures is incapable of entering into the dialogue of cultures. At the same time, as I have attempted to show, modern scientific reason with its intrinsically Platonic element bears within itself a question which points beyond itself and beyond the possibilities of its methodology. Modern scientific reason quite simply has to accept the rational structure of matter and the correspondence between our spirit and the prevailing rational structures of nature as a given, on which its methodology has to be based. Yet the question why this has to be so is a real question, and one which has to be remanded by the natural sciences to other modes and

346

planes of thought—to philosophy and theology. For philosophy and, albeit in a different way, for theology, listening to the great experiences and insights of the religious traditions of humanity, and those of the Christian faith in particular, is a source of knowledge, and to ignore it would be an unacceptable restriction of our listening and responding. Here I am reminded of something Socrates said to Phaedo. In their earlier conversations, many false philosophical opinions had been raised, and so Socrates says: "It would be easily understandable if someone became so annoyed at all these false notions that for the rest of his life he despised and mocked all talk about being—but in this way he would be deprived of the truth of existence and would suffer a great loss." The West has long been endangered by this aversion to the questions which underlie its rationality, and can only suffer great harm thereby. The courage to engage the whole breadth of reason, and not the denial of its grandeur—this is the program with which a theology grounded in Biblical faith enters into the debates of our time. "Not to act reasonably, not to act with *logos*, is contrary to the nature of God," said Manuel II, according to his Christian understanding of God, in response to his Persian interlocutor. It is to this great *logos*, to this breadth of reason, that we invite our partners in the dialogue of cultures. To rediscover it constantly is the great task of the university.

CHAPTER 54

The Development of Peoples and Technology

In this excerpt from his 2009 social encyclical *Caritas in Veritate* (*Charity in Truth*), Benedict XVI discusses both the promises and the dangers of technological progress in its relation to the development of peoples around the world. He emphasizes the primary place of morality in such development, writing that it "must include not just material growth but also spiritual growth."

The development of peoples is intimately linked to the development of individuals. The human person by nature is actively involved in his own development. The development in question is not simply the result of natural mechanisms, since as everybody knows, we are all capable of making free and responsible choices. Nor is it merely at the mercy of our caprice, since we all know that we are a gift, not something self-generated. Our freedom is profoundly shaped by our being, and by its limits. No one shapes his own conscience arbitrarily, but we all build our own "I" on the basis of a "self" which is given to us. Not only are other persons outside our control, but each one of us is outside his or her own control. *A person's development is compromised, if he claims to be solely responsible for producing what he becomes.* By analogy, the development of peoples goes awry if humanity thinks it can re-create itself through the "wonders" of technology, just as economic development is exposed as a destructive sham if it relies on the "wonders" of finance in order to sustain unnatural and consumerist growth. In the face of such Promethean presumption, we must fortify our love for a freedom that is not merely arbitrary, but is rendered truly human by acknowledgment of the good that underlies it. To this end, man needs to look inside himself in order to recognize the fundamental norms of the natural moral law which God has written on our hearts.

The challenge of development today is closely linked to *technological progress*, with its astounding applications in the field of biology. Technology—it is worth emphasizing—is a profoundly human reality, linked to the autonomy and freedom of man. In technology we express and confirm the hegemony of the spirit over matter. "The human spirit, 'increasingly free of its bondage to creatures, can be more easily drawn to the worship and contemplation of the Creator.'"[1] Technology enables us to exercise dominion over matter, to reduce risks, to save labor, to improve our conditions of life. It touches the heart of the vocation of human labor: in technology, seen as the product of his genius, man recognizes himself and forges his own humanity. Technology is the objective side of human action[2] whose origin and *raison d'etre* is found in the subjective element: the worker himself. For this reason, technology is never merely technology. It reveals man and his aspirations towards development, it expresses the inner tension that impels him gradually to overcome material limitations. *Technology, in this sense, is a response to God's command to till and to keep the land* (cf. Gen. 2:15) that he has entrusted to humanity, and it must serve to reinforce the covenant between human beings and the environment, a covenant that should mirror God's creative love.

Technological development can give rise to the idea that technology is self-sufficient when too much attention is given to the "*how*" questions, and not enough to the many "*why*" questions underlying human activity. For this reason technology can appear ambivalent. Produced through human creativity as a tool of personal freedom, technology can be understood as a manifestation of absolute freedom, the freedom that seeks to prescind from the limits inherent in things.

---

1. Paul VI, Encyclical Letter *Populorum Progressio*, 41: loc. cit., 277–278; cf. Second Vatican Ecumenical Council, Pastoral Constitution on the Church in the Modern World *Gaudium et Spes*, 57.

2. Cf. John Paul II, Encyclical Letter *Laborem Exercens*, 5: loc. cit., 586–589.

The process of globalization could replace ideologies with technology,[3] allowing the latter to become an ideological power that threatens to confine us within an *a priori* that holds us back from encountering being and truth. Were that to happen, we would all know, evaluate, and make decisions about our life situations from within a technocratic cultural perspective to which we would belong structurally, without ever being able to discover a meaning that is not of our own making. The "technical" worldview that follows from this vision is now so dominant that truth has come to be seen as coinciding with the possible. But when the sole criterion of truth is efficiency and utility, development is automatically denied. True development does not consist primarily in "doing." The key to development is a mind capable of thinking in technological terms and grasping the fully human meaning of human activities, within the context of the holistic meaning of the individual's being. Even when we work through satellites or through remote electronic impulses, our actions always remain human, an expression of our responsible freedom. Technology is highly attractive because it draws us out of our physical limitations and broadens our horizon. *But human freedom is authentic only when it responds to the fascination of technology with decisions that are the fruit of moral responsibility.* Hence the pressing need for formation in an ethically responsible use of technology. Moving beyond the fascination that technology exerts, we must reappropriate the true meaning of freedom, which is not an intoxication with total autonomy, but a response to the call of being, beginning with our own personal being.

This deviation from solid humanistic principles that a technical mindset can produce is seen today in certain technological applications in the fields of development and peace. Often the development of peoples is considered a matter of financial engineering, the freeing up of markets, the removal of tariffs, investment in production, and institutional reforms—in other words, a purely technical matter. All these factors are of great importance, but we have to ask why technical choices made thus far have yielded rather mixed results. We need to

---

3. Cf. Paul VI, Apostolic Letter *Octogesima Adveniens*, 29: loc. cit., 420.

think hard about the cause. Development will never be fully guaranteed through automatic or impersonal forces, whether they derive from the market or from international politics. *Development is impossible without upright men and women, without financiers and politicians whose consciences are finely attuned to the requirements of the common good.* Both professional competence and moral consistency are necessary. When technology is allowed to take over, the result is confusion between ends and means, such that the sole criterion for action in business is thought to be the maximization of profit, in politics the consolidation of power, and in science the findings of research. Often, underneath the intricacies of economic, financial, and political interconnections, there remain misunderstandings, hardships, and injustice. The flow of technological know-how increases, but it is those in possession of it who benefit, while the situation on the ground for the peoples who live in its shadow remains unchanged: for them there is little chance of emancipation.

Even peace can run the risk of being considered a technical product, merely the outcome of agreements between governments or of initiatives aimed at ensuring effective economic aid. It is true that *peacebuilding* requires the constant interplay of diplomatic contacts, economic, technological, and cultural exchanges, agreements on common projects, as well as joint strategies to curb the threat of military conflict and to root out the underlying causes of terrorism. Nevertheless, if such efforts are to have lasting effects, they must be based on values rooted in the truth of human life. That is, the voice of the peoples affected must be heard and their situation must be taken into consideration, if their expectations are to be correctly interpreted. One must align oneself, so to speak, with the unsung efforts of so many individuals deeply committed to bringing peoples together and to facilitating development on the basis of love and mutual understanding. Among them are members of the Christian faithful, involved in the great task of upholding the fully human dimension of development and peace.

Linked to technological development is the increasingly pervasive presence of the *means of social communications.* It is almost impossible today to imagine the life of the human family without them. For better or for worse, they are so integral a part of life today that it seems quite absurd to maintain that they are neutral—and hence unaffected by any moral considerations concerning people. Often such views, stressing the strictly technical nature of the media, effectively support their subordination to economic interests intent on dominating the market and, not least, to attempts to impose cultural models that serve ideological and political agendas. Given the media's fundamental importance in engineering changes in attitude towards reality and the human person, we must reflect carefully on their influence, especially in regard to the ethical-cultural dimension of globalization and the development of peoples in solidarity. Mirroring what is required for an ethical approach to globalization and development, so too the *meaning and purpose of the media must be sought within an anthropological perspective.* This means that they can have a *civilizing effect* not only when, thanks to technological development, they increase the possibilities of communicating information, but above all when they are geared towards a vision of the person and the common good that reflects truly universal values. Just because social communications increase the possibilities of interconnection and the dissemination of ideas, it does not follow that they promote freedom or internationalize development and democracy for all. To achieve goals of this kind, they need to focus on promoting the dignity of persons and peoples, they need to be clearly inspired by charity and placed at the service of truth, of the good, and of natural and supernatural fraternity. In fact, human freedom is intrinsically linked with these higher values. The media can make an important contribution towards the growth in communion of the human family and the *ethos* of society when they are used to promote universal participation in the common search for what is just.

A particularly crucial battleground in today's cultural struggle between the supremacy of technology and human moral responsibility is the field of *bioethics*, where the very possibility of integral human development is radically called into question. In this most delicate and critical area, the fundamental question asserts itself forcefully: is man the product of his own labors or does he depend on God? Scientific discoveries in this field and the possibilities of technological intervention seem so advanced as to force a choice between two types of reasoning: reason open to transcendence or reason closed within immanence. We are presented with a clear *either/or*. Yet the rationality of a self-centered use of technology proves to be irrational because it implies a decisive rejection of meaning and value. It is no coincidence that closing the door to transcendence brings one up short against a difficulty: how could being emerge from nothing, how could intelligence be born from chance?[4] Faced with these dramatic questions, reason and faith can come to each other's assistance. Only together will they save man. *Entranced by an exclusive reliance on technology, reason without faith is doomed to flounder in an illusion of its own omnipotence. Faith without reason risks being cut off from everyday life.*[5]

Paul VI had already recognized and drawn attention to the global dimension of the social question.[6] Following his lead, we need to affirm today that *the social question has become a radically anthropological question*, in the sense that it concerns not just how life is conceived but also how it is manipulated, as bio-technology places it increasingly under man's control. *In vitro* fertilization, embryo research, the possibility of manufacturing clones and human hybrids: all this is now emerging and being promoted in today's highly disillusioned culture, which believes it has mastered every mystery, because the origin of life is now within our grasp. Here we see the clearest expression of technology's supremacy. In this type of culture, the conscience is simply invited to take note of technological possibilities. Yet we must not underestimate the disturbing scenarios that threaten our future, or the powerful new instruments that

4. Cf. Benedict XVI, Address to the Participants in the Fourth National Congress of the Church in Italy, Verona, October 19, 2006; Ibid., Homily at Mass, Islinger Feld, Regensburg, September 12, 2006.

5. Cf. Congregation for the Doctrine of the Faith, Instruction on certain bioethical questions *Dignitas Personae* (September 8, 2008): AAS 100 (2008), 858–887.

6. Cf. Encyclical Letter *Populorum Progressio*, 3: loc. cit., 258.

the "culture of death" has at its disposal. To the tragic and widespread scourge of abortion we may well have to add in the future—indeed it is already surreptitiously present—the systematic eugenic programming of births. At the other end of the spectrum, a pro-euthanasia mindset is making inroads as an equally damaging assertion of control over life that under certain circumstances is deemed no longer worth living. Underlying these scenarios are cultural viewpoints that deny human dignity. These practices in turn foster a materialistic and mechanistic understanding of human life. Who could measure the negative effects of this kind of mentality for development? How can we be surprised by the indifference shown towards situations of human degradation, when such indifference extends even to our attitude towards what is and is not human? What is astonishing is the arbitrary and selective determination of what to put forward today as worthy of respect. Insignificant matters are considered shocking, yet unprecedented injustices seem to be widely tolerated. While the poor of the world continue knocking on the doors of the rich, the world of affluence runs the risk of no longer hearing those knocks, on account of a conscience that can no longer distinguish what is human. God reveals man to himself; reason and faith work hand in hand to demonstrate to us what is good, provided we want to see it; the natural law, in which creative Reason shines forth, reveals our greatness, but also our wretchedness insofar as we fail to recognize the call to moral truth.

One aspect of the contemporary technological mindset is the tendency to consider the problems and emotions of the interior life from a purely psychological point of view, even to the point of neurological reductionism. In this way man's interiority is emptied of its meaning and gradually our awareness of the human soul's ontological depths, as probed by the saints, is lost. *The question of development is closely bound up with our understanding of the human soul,* insofar as we often reduce the self to the psyche and confuse the soul's health with emotional well-being. These over-simplifications stem from a profound failure to understand the spiritual life, and they obscure the fact that the development of individuals and peoples depends partly on the resolution of problems of a spiritual nature. *Development must include not just material growth but also spiritual growth,* since the human person is a "unity of body and soul,"[7] born of God's creative love and destined for eternal life. The human being develops when he grows in the spirit, when his soul comes to know itself and the truths that God has implanted deep within, when he enters into dialogue with himself and his Creator. When he is far away from God, man is unsettled and ill at ease. Social and psychological alienation and the many neuroses that afflict affluent societies are attributable in part to spiritual factors. A prosperous society, highly developed in material terms but weighing heavily on the soul, is not of itself conducive to authentic development. The new forms of slavery to drugs and the lack of hope into which so many people fall can be explained not only in sociological and psychological terms but also in essentially spiritual terms. The emptiness in which the soul feels abandoned, despite the availability of countless therapies for body and psyche, leads to suffering. *There cannot be holistic development and universal common good unless people's spiritual and moral welfare is taken into account,* considered in their totality as body and soul.

The supremacy of technology tends to prevent people from recognizing anything that cannot be explained in terms of matter alone. Yet everyone experiences the many immaterial and spiritual dimensions of life. Knowing is not simply a material act, since the object that is known always conceals something beyond the empirical datum. All our knowledge, even the most simple, is always a minor miracle, since it can never be fully explained by the material instruments that we apply to it. In every truth there is something more than we would have expected, in the love that we receive there is always an element that surprises us. We should never cease to marvel at these things. In all knowledge and in every act of love the human soul experiences something "over and above," which seems very much like a gift that we receive, or a height to

7. Second Vatican Ecumenical Council, Pastoral Constitution on the Church in the Modern World *Gaudium et Spes*, 14.

which we are raised. The development of individuals and peoples is likewise located on a height, if we consider *the spiritual dimension* that must be present if such development is to be authentic. It requires new eyes and a new heart, capable of *rising above a materialistic vision of human events*, capable of glimpsing in development the "beyond" that technology cannot give. By following this path, it is possible to pursue the integral human development that takes its direction from the driving force of charity in truth.

SOURCES

❖

For permission information, see the copyright page.

PART I: LIFE

Chapter 1: Early Childhood and Vocation

Joseph Ratzinger and Peter Seewald, *Salt of the Earth: The Church at the End of the Millennium*, trans. Adrian Walker (San Francisco: Ignatius Press, 1997), 41–44, 54–56.

Chapter 2: The Young Professor

Joseph Ratzinger and Peter Seewald, *Salt of the Earth: The Church at the End of the Millennium*, trans. Adrian Walker (San Francisco: Ignatius Press, 1997), 59–63.

Chapter 3: A *Peritus* at Vatican II

Benedict XVI and Peter Seewald, *Last Testament: In His Own Words*, trans. Jacob Phillips (London: Bloomsbury, 2016), 127–134, 141–142.

Chapter 4: Prefect of the Congregation for the Doctrine of the Faith

Benedict XVI and Peter Seewald, *Last Testament: In His Own Words*, trans. Jacob Phillips (London: Bloomsbury, 2016), 167–175.

Chapter 5: *Habemus Papem*

Benedict XVI and Peter Seewald, *Light of the World: The Pope, the Church, and the Signs of the Times*, trans. Michael J. Miller and Adrian J. Walker (San Francisco: Ignatius Press, 2010), 69–78.

Chapter 6: The Resignation

Benedict XVI and Peter Seewald, *Last Testament: In His Own Words*, trans. Jacob Phillips (London: Bloomsbury, 2016), 15–26.

PART II: GOD

Chapter 7: Prolegomena on the Subject of God

Joseph Ratzinger, *Introduction to Christianity*, rev. ed., trans. Michael J. Miller (San Francisco: Ignatius Press, [1968] 2004), 103–115.

Chapter 8: God: The Essential Matter

Joseph Ratzinger and Peter Seewald, *God and the World*, trans. Henry Taylor (San Francisco: Ignatius Press, 2002), 103–109.

Chapter 9: One God in Three Persons

Joseph Ratzinger, *The God of Jesus Christ: Meditations on the Triune God*, trans. Brian McNeil (San Francisco: Ignatius Press, 2008), 29–37.

PART III: JESUS CHRIST

Chapter 10: Jesus Christ: The Incarnate Love of God

Pope Benedict XVI, *Deus Caritas Est*, 9–15 (Vatican City: Libreria Editrice Vaticana, 2005).

Chapter 11: The Birth of Jesus

Joseph Ratzinger, *Jesus of Nazareth: The Infancy Narratives*, trans. Philip Whitmore (New York: Image Books, 2012), 58–67.

Chapter 12: Jesus on the Cross

Joseph Ratzinger, *Jesus of Nazareth: Holy Week* (San Francisco: Ignatius Press, 2011), 223–226.

Chapter 13: The Resurrection

Joseph Ratzinger, *Jesus of Nazareth: Holy Week* (San Francisco: Ignatius Press, 2011), 241–248.

Chapter 14: Eschatology: The True Shape of Christian Hope

Pope Benedict XVI, *Spe Salvi*, 24–31 (Vatican City: Libreria Editrice Vaticana, 2007).

PART IV: THE CHURCH

Chapter 15: The Holy, Catholic Church

Joseph Ratzinger, *Introduction to Christianity*, rev. ed., trans. Michael J. Miller (San Francisco: Ignatius Press, [1968] 2004), 338–347.

Chapter 16: The Church in the Third Millennium

Joseph Ratzinger, *Pilgrim Fellowship of Faith: The Church as Communion*, trans. Henry Taylor (San Francisco: Ignatius Press, 2005), 284–290

Chapter 17: Remaining in the Church

Joseph Ratzinger, *Credo for Today: What Christians Believe* (San Francisco: Ignatius Press, 2009), 193–200.

Chapter 18: Christianity and the World Religions

Joseph Ratzinger, *Many Religions—One Covenant: Israel, the Church, and the World*, trans. Graham Harrison (San Francisco: Ignatius Press, 1999), 106–113.

PART V: THE SECOND VATICAN COUNCIL

Chapter 19: A Council to Be Rediscovered

Joseph Ratzinger and Vittorio Messori, *The Ratzinger Report: An Exclusive Interview on the State of the Church*, trans. Salvator Attanasio and Graham Harrison (San Francisco: Ignatius Press, 1985), 27–40.

Chapter 20: The Meaning of *Subsistit In*

Joseph Ratzinger, *Pilgrim Fellowship of Faith: The Church as Communion*, trans. Henry Taylor (San Francisco: Ignatius Press, 2005), 144–149.

Chapter 21: The Hermeneutic of Continuity

Pope Benedict XVI, "Address of His Holiness Benedict XVI to the Roman Curia Offering Them His Christmas Greetings," Vatican website, December 22, 2005, http://www.vatican.va/content/benedict-xvi/en/speeches/2005/december/documents/hf_ben_xvi_spe_20051222_roman-curia.html.

PART VI: THE BIBLE

Chapter 22: The Limits of the Historical-Critical Method

Joseph Ratzinger, *Jesus of Nazareth: From the Baptism in the Jordan to the Transfiguration*, trans. Adrian Walker (New York: Image Books, 2007), xv–xxi.

Chapter 23: The Senses of Scripture

Pope Benedict XVI, *Verbum Domini*, 37–41 (Vatican City: Libreria Editrice Vaticana, 2010).

Chapter 24: *Lectio Divina*

Pope Benedict XVI, *Verbum Domini*, 86–87 (Vatican City: Libreria Editrice Vaticana, 2010).

PART VII: LITURGY, THE SACRAMENTS, AND THE PRIESTHOOD

Chapter 25: Liturgy and Life: The Place of the Liturgy in Reality

Joseph Ratzinger, *The Spirit of the Liturgy*, trans. John Saward (San Francisco: Ignatius Press, 2000), 13–22.

Chapter 26: The Eucharist and the Sacraments of Mission

Pope Benedict XVI, *Sacramentum Caritatis*, 23–29 (Vatican City: Libreria Editrice Vaticana, 2007).

Chapter 27: On Being a Priest

Pope Benedict XVI, "Letter of His Holiness Pope Benedict XVI Proclaiming a Year for Priests on the 150th Anniversary of the 'Dies Natalis' of the Curé of Ars," Vatican website, June 19, 2009, http://www.vatican.va/content/benedict-xvi/en/letters/2009/documents/hf_ben-xvi_let_20090616_anno-sacerdotale.html.

PART VIII: MARY

Chapter 28: The Place of Mariology in the Bible

Joseph Ratzinger, *Daughter Zion: Meditations of the Church's Marian Belief*, trans. John M. McDermott, SJ (San Francisco: Ignatius Press, 1983), 16–27.

Chapter 29: The Mother of God

Joseph Ratzinger and Peter Seewald, *God and the World*, trans. Henry Taylor (San Francisco: Ignatius Press, 2002), 293–297.

Chapter 30: The Faith of Mary

Pope Benedict XVI, "General Audience," Vatican website, December 19, 2012, http://www.vatican.va/content/benedict-xvi/en/audiences/2012/documents/hf_ben-xvi_aud_20121219.html.

PART IX: THE CHURCH FATHERS

Chapter 31: St. Clement of Rome

Pope Benedict XVI, "General Audience," Vatican website, March 7, 2007, http://www.vatican.va/content/benedict-xvi/en/audiences/2007/documents/hf_ben-xvi_aud_20070307.html.

Chapter 32: St. Ignatius of Antioch

Pope Benedict XVI, "General Audience," Vatican website, March 14, 2007, http://www.vatican.va/content/benedict-xvi/en/audiences/2007/documents/hf_ben-xvi_aud_20070314.html.

Chapter 33: St. Justin Martyr

Pope Benedict XVI, "General Audience," Vatican website, March 21, 2007, http://www.vatican.va/content/benedict-xvi/en/audiences/2007/documents/hf_ben-xvi_aud_20070321.html.

Chapter 34: St. Irenaeus of Lyons

Pope Benedict XVI, "General Audience," Vatican website, March 28, 2007, http://www.vatican.va/content/benedict-xvi/en/audiences/2007/documents/hf_ben-xvi_aud_20070328.html.

Chapter 35: Origen of Alexandria

Pope Benedict XVI, "General Audience," Vatican website, April 25, 2007, http://www.vatican.va/content/benedict-xvi/en/audiences/2007/documents/hf_ben-xvi_aud_20070425.html.

Chapter 36: St. Athanasius

Pope Benedict XVI, "General Audience," Vatican website, June 20, 2007, http://www.vatican.va/content/benedict-xvi/en/audiences/2007/documents/ hf_ben-xvi_aud_20070620.html.

Chapter 37: St. Basil

Pope Benedict XVI, "General Audience," Vatican website, July 4, 2007, http://www.vatican.va/content/benedict-xvi/en/audiences/2007/documents/ hf_ben-xvi_aud_20070704.html.

Chapter 38: St. Gregory Nazianzus

Pope Benedict XVI, "General Audience," Vatican website, August 8, 2007, http://www.vatican.va/content/benedict-xvi/en/audiences/2007/documents/ hf_ben-xvi_aud_20070808.html.

Chapter 39: St. John Chrysostom

Pope Benedict XVI, "General Audience," Vatican website, September 19, 2007, http://www.vatican.va/content/benedict-xvi/en/audiences/2007/ documents/hf_ben-xvi_aud_20070919.html.

Chapter 40: St. Hilary of Poitiers

Pope Benedict XVI, "General Audience," Vatican website, October 10, 2007, http://www.vatican.va/content/benedict-xvi/en/audiences/2007/documents/ hf_ben-xvi_aud_20071010.html.

Chapter 41: St. Ambrose

Pope Benedict XVI, "General Audience," Vatican website, October 24, 2007, http://www.vatican.va/content/benedict-xvi/en/audiences/2007/documents/ hf_ben-xvi_aud_20071024.html.

Chapter 42: St. Jerome

Pope Benedict XVI, "General Audience," Vatican website, November 7, 2007, http://www.vatican.va/content/benedict-xvi/en/audiences/2007/documents/ hf_ben-xvi_aud_20071107.html.

Chapter 43: St. Augustine

Pope Benedict XVI, "General Audience," Vatican website, January 9, 2008, http://www.vatican.va/content/benedict-xvi/en/audiences/2008/documents/ hf_ben-xvi_aud_20080109.html.

Chapter 44: St. Leo the Great

Pope Benedict XVI, "General Audience," Vatican website, March 5, 2008,
http://www.vatican.va/content/benedict-xvi/en/audiences/2008/documents/
hf_ben-xvi_aud_20080305.html.

Chapter 45: St. Benedict

Pope Benedict XVI, "General Audience," Vatican website, April 9, 2008,
http://www.vatican.va/content/benedict-xvi/en/audiences/2008/documents/
hf_ben-xvi_aud_20080409.html.

Chapter 46: St. Gregory the Great

Pope Benedict XVI, "General Audience," Vatican website, May 28, 2008,
http://www.vatican.va/content/benedict-xvi/en/audiences/2008/documents/
hf_ben-xvi_aud_20080528.html.

PART X: PRAYER

Chapter 47: Prayer and the Natural Desire for God

Pope Benedict XVI, "General Audience," Vatican website, May 11, 2011,
http://www.vatican.va/content/benedict-xvi/en/audiences/2011/documents/
hf_ben-xvi_aud_20110511.html.

Chapter 48: Prayer and the Holy Spirit

Pope Benedict XVI, "General Audience," Vatican website, May 16, 2012,
http://www.vatican.va/content/benedict-xvi/en/audiences/2012/documents/
hf_ben-xvi_aud_20120516.html.

Chapter 49: The Nature of Christian Prayer

Pope Benedict XVI, "General Audience," Vatican website, May 23, 2012,
http://www.vatican.va/content/benedict-xvi/en/audiences/2012/documents/
hf_ben-xvi_aud_20120523.html.

PART XI: FAITH IN THE MODERN WORLD

Chapter 50: The Dictatorship of Relativism

Pope Benedict XVI, "Homily at Mass 'Pro Eligendo Romano Pontifice,'" Vatican website, April 18, 2005, http://www.vatican.va/gpII/documents/homily-pro-eligendo-pontifice_20050418_en.html.

Chapter 51: The Two Levels of Conscience

Joseph Ratzinger, *On Conscience* (San Francisco: Ignatius Press, 2007), 30–38.

Chapter 52: The Problem of Practical Atheism

Pope Benedict XVI, "General Audience," Vatican website, November 14, 2014, http://www.vatican.va/content/benedict-xvi/en/audiences/2012/documents/hf_ben-xvi_aud_20121114.html.

Chapter 53: Defending the Rationality of Faith

Pope Benedict XVI, "Regensburg Address: Faith, Reason, and the University," Vatican website, September 12, 2006, http://www.vatican.va/content/benedict-xvi/en/speeches/2006/september/documents/hf_ben-xvi_spe_20060912_university-regensburg.html.

Chapter 54: The Development of Peoples and Technology

Pope Benedict XVI, *Caritas in Veritate*, 68–77, encyclical letter, Vatican website, June 29, 2009, http://www.vatican.va/content/benedict-xvi/en/encyclicals/documents/hf_ben-xvi_enc_20090629_caritas-in-veritate.html.